BURGLAR

TO

BUDDHA

ALSO BY SIMON

Self Love Now
(Published by ReLoveution)

BURGLAR

TO

BUDDHA

Transforming From The Inside Out

SIMON PAUL SUTTON

First published in Great Britain in 2021 by Labradorite Press, an imprint of Not From This Planet

Copyright © 2021 by Simon Paul Sutton
Cover Design by The Amethyst Angel
Cover photo by Erick Tejas

Interior images:
Patrick Glaize
Dhamma Dipa

ISBN: 978-1-912257-26-3

GRATITUDE

Gratitude is the greatest form of receivership, and what we appreciate appreciates. I am deeply grateful to all my ancestors who have lived and died before me. Everything has had to happen in the exact way it has unfolded in order for me to have lived and written this book and for you to be here now reading these words.

I am grateful for all of you who I have had the gift of hugging, smiling, laughing, crying, dancing, discussing, learning, challenging, creating, playing, kissing and loving with so far.

I am extremely grateful for all those who have shared longer moments with me, those who have loved me through thick and thin. So grateful for each and every interaction that has happened up until this moment and I am gratefully excited for all that is yet to come.

FOREWORD

I've been lucky enough to know Simon for many years now, and I am so excited for you to meet him through the following pages.

I remember at one of his early *Language of Love* events, Simon set us a task to complete over lunchtime. He told us to go out onto the bleak, wet streets of South London, find someone we didn't know and tell them that we loved them. There weren't that many people about, so I found myself tentatively approaching a young man with a hoodie and hard stare. I was scared, hoodies are scary, right?

'Hello,' I called to him. 'I love you.'

He looked at me for a moment and then he seemed to melt. 'I love that!' he raised his arms, 'I love you too, man!' He showed me the most beautiful smile and continued to shout 'I love you too!' as I walked down the road.

The magic of love is something you experience again and again with Si. Hanging out with him, be it in person or on the page, is energizing and inspiring. You will definitely laugh, you might well cry, and you will leave feeling a little bit closer, not just to him, but to yourself and the beautiful heart and truth at the core of you. You may well find yourself stepping towards your dreams or getting over something that has been holding you back. It is of no surprise to me that the more brave and brilliant things I have done in my life (becoming a writer, starting a campaign against a powerful newspaper) I did when Simon and I lived together as house mates, when his cheery 'you can do it, you're amazing' was a daily echo in my life.

And now he has (finally!) written his story. It's a great yarn, the ultimate hero's journey, from a lad doing crime on an estate to a man travelling the world helping people to fall in love with themselves and their lives. Via prison, existential crisis and selling tequila-based drinks served in realistic plastic cocks (I still have one of those somewhere) he tells his story with humour as well as glorious and often gulp-making honesty.

Reading it allowed me to reflect on my own story and life with equal candour. I looked at the beliefs I held, but wasn't living true to, and the longings I had but wasn't making any steps towards fulfilling. It was an empowering experience for me and I'm pretty sure I won't be the only one who will be moved by his words.

In so many ways, Simon's story of moving from fear to love, from delusion to truth couldn't be more timely. Humanity is at a tipping point right now and the world is unstable; wars, pandemics, natural disasters, and so many having to flee their homes. We appear to be becoming ever more divided as people. If we are going to be able to save our beautiful planet and come together as a global people, we need men and women showing us a new way, and Simon is one of the light bearers.

Simon says, 'fear takes and love gives' and he lives to show people the magic of this love. I personally find that so bloody amazing.

I am raising a son, and it's an odd experience. He's 5 now and I go to the toy shop and confront a whole wall where all the toys enticing him are male characters holding weapons. From such a young age he's absorbing that to be a man is to be dominant, violent and aggressive.

We are so used to and desensitised to seeing men pick up arms, that it becomes almost radical for a man to write a story about how, despite growing up on a rough estate and going to prison at a young age, he learnt to open his arms.

Proud to know you, Si. x

Lucy-Anne Holmes
Author of *Don't Hold My Head Down,
50 Ways to Find a Lover
& How to Start a Revolution.*

'Let our worries disperse
like clouds in a clear blue sky.
Like a thief entering
an empty house,
bad thoughts can do no harm
to an empty mind.'

Adapted from Padmasambhava
(c.8th Century)

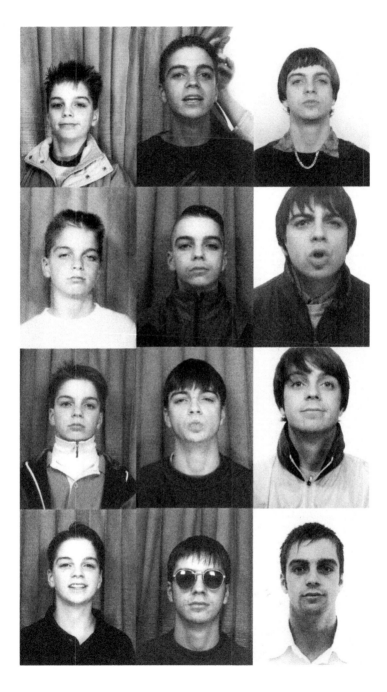

THEY WERE HOME - AND SO WERE WE!

'They're home! Run!'

'STOP! Police!'

'Aarrrgggghhhhh!'

That was all we heard from the barrage of noise and screaming that suddenly arose from downstairs. When you're on a job and you hear the word 'Police', it means 'run like fuck, we're in trouble.'

The bedroom windows were our best escape route, but they were locked, so I frantically looked for the keys, which were usually on the window sills or in little jars close by. Vic and I were both tugging at the window handles, hoping one of them would open.

My heart was beating fast, adrenalin was released and panic rose quickly. I tried the handles again and then to my relief, the lock broke free. If that hadn't happened, smashing the window would have been the next option. My only focus was on getting out.

Our other friend, Mike, was still downstairs but there

was no telling what was happening; everything went crazy and I couldn't think straight. It was every man for himself at that stage. Vic and I quickly climbed out of the window which led to the conservatory roof and as gently as possible walked along the wooden beams and then jumped down fifteen feet or more onto the ground, rolling as we landed. Then we sprinted to the end of the garden, climbed the six-foot fence and kept running until we had to stop to gulp in deep breaths. We listened for Mike or anybody else who may have been chasing us. I couldn't hear anything. It was totally silent, but I could see all the lights in the house were now on. We had no clue where we were and had to trust our intuition and continued running in the dark. There was obviously no turning back, we had to find our way home. I was scared, fear rushing through my veins. The alleyway we found ourselves in soon led us onto the main brightly lit street and we saw a bus station. I checked the timetable, and there were no buses due, but luckily some taxi cabs were sitting nearby.

In this situation, our only focus was getting home. The police would be on their way to the area so waiting around to get caught was not a good idea. After all, being on the run means running away and we felt anxious enough and didn't need to attract any further attention. I could feel the taxi driver could sense something was wrong and I couldn't look him in the eye. I was paranoid and it showed. It's difficult to hold eye-contact when you have something to hide.

When the taxi driver asked "Where to?" I stupidly replied with the name of a street very close to where we were going. You never get dropped off to where you are actually going.

I should have known better, but I wasn't thinking clearly. I was flustered.

Those were the early days for me as a criminal. And in that moment, all I wanted was to be home and safe. I was tired and it's often tiredness that gets you caught. We got dropped off and made our way to the Topman's house. Topman was the main gang leader and who we reported back to after a night of crime. It was common to go there and meet up with friends and show our stolen treasures. This was a highlight of the experience. Expressing what happened created group connection and boosted the ego.

But tonight, we weren't interested in boosting our egos, we just hoped Mike was okay.

Vic and I were both still shaken up and pumped with adrenalin, but happy to be knocking on this familiar door, because it represented safe pastures. The evening had been quite an ordeal.

There was a surprise waiting for us when we arrived. Mike. He'd made it back before us and had a spliff in one hand and a cup of tea in the other, sat there all cosy and warm.

"He doesn't need your help does he?" Topman said. "He's fucking hard, mate. Look at his bruises, fucking guy tried to kill him, look at this!"

Mike had red burn marks and a bruised body from the struggle he'd endured with the owner of the house. Mike hadn't been attacked like that before, but didn't seem too fazed. He wasn't scared of fighting. He practiced boxing and martial arts and had fought a few people in his time. We all sat down and rolled a few joints to chill out a bit. I poured

3

myself a tea and Mike told us his side of the story.

The owners unexpectedly entered their house without any of us hearing them arrive. Usually the 'lookout' would have spotted a car coming into the drive and alerted the other thieves, but not on this occasion.

Instead, a man and a woman, presumably the owners, entered their house, and the man caught Mike as he tried to run away and a grapple took place. The woman was hysterical, screaming and shouting in panic while Mike was struggling for his life. The whole house was in turmoil.

Imagine for a second, returning home to your safe abode and in an instant, it becomes a violent crime scene. It's an alarming experience for all concerned, because a thief does not want confrontation either. It's no different than when we see a rat, snake or cockroach come out of nowhere; they are just as scared as we are, if not more.

It's fight, flight or freeze, as the nervous systems goes into survival mode and a massive release of adrenalin flows into the bloodstream. Which the body then uses to either to get away as fast as humanly possible, freeze in shock or stay put and use the power from the adrenalin in a fight.

This is what happened to Mike. He didn't know how he got away, but he managed to free himself from the man's hold, run out the house and to the car as fast as he could. The police had been called, so he knew he didn't have long.

Frantically, he drove off into the darkness and headed home beaten and scarred, but relieved, so relieved! And I thought my experience had been an ordeal.

It was soon time for us to clean up our tracks. When you're a criminal, you are always covering your trail and how well you do this can be the difference between getting caught and staying free. We would always discard the scrap (the fake treasure that has no value) often dropping them down the drains in the road, then change and clean our clothes, park the car somewhere safe and away from where we lived and then clean up the house of any criminal paraphernalia, because you never knew when you may be in for a spin (your house being raided by the police).

BANG! BANG! BANG!

At 6am a few days later, my house got raided. The police smashed down the front door and rushed in. It seems my instincts were right, never tell a taxi driver where you are actually going. I was woken by the noise and saw the police van outside my window, so I scrambled up into the loft to hide. I listened from the loft, the sensations of fear rising fast. By now, I was becoming familiar with the feeling of fear rushing through my veins.

The police checked all the rooms and then sent a dog into the house to sniff me out. Eventually, the dog started barking up at the loft hatch in the ceiling. They sent the dog up and I was found hiding in the corner underneath some boxes and old carpet. The loft was like my spare room, my camp, my hideout (although clearly not a very good one). I had converted it into a space for hanging out with friends, listening to music and playing games. The police pulled me downstairs and one of them pulled up my t-shirt and checked my body for marks. I knew then why they had called by.

I was taken to the police station, locked up for 24 hours

and questioned numerous times. I gave no comment. They tried to make me talk, telling me it was a serious crime and I was going to jail. They knew it wasn't me they were looking for based on the description from the family and the fact I had no bruises on my body. But they were trying to break me so I would tell them who it was. They had linked the crime to me because I was on their hit list and the taxi driver reported two suspicious boys being dropped off in our area close to my home. I can only assume this is how they made their choice to raid me. But I wasn't about to ask.

When being interrogated by the police, we always gave the same reply to all questions: "No comment." Because if you didn't, you were either a grass (snitch), or you might have said something which couldn't be retracted later in court.

There was no point trying to outsmart the police and tell a fabricated story, because they would never have believed me. They were trained to make people talk. I had tried fabricating a story in the past and was caught out good and proper.

I find it fascinating how life is created through our choices and how those choices affect the lives of others around us. Back then, I was just doing what I felt I had to, to survive.

The experience and decision of ours that evening to earn some money, the only way we knew how, or at least, the way we chose to at the time, had in fact created a life experience for that family, which could have transformed their beliefs and actions forever.

The ripple effect of our choices is powerful. Yet it wasn't going to be this experience that would deter me from burgling again, because I wasn't yet conscious of my actions.

This is my journey from Burglar to Buddha. It's my personal experience from an unconscious life of crime and drugs, driven by fear, to a conscious life of awareness, living high on love and truth in service to that which is greater than me. From crime to the divine.

In order to share this personal transformation and some of the insights I've collected along the way, I feel it's best to answer the question – how did I become a burglar in the first place?

CASTLEFIELD

I grew up in High Wycombe and lived on a government housing estate called Castlefield with my Mum, Dad and two brothers. Stephen was five years older and Lloyd was four years younger. The man I called my dad wasn't mine and Stephen's biological father, who left when I was nine months old. Lloyd's dad, Roger, did the best he could for us in the time he was around. But my mum filed for a divorce when I was about eleven years old, and then it was just the four of us.

From the outside looking in, Castlefield was bleak and it appeared that most people living there were dysfunctional in some way. The crime rate was higher than the national average, domestic violence was evident in many homes, including my own, school drop-outs were the norm and most families were living off government benefits. We were too, especially after both fathers had left us.

There is a stigma around council estate life which carries a negative energy that can be quite depressing. The whole estate had various levels of poverty and this created states of inferiority and deprivation. A lack and scarcity mentality is born out of struggle and this was the default psychology of the residents, including my family. But I never really noticed the extent of the struggles my family or friends' families were experiencing. I'm sure there were feelings of resentment, unworthiness and class division and if so, it was just the norm for me as I don't recall ever consciously thinking about these things. As the saying goes, when you're in the shit, you can't smell it.

The police feared the area and had regular surveillance operations running. A TV documentary was produced highlighting Castlefield as one of the roughest estates in the UK. This was of course good for the crime world, good marketing of fear, you could say.

To give you a more present day idea, while writing this book I looked up my old estate to see if anything had changed after 24 years. This was one article I found in the *Bucks Free Press* newspaper online, dated 31st July 2018:

'Residents in Castlefield have been left fearing for their lives and their homes amid an alleged drug "turf war". The terrified resident from Spearing Road (where I lived)*, did not want to be named for fear of repercussions, they said his neighbours are being tormented by gangs who are running rife on the streets. Some of the gangs are even armed with weapons including hammers and bricks as they go head-to-head over drug disputes.*

The resident said: "People are coming from all over town and drugs are being sold in the streets. They even put a fishing chair out on the pavement and sold them from there. It has got really bad here recently. And some of my neighbours are scared they could get a stray bullet through their windows." He also recalled a terrifying incident three months prior where armed youths descended on his road.

"I looked out the window and saw around 15 of them coming up the road with axes and hammers and then they started throwing bricks through car windows.""

It's not advisable to believe everything you read in the newspapers, as journalists often hype up stories for better readership, but my reason for doing this research was a genuine curiosity and a little hope that the estate had changed as I had. The events in this article are probably not going on every day, but what this confirmed for me was that for an environment to change, the people within it need to change, and while poverty and lack prevail, that kind of lasting change is unlikely. The environment we live in plays a huge role in shaping our behaviour and attitudes to life.

Although I could say I was destined to become a criminal because I grew up in such harsh and hostile conditions, not everyone who grew up on the estate became criminals. There were other factors at play.

CHOCOLATE BARS TO GARDEN SHEDS

In 1991, at the age of fourteen, I committed my first criminal act – shoplifting. It started on my paper round. I would steal a few bars of chocolate and stash them in my paper bag before heading out to do my morning deliveries. I saw it as a little extra for my time and a snack along the way. My belief was, it wasn't hurting anyone and they had many bars on the shelf, right? This little 'harmless' act soon grew into a habit and I would pretty much take something from every shop I went in.

I loved hanging out in the town centre on Saturdays. I'd wear my best clothes, take my pocket money and get the bus to town with friends. I felt grown-up and cool, especially as mum always dressed me fashionably in branded clothes and trainers. If you had style when growing up, it helped your image.

The older boys would hang out inside the Octagon shopping centre, around the circle above the spiral staircase.

They didn't do the stealing, they were the clients who would buy the stolen goods. They used to pay either a pound or fifty pence for Lynx deodorants, and Garfield teddies sold quite well too. Anything and everything was potentially sellable. They were the demand and I was the supplier, and as you know, consumerism is all about supply and demand.

Shoplifting was a quick adrenalin rush for me, a game of wits which felt exciting. It gave me a buzz, status and paid fast. It felt somehow like a dangerous and intense psychological game between the shop and me.

Woolworths was a prime target of mine. They had ten glass doors at the front of the shop. They were the threshold, the divide between right and wrong, good and bad. They represented freedom. Once I got past those doors, I knew I was home free. It was a challenge, a confrontation of fear, an adrenalin release. I can see the aisles now, and the slow walk through them, moving closer towards the glass exit doors knowing I had stolen property in my pockets. I would try to be calm but my heart would be racing. My body would become overpowered by the cocktail of emotions and I'd be ready to run. My senses were heightened as I listened attentively. I'd push the doors open, almost waiting for someone to stop me, and then the door would swing back, and I'd feel the air on my face, which felt hopeful.

Outside, I'd walk faster, down the high street, past the market stalls, turn the corner, and run, not too fast though, then as I reached the church yard, the adrenalin would subside. I'd made it! Home free... this time.

It wasn't long before I was caught for the first time. A sly store detective nabbed me after stealing a bar of chocolate and some aftershave. The police were called into the store while I was held in the office. I was given a warning and slapped on the wrist (metaphorically). You could say this was the day I was labelled as a 'petty thief'. It was inevitable from my actions and the environment I lived in that I was going to continue down the path of crime. I kept chasing the high of adrenalin and went from stealing sweets, teddies, deodorant, tapes, CDs and clothes to larger items like bikes, lawnmowers and garden sheds.

If you're wondering, it requires a fair bit of time to steal garden sheds. Especially those that are already built. The council had been commissioned to install new sheds for many of the residents on the estate, even the houses that were currently empty. It turned out that these could be dismantled again. So, one night a few of us would go into the shed and undo all the bolts connecting the shed side panels to the concrete bases. And the next night we would go back and take the panels and walk them down the backroads (service roads behind the houses) and then store them in a safe place. Even now I have to chuckle at the absurdity of the things we got up to.

Thankfully this only happened a few times before the council noticed their sheds were going missing and began installing with them with safety measures and undoable bolts. I wasn't disappointed as the amount of labour for the amount of pay was completely imbalanced. It was no surprise that I moved onto stealing cars and then burgling houses. You name it, I'd steal whatever would earn some cash to buy drugs and fuel the lifestyle I was becoming identified with. It was the beginning of a downward spiral.

BOYS JUST WANT TO HAVE FUN

I remember my early teens when I didn't have a care in the world, just going out to play each day and meeting up with different boys from around the estate.

In those days, mobile phones didn't exist in our world so one of our main forms of communication was whistling. There was a code whistle that helped us to find each other around the estate. It could be heard for at least a half mile radius depending on how good you could whistle. I couldn't whistle, so I would walk to friends' houses and knock on their doors or use the telephone boxes to call home phones if they had one. Not everyone had a phone. Often, I had to call different houses to find out how long it had been since my friend had left home and ask if their parents, brothers or sisters knew where they were heading.

We would play street games like pom pom, which was sort of like hide and seek mixed with tag, and you had to try and touch a specific lamppost without getting caught. Or kerbsie, where two people play with a football or tennis

14

ball and you stand either side of the road and have to throw the ball and hit the opposite kerb and when done right, the ball will come back to the person throwing it, and that's one point to you. Then there was man hunt, that's when one person is the fugitive and however many others are playing, have to hunt them down and catch them. That's a lot of fun and I just realised as I write this that ironically this game became more real when I became a criminal. And finally there was hedge hopping. Hedge hopping was a favourite. Many gardens at the back of the houses had small hedges from approximately four or five feet and it was possible to run from garden to garden jumping hedges, or just crashing into them and falling over. We had so much fun just jumping through and over hedges. (Not so much fun for the owners though.)

We were young boys just being boys, entertaining ourselves and making the most of any situation. We would also go bike riding, build go-carts and fly around the pavements, or hang out in the local woods building camps and swinging on rope swings created by the older boys. Autumn was our favourite time of year, when Halloween came around and we could go trick or treating to get sweets and money. If a house didn't give us any money or sweets, we would play a trick on them which could mean egging the house or putting a dog poo in a paper bag and setting it on fire outside the front door, then knocking the door and running away.

Then there was fireworks night or Guy Fawkes night. How cool was that, full permission to play with fire. I loved building bonfires and the anticipation of all the pretty lights and sparkles in the sky from the many firework displays from all the different houses around the estate. The local shops would often let us buy whatever we needed and if they didn't, we would ask the older boys to get them for us. We would have our own firework display, but after getting bored of firing them into the sky, we realised we could fire them at each other. It wasn't with the real intention of hitting each other, although it was funny watching your friend running away from a firework. Bloody scary for the one running away of course. Just to be clear, I'm not in any way advocating you try this, it was dangerous and pretty stupid, but seemed completely normal at the time. We were mischievous boys at times, that's for sure.

Oh and I mustn't forget my passion for football.

It's hard to describe how much of a big event football games were on the estate. We would meet up regularly and play long games in the school playground or on the local recreational fields. And as they went on, the teams would grow as more people arrived and joined in. These matches were quite a spectacle. My brother Steve and his friend Matthew taught me how to play football very well. These games would go on for hours. The bonding and banter that occurred from the games was quite special too. I have never forgotten the day I got a ball kicked straight into my face, from Johnny, one of the older boys who had a seriously powerful kick. I can still feel the sting.

Steve and I dreamed of being professional footballers and had the hope that we would be scouted by a manager and attend soccer school to realise our dream. It never happened though. The furthest we got was playing in school teams and the local Saturday and Sunday league.

We were known around town as the Sutton brothers. People often commented on how alike we were, which really pleased me at the time and gave me a sense of belonging.

Naturally, I was culturally conditioned by the environment and I mimicked the language and behaviours of those closest to me: my parents, family and friends. I really respected my older brother Steve, and wanted to be like him. I thought he dressed stylishly, listened to great music, played football really well, and had cool friends that drove cool cars. He was my main role model and the estate was my world. At that point, I had no idea how vast the wider world really was.

UP IN SMOKE

Steve and a core group of his friends were smoking marijuana and committing crimes way before I realised. I knew they were going to nightclubs and drinking alcohol because they all dressed me up one night and thought it would be fun to sneak me into the local club.

Their world was becoming more attractive to me. I often listened to them through the thin walls when they all gathered in Steve's bedroom. They seemed to be having fun and living an exciting life. They'd often meet up in the morning and hang out all day together, or I would hear the horn of a car outside which signalled to Steve to go out and then they were off somewhere into the unknown. I kept my eye on them from my bedroom window and wondered where they were going and what they were up to. At times, I would be asked to do errands for Steve, which made me feel appreciated and included. I would make his friends cups of tea or tidy his room when they had all left after their smoking sessions.

One day, I was invited into his room by Jason, one of Steve's closest friends. I was hovering curiously close by and he said,

"You can come in if you want?"

I had no idea what this invite would lead to and what influence Jason would have on my life. I walked in and climbed up on to the top bunk bed. I just sat up there, listening and observing the conversation. It was smoky in the room from the joints being passed around. After a while I was offered a joint to try. Apprehensively I accepted and attempted to smoke it. I'm not sure my brother was very happy about it, but I think it was probably fun for them all to see me stoned.

That afternoon after my first spliff, which made me cough for quite some time, I felt light-headed and nauseous, and then passed out on the bed. I woke some hours later, feeling very hungry, to find everybody had left. I went downstairs and Mum said:

"Hello, Simon, where have you been, love? I didn't know you were home." (Mum often didn't have a clue to what was going on). I can't remember what I replied, but I know I went straight for the cornflakes and added heaps of white sugar. This was going to be a new delicacy of mine and 'munchies' (sugar cravings) was a new term in my vocabulary.

Now I had a taste of smoking weed, I was curious to try it again. The last year of school was a smoky affair, and instead of gaining high grades, I was smoking high grades of skunk. I tried smoking a normal cigarette and it tasted disgusting. So much so that I firmly said no to cigarettes alone and yes to ganja. It didn't make sense to me why people would put those ugly chemical sticks in their mouths, but for some reason, I saw no problem with weed mixed with tobacco, and continued to smoke those instead.

Now that I was in the smoking posse at school, I started to hear about the 'Cellar Dwellers'. They were a gang of guys who lived on another estate not too far from Castlefield. They had converted a four-foot high cellar into a smoking den. It was carpeted and had cushions, a stereo, mini fridge for the beers and a TV. They made it really homely with Bob Marley posters and all sorts of weed related paraphernalia. You had to be accepted into the gang before you even got a sniff at visiting the Cellar. One of the boys at school who was my closest friend knew about the Cellar, so he invited me once and over time, I was slowly introduced to all the Cellar Dwellers and soon accepted into the gang. Some of the boys didn't like me at first. They thought I was too cocky. I was Jack the lad and they were a bit apprehensive and paranoid because I was the new guy from another estate. Could I be trusted?

I noticed this process of acceptance into the gang was very similar across all the different estates around town and I was thankful to be accepted into this particular group. They were good guys, not really hard-core criminals. In fact, most of them had regular jobs. The Cellar was an intense space and smoking sessions down there were fierce with several boys smoking drugs, listening to music, laughing, joking and drinking. Whenever I finally crawled out of there, I was seriously stoned. Many a time I would throw 'whitees' (which is extreme loss of blood to the head and you almost faint and/or puke up). Oh the joys of getting high.

The stories from the cellar always leaked around school and the local estates. Many wanted to be part of it. From the cellar we emerged onto the streets and into the local parks. Smoking drugs, drinking and hoping to get some female attention or hustle a space in the cars with those who were old enough to drive and were heading to illegal raves. We drank all sorts of cheap alcohol like cider, diamond white, dynamite and pink lady wine and any kind of beer. It was one of the Cellar Dwellers who introduced me to my first pill of ecstasy. And of course you know what they say - one thing leads to another...

Smoking Dope at 17

Smoking that first spliff on the bunk bed that day in my brother's room, was the beginning of a whole new journey. One that included a lot of drugs. You name it, I've smoked it: marijuana, solids, green, hash, black, diesel, skunk, and resin. I've even smoked what wasn't supposed to be smoked. After many smoking sessions with different people and sacrificing thousands of brain cells, I was hooked and so it obviously seemed like a good idea to continue. I soon become addicted and it wasn't long before I was following the footsteps of my brother and his friends. I went from smoking it, to selling it, to smuggling it, and making many trips to Amsterdam, the drug dealers' paradise.

ON THE MISSION

Burglary was commonly known as 'drumming' or 'on the mission' and it brought with it many highs and lows. Stealing was easy if you didn't get caught and a nightmare if you did.

Having money was a big benefit and the world I broke into consumed my life. If I wasn't stealing, I was selling something stolen or selling drugs and running around doing deals left, right and centre. We called this 'Runnings', a daily run around doing what needed to be done. Running here and running there. When I had what people needed, I was a busy boy and if I didn't, I was busy trying to get what people needed.

Being involved in burglary began for me sometime in 1993, during my sixteenth year alive, when two close friends at the time were burgling partners and they invited me along to be a 'lookout'. My role was to stand outside in the garden while they broke into the house to get a video player or TV or anything else that could earn us some money to buy some hash and alcohol. All I had to do was shout if somebody was coming home or the police were seen patrolling.

Nobody in our close group was driving yet, which meant that many crimes were committed on foot. The estate wasn't that big so we had to be careful as we never knew if others had already committed a crime near us. If they had, then it was quite likely the police would have been patrolling the area which meant it was 'hot'. That was not good because if somebody had spotted us, the police could respond much faster and this would have limited our getaway time. Of course, it worked both ways, it meant we were also potentially a problem for other thieves.

A lot of burglaries started to occur around the estate. 'Shitting on your own doorstep' is the term for that. News travelled fast, even without the use of the internet or mobile phones, and the estate was becoming a hot spot of crime.

All the roads around the estate interlocked with each other with alleyways and certain gardens serving as short cuts. At the back of some houses there was a service road which we called the 'back roads'. These back roads, alleys and garden routes helped us get to different locations around the estate with stolen goods (remember the sheds?) and drugs without having to walk the main lit-up streets and risk being seen by patrolling police vehicles or the local bobby walking the streets. These routes played havoc for the coppers when trying to chase criminals.

As well as us full-timers, there were part-time burglars. They were either not very good at it or just scared. Most people didn't have the bottle to actually steal. You either like the buzz and cope with the fear or don't do it. The part-timers could fill in if no one else was around or the full-timers were off sick. There were also leeches, or hanger-ons, as they were called. They would wait until everyone arrived back from the mission to see what had been stolen and what they could get out of someone else's crimes. Sometimes they sold the goods, if there were any, or they would store the goods for a cut.

After a night out it was typical for the thieves to buy dinner, beers and a bag of weed. Somebody would make money from selling the goods, someone would make money from buying the gold and silver, and those buying the goods would be getting a deal much cheaper than in the shops. The leeches would get a smoke, drink and food. Somewhere along the dirty trail everyone got something.

MIDGETS ON THE RUM

It wasn't long before I began receiving more invitations to hang with my brother's circle. I would buy drugs from them and at times they would take me with them to their dealers on different estates. I was able to invite a couple of my close friends too. It was very exciting for me to explore new places, meet new people and be in the presence of the older guys. Seeing their world and how they acted.

They took me once to the Smoking Men's Club in another town, which provided a different place to buy weed or hash. It was a rugby club for men. It had an old bar, pool table and wooden chairs. There was a very dodgy crowd in there, and it was not the most welcoming of places. We had to go there under cover, and were only allowed in by invitation.

One time we were having a few beers while waiting for a delivery of weed, when an old black guy pulled out some 100% proof Jamaican rum and asked if we wanted a shot? Of course, I said yes. Oh, Mary, that's strong shit. I had never drunk anything so strong. I had one shot and the next thing you know, I'm up dancing on a chair. Everyone was laughing, and I was centre stage, pissed, dancing around like a crazy man. Which wasn't exactly keeping things under cover was it? Suddenly, the door flew open and in walked a group of bikers and two midgets.

Of course, big mouth here said, laughing, "Who invited the midgets?" and "Look! Look! Midgets!"

It turned out that they were the Top Men and the dealers that we were waiting for, to deliver our weed. Jason and Steve were told they had better get me out of the Men's Club sharpish, afraid it could kick off, because I was being way too loud and lippy. I was ushered out and for some reason, I couldn't stop laughing.

As I opened the car door to get inside, I fell out again. That rum was lethal. I've never drunk it since.

The next day I was told what had happened which made me chuckle but more importantly I felt very lucky that we all didn't get into a big fight with the midgets or experience any real trouble as a result of my drunken behaviour.

Obviously, I was never invited back, and I decided to stay low in the car whenever we returned to the club.

It's hard to describe how it was for me being invited into the older gang. I was lost in the adventure, the curiosity and the excitement. Being with them was hypnotic. As time went on, I was able to hang out all day, cruising around in their flash cars, getting high while listening to Hip Hop, R&B and Drum & Bass blaring from the speakers. My interest in their life and my wish to be like them was taking shape. I had manifested myself into their world.

Getting stoned with them in their cars was the next

level of the term smashed. Take the intensity of the Cellar I mentioned and multiply it tenfold. The car became a large 'bong' that we were literally sat in. Windows were rarely allowed down unless in extreme circumstances, like the police coming or someone having to evacuate the vehicle. The purpose was to get high, the only question was, how high? This is what it means to be 'up in smoke'.

Although it felt like I was progressing and experiencing a new-found status, I could also feel resistance and jealousy coming from other friends. Even though we met up from time to time at different places, there was still a divide between the groups, like a subtle hierarchy being played out. I was now hanging out with the older, more established gang members; and my friends, even if they were not aware of their feelings, felt let down and that I had abandoned them in some way. I am guessing that some thought I was definitely getting too big for my boots. And from my selfish perspective, there was a sense of it being more beneficial for my personal growth to learn from those who were older and more experienced.

It wasn't just my friends though; my brother was also unhappy about me being around more often. He said on a few occasions that I should "be careful". He didn't like it when one day, Jason said, "Let's take Si with us on the next mission."

ROBBING HOOD PRINCE OF THIEVES

This was a welcome surprise for me and felt super exciting. I felt like I was being trusted and my ego was boosted. I could feel Steve's resistance, but I went against his wishes and started going on missions with them. This was a huge initiation. It was a whole different ball game to what I was used to. They were way more professional, more calculated and targeted much bigger houses. We were travelling out of our poor estates to rich areas. Detached houses with four or five bedrooms, two garages and Porsches, Lamborghinis and other expensive cars on the driveway. I had never seen houses like them. It was all new to me. I could feel that familiar adrenalin moving through my body. This was an upgrade in responsibility. I was definitely out of my comfort zone, but that's the only place we learn and grow, right?

Going on a mission with them was like my first day at a new job. That feeling of wanting to impress was strong, so I did exactly what I was told and kept quiet the rest of the time. I was scared, but wanted to see how it was done by the professionals. I was told I would be the 'lookout'. As I'd had a little experience of this role before, I felt ready to take on the new job vacancy. That first mission was a success in my eyes and I think they appreciated my courage and fearlessness to get the job done. To get in and get out as smooth as possible. The thing I learned from them was the process and planning that made the crime easier. Where to store the tools in the car, what to wear, how to pop open the windows faster. Also, small details like checking the surrounding areas and escape route before entering the dwelling. The decision to take only gold most of the time. They saw themselves as jewel thieves because stealing gold and jewels was how the real money was made. They taught me that video recorders, and other electrical goods were small fry. And that stealing them could be more hassle than they were worth.

A 'lookout' is an especially important part of the team. As soon as everyone has entered the house, the lookout would go to the best lookout point at the front of the house or where the owner's point of entrance would be. They are the eyes and they make the decision when to leave the house if someone is coming home or it's dangerous and there's the potential of getting caught.

It was intense being the lookout, because I could hear what was going on in the house and I could also see everything going on outside. My mind would be awash with thoughts. The art to this role was calculating what was going on outside, what lights were on in other houses, who was home or not home.

A good lookout could spot another house to burgle from the one they were in; everybody involved liked it if this happened. The lookout also had to be aware of the subtle dangers too. For example, too many torch lights flashing around in the house could alert the neighbourhood watch crew; we nicknamed them "flat caps" because they were often old men walking around surveying the estate with their dogs and many of them wore flat caps. To us they were just nosey buggers causing us problems.

The lookout also had to have a good judgment of the escape time. It was all about communication and sometimes it might appear that the owners had returned home, and the lookout would say "Let's chip!" (chip = run). Only to find when you were outside running like crazy, it was the next-door neighbours returning home. Then everyone would have to make the decision of whether to go back in or not, depending on what had been found.

In my experience, as many as four people would go out on a mission together and this could amplify the danger, especially if nobody was on lookout, due to lack of trust. In the less professional groups, nobody really wanted to be the lookout because the dominating thought in these circles was: "If I'm the lookout, I'm going to get robbed myself." Because if you're the lookout, you're not searching for things to steal, and if a great piece of gold or diamonds were found, they would often go in a separate pocket and not shared with the group. So the lookout's swag could end up being considerably less, for the same level of risk.

Never trust a thief was the rule of thumb, it was a dog eat dog, every man for himself, eat or be eaten world.

However, finding someone to work with who you trusted was essential, otherwise it could mean ending up in jail on a regular basis. Imagine four or more people searching a house in the dark with no one looking out, while all making noises and each with a torch light flashing around as they move around the space. When there's nobody on look out, it's very hard to hear the front door opening or any approaching vehicles, and this situation would create a more frantic energy in the space. It's disorientating and you can't focus fully. Every now and then someone would say, "Shush! Shush! Who's that? Is that you? Everyone cool? Someone have a quick look, who's at the front? Alright? Alright? All clear! Anyone got anything? Let's hurry up!" And so on. It was nerve-wracking.

One time, I was out with three guys I got on great with. We would have a lot of fun cracking jokes all the time and taking the piss out of one another. This joker mentality also helped ease the stress of the situations we were putting ourselves into. One time my friend walked into the room I was checking, it was pitch black apart from my torch light, he said, "You got anything?" I said, "Yeah! Yeah hold this!"

I had just found a vibrator in the top bedside drawer and passed it to him as I walked out the room. He grabbed it and said "What is it?" Then he looked closely and realised what was in his hands and said, "Aarrgh Simon, man! Fuck that shit, you joker." I said, "You fuck it!" He dropped it on the floor, and it started vibrating as I ran off laughing.

When out on a mission, this crew liked taking everything. I lost count of how many times I said, "Leave the TV and anything big and just take the gold, that's where the money is." (But they didn't always listen). On one particular mission, it was time to leave, so we had all vacated the house and headed back to the vehicle. But one guy was missing and no one knew where he'd gone. We were all waiting in the car, feeling like sitting ducks for the police to find. I was panicking a little and said, "I'm going to drive up the road to see where he is, or we have to leave him." We couldn't find him on the first sweep, so I did one more turnaround and then just as we drove away he came running down the road from behind some trees with a portable TV in his arms. I had told them all before I wouldn't drive with TVs because it was like playing with fire. He jumped in the car and said "Come on, Si, mine has blown up and stopped working man." What can you do when a friend needs a TV and just happens to have one in his hands?

Maybe you are getting the feeling of how scary burgling is? It's even more alarming if you get seen or chased from the dwelling. Being chased literally feels like a life or death situation. If you get caught, it means you have to face the consequences of your actions and that's the last thing you want. Pure survival instincts are triggered and your whole body goes into a different state of being, and when that adrenalin takes over, there is no stopping it. If we got away from these chases, then how we acted during the chase made great stories to entertain friends with later.

I wasn't there, but I heard the story of when 'Pickle' (that was his nickname), was on the run from a crime. It was very dark as he ran through multiple gardens to get away, then he jumped over a six foot fence, not knowing what was on the other side and landed feet first into a small pond. Of course, that didn't stop him, he had to keep running with wet trousers and soggy trainers to get back to the car. Luckily he got away and this little incident birthed another nickname for him, 'Swamp foot'.

I have heard a saying that the mind is a servant to whatever it wants. It makes sense, because my mind definitely learned how to justify my actions when I was committing crime. For example, I didn't want my own home to be burgled, but it felt okay to steal from others. I became numb and desensitized to my true feelings. I was in denial. I thought I was doing the right thing to survive, because I needed to be above the rest and not the downtrodden, poorest person on the estate. The rich could afford it, was my motto. Even though the truth of it was, many were not rich either. They were middle class and often struggling to survive in society just like me. And the things we were stealing were likely paid for with credit cards and loans. At that time I had no concern for the people I was stealing from because the only thing I was concerned with was me, myself and my survival.

As time went on Steve was not happy with my deeper involvement. I thought it was because he was jealous, like my friends, but I know that wasn't the whole truth. I think part of him didn't want me getting into this world, and that he wanted to protect me. Yet at the same time, he was one of the main influences for me to enter this world in the first place.

My ego was thriving, and though I can see now that Steve felt let down by me and Jason, in those early days I didn't seem to have a care in the world. I was enjoying myself, I thought I was free and didn't think of the consequences my actions had on others.

In my warped mind, I was 'Robbing Hood'. I thought I was stealing from the rich to pay the poor, the poor being me. Robin Hood was a truth crusader who rebelled against society and stood for freedom and justice. This is exactly what I was doing in my unconscious way. I wanted to free my family from our life situation. I was an upset teenager in conflict with the police who represented control and power. I was putting my fist up to society. Power to the people and all that. I didn't know how to articulate my feelings, nobody showed me how, so I communicated them the best I could through my actions.

Paradoxically, by choosing the path I chose, I was only creating more pain and suffering. Conflict only fuels conflict. But I would not recognise this for many years. I was burgling with the best, gaining higher respect and a greater identity. It wasn't long before I would be officially introduced to the Topman.

There was no turning back now.

TOPMAN - KING OF THE CASTLE

On many of the estates around town, there were 'Topmen' who were the gang leaders. They were like Fagin from Oliver Twist. Everyone in the crime circles knew who they were and if you didn't know them, you wanted to. They were the main dealers on the estates and supposedly in the know, which meant they were the most connected and the most dangerous. Being introduced and accepted into the Topman's set-up was a big deal.

Topmen were feared and as the name describes, they were at the top of the food chain; the top cats, the King of the Castle. Everyone wanted to be in with the Topmen and accepted into their circles. They had a lot to offer, like connections to drugs, money, stolen goods, opportunities and protection.

To be invited into a dealer's domain, you had to be trusted and have passed a few tests. Firstly, you're not a 'Grass' (somebody who breaks under police interrogation) Secondly, a few people within the 'gang' who were already allowed in the Topman's circle had to give the green light. That could be a connection through friends, relatives, or a recommendation from someone the Topman trusted.

Turning up uninvited and knocking on a Topman's door could lead to getting hit over the head with a lethal weapon (trust me, shit like that happened). I can recall when I was first told I could enter the Topman's domain. I felt extremely nervous but also respected and accepted by the group. It was a step up the ladder, which did wonders for my ego.

Topmen created their own world and wanted to be in control of everything and everyone in it. Once accepted, you had to check in most days; they needed to know what people were doing. Most guys in the tight circles would visit every day or so, to sit around and keep the Topman company. A key thing to realise here is that this was a dealer's den and their full-time job. Once you were in, it created opportunity but at the same time, once you were in, there was no easy way out.

Knowing a big dealer gave me extra status. Scoring drugs from a Topman made me the man that everyone else wanted to know, because I could now get a properly weighed draw (bag of weed) and not be ripped off by the street dealers who worked from one ounce or less. Dealing with a Topman meant getting good value, good quality, the precise weight and being treated with a little more respect. Lower down the food chain, the value, quality and respect diminished, because everyone had to make their 'drink' (percentage) for doing their bit.

In Castlefield, there were a few Topmen; some who thought they were top of the chain and those who actually were. Topmen, in my opinion (and most criminals for that matter), were ruled by paranoia. They experienced heightened stress, anxiety and sleep deprivation, which arose from constantly thinking about the police, money and/or getting caught for their crimes. You've heard the term 'guilty conscience' and although you may not see yourself as a criminal, we all know that feeling of lying and doing something we shouldn't have. Guilt is a powerful energy that effects the body in ways we are not fully aware of. Most Topmen only got high when they felt safe enough to do so, and some would rarely take their own drugs, as this could impair the concentration they needed to keep on top of the operation they were controlling.

Topmen lived in fear, yet paradoxically, used fear as their most powerful weapon to control and manipulate everyone around them. You may ask why they would be in fear if they were at the top of the food chain, but just because you are at the top of some hierarchical ladder doesn't mean you don't experience fear. In fact, I would say you experience a deeper sense of fear and terror from getting caught or losing money, power or status. Money was the drug of choice for Topmen, and I too became addicted to the idea of money and what it could give me. Having money made me crave more. I could never get enough. I know the others were the same. Jason would constantly count it, iron it and stash it safely in £1000 bundles.

This habit of wanting and striving for money made sense to me. I had witnessed my mum, and other families on the estate, struggle to make ends meet. Money is one of our main means of survival, so it stands to reason humans blatantly or subtly desire it. Making money was my motivation. And yet I had a deep-seated lack mentality with limiting beliefs that money was scarce and could run out at any time. I had been taught that money doesn't grow on trees, which was why it made sense to me to steal it.

Topmen were also known for carrying various lethal weapons and had used them many times. From axes to hammers, baseball bats to CS gas (known also as mace or tear gas). When a weapon was used in any way, everyone would be made aware of it, as this helped to spread fear which sustained their power and status. Most Topmen also had guns for protection and to give them internal confidence. Think of it like nuclear warfare: no one wants to use the gun because of the ramifications, but the one who has the gun gets a little more respect. I viewed the gun as a physical creation birthed from the idea that everyone is against us and we must protect ourselves from attack.

If a Topman felt that his power over others was slipping, he would set up the opportunity to use a weapon and do so with intent. I recall there was a handgun found in the playground of our local school. This was planted there to spread fear and drama amongst the teachers, knowing the school would report this instantly to the police and it would gain a feature in the local newspapers. Most mainstream news channels love a dramatic story of fear to spread around, which get more viewers than feel-good stories. Topmen used this knowledge to their advantage.

Topmen would also make it their business to know where the local policeman patrolling the area lived. Once this information was found out, it could then be dropped into random conversations with either that particular person or other policemen to scare them off. Gang members could then vandalise their property, spray-paint policemen's names on walls and even smash the police lights off the top of their cars. Shouting out to policemen the name 'nonce' (paedophile) was the norm. This is just one of the abusive words used to belittle them. It was a game of wits, a mini war; the police versus the criminals. All these actions were used to instil fear around the estate. These actions caused people to be afraid of fear itself. This was psychological warfare at its finest.

People from our estate would often ask Topmen for help or protection. If, for example, someone was causing trouble for them, or their car had been broken into, or their house burgled, then they would ask the Topman if he knew anything. Of course, his first response would be, "No, not heard anything, I'll ask around though." If the Topman liked the person asking, he would then mention this to his cronies (gang members) by saying "Take care and don't shit on your own doorstep." If he didn't like or care about them then it would be a running joke among the clan.

On the flip side, if anyone had pissed him off personally, he could, and would, quite easily plan to get their houses burgled or vandalised in some way. Maybe put a few bricks through a window or burn a car out. Whatever came to mind in that moment.

The fear of violence is a powerful weapon when used effectively, even a single incident can spread a huge amount of fear. The following story is an example of that.

Before I was old enough to be welcomed into the higher

circles, I heard about a savage street fight which took place between a Topman and his gang versus two men from another estate. As the story goes, there had been a feud going on for a number of years with some minor chases and confrontations between them. Some verbal abuse, gossip and vandalism, that sort of thing. Then it all came to a climax one day, ending up with the two men from the other estate seriously wounded in hospital. They had been battered with baseball bats and other blunt instruments and one of them got stabbed in the leg with a garden fork. These are the type of stories which give people a reason not to get too cocky or try to take advantage of a gang. This is how gangs communicate, through terror and control.

An event of this magnitude created a vibration of fear so strong, it boosted the gang's confidence to do it again if needed. I'm guessing that most people, if they'd had a choice, would rather have sat at home in comfort than commit violence, but there are some who loved violence, because the bloodlust and bodily sensations from feeling dominant can become addictive. When in these types of criminal circles, anyone could be called upon and required to take part in protecting the gang. Backing out or running away in the heat of conflict would class a person as a coward and this could mean a quick-fire exit out of the group.

I wasn't aware of physical violence on this level happening every day, however there was a lot more non-physical, psychological violence taking place, which can be just as damaging. Violence is the destructive response to toxic emotions and the conflict that spreads from violent behaviour is infectious. Consider the minority who manifest the bigger global wars, in relation to the billions of us on this planet who experience the suffering of its ripple effects. Wars are happening all the time in more ways than we are aware of.

The Topmen were also the main buyers for stolen goods, though of course they were mostly interested in gold and diamonds. In my early days as a thief, nobody in our little group knew much about gold and even less about diamonds and their real worth. We had no idea what carat they were or how to tell the difference between a cubic zirconia and a real diamond. The only carrot I knew was the vegetable! However, The Topman I mainly dealt with (who I will call 'TC' - Top Cat) did know, because he took his gold to 'The Garden' (Hatton Garden) in London to a few older gold dealers. The professionals in London had taught TC what he needed to know, and over time, Jason learnt from him too.

There was good money in gold and especially in diamonds. If the buyer could blag a few 18ct rings then they would be on an extra bonus. If somebody was offering £1.20 for 1 gram of 9ct Gold then it was probably worth £2. This way they made something on the deal too. Not many criminals checked out the current gold and silver rate, or even knew how, they just took what was offered. Although later on when we got savvier with experience, we made a lot more money once we were in the know. One good thing about TC, was he always had cash and could pay out for the gold there and then, job done. It seemed fair if he was making a bit of profit on top, that's the food chain. No point in getting grief messing around with other dealers wanting to rip you off or that didn't even have the cash to pay out on the spot. 'Cash rules everything' was the motto. Everyone was out to make money from everyone else. That was the nature of the beast.

THE ROCK STAR

Another fear for any Topman was getting robbed by RockStars. Not the kind that played in rock bands, but the kind that were heavily addicted to crack. They were known for robbing houses and people to fulfil their addiction to crack cocaine. The drug was also known as 'rock', hence being called a RockStar. They targeted drug dealers because they knew they could get drugs, money (or both) and of course a drug dealer couldn't grass to the police could they?

These crackheads' manic and unpredictable behaviour stood out and was best avoided. Jason had become quite well known around town for a multitude of reasons, including drug dealing. A known RockStar had cottoned onto his operation and was trying to get hold of him. It wasn't difficult to find out who was dealing on the estates, doing well and primed to be robbed.

One day, the 'Star came looking to score a draw. Jason knew he was a crackhead and on opening the door decided it wasn't a good idea to sell anything to him. Instead, he offered him a telephone number of somebody else he may be able to visit. (Pass on the fear, as it were.) At this point, the 'Star stepped in and followed Jason upstairs as he went to get a pen and write down the number.

As Jason walked into the kitchen, the 'Star put a knife to his belly, and said, "Where is it? Where's the cash?"

Jason said, "I ain't got any." Meanwhile, the 'Star was patting him down looking for cash. Jason pulled out his wallet and there was only £5 inside. The 'Star took it and ran into the front room where he ripped the video recorder from under the TV and ran off down the stairs and out the door. He didn't even take the remote control!

The crackheads we knew were running on high levels of anxiety. What is anxiety at the core? Fear. The next 'hit' (drug intake) for them was life or death. They were so hooked on the drug that they were quite literally out of control. This is why they were so dangerously unpredictable. Just being in the presence of a person like this made me feel on edge and nervous.

In the early hours of the next morning, Jason's girlfriend woke him up and said that somebody was in the flat. Yes, you guessed it, the RockStar was back for the TV and the remote control! Diana and Jason stayed in the bedroom with the door shut and just waited, listening. They could hear the intruder making their way around the flat and heading towards the bedroom.

On hearing him approach, Jason opened the door just wide enough to stab a samurai sword through the crack in the door. The sword went straight through the 'Star's arm. But they didn't know this at the time. All they knew was that he didn't go any further towards the bedroom, but instead, bleeding heavily, he made his way back to the front room and took the TV. Let's pause for a minute just to put this into perspective; it was a 35" screen TV, very big and very heavy. No lightweight flat screens in those days. It took two men to carry it into the flat, but only one man on crack to take it out. That's what crack does to a person. They're only interested in the next hit. All he left behind was a blood stain down the walls of the flat leading to his exit. It would not have been very hard for Sherlock Holmes to figure out who was the culprit! I wondered what must have happened to him after he left the flat. How far he got with that huge TV and if anybody else saw him, and what they must have thought if they did. I was shocked to witness the extent of what humans will do to maintain their destructive and addictive habits.

DRIVING ME CRAZY

Jason had taken me on as his protégé. He enjoyed teaching me new things, because I listened. One day, he said to me "Come around tomorrow if you want, and I'll teach you how to drive."

I was almost 17 and too young to drive but this sounded exciting. I learned to drive in a Gold Mark 2 escort. That was a crazy day. Driving around the block, with Jason saying: "You ain't stopping till you get it," and "Get them feet working boy, clutch! Easy! Steady!" The car was bouncing around and I was holding up traffic. People were looking at me as I bounced past, revving the engine high. I kept stalling the car while thinking the police could pull me over at any minute.

But eventually, I got it and passed my driving test with flying colours. It was really easy to pass illegally, no paperwork or tests or anything like that.

My first car was an automatic 3ltr Ford Capri with leather 'Ricaro' bucket seats and 'pepper pot' wheels. Alloy wide rim wheels were all the rage at the time. The fatter the tyre the fatter your wallet. The Capri has the longest chassis known to man, and I couldn't see over the steering wheel, let alone the end of the bonnet. (Remember though, I thought I was a man.) I had to use a child booster seat and cushions just to see out of the windscreen.

Ford Capri - My First Car

This was the first of many cars to follow. Some of the cars we owned we couldn't keep for long because they became hot, meaning they were involved in a crime or being driven illegally. And we never knew who was watching our actions. There was one car we purchased that caused me more hassle than it was worth. A red Cortina to be exact, it was a right old banger and it was huge. A beast it was. I hadn't been driving manual shift much and this Cortina's clutch was aggravating the fuck out of me because I just couldn't consistently find the biting point.

One day, we were on 'runnings' and had to see an associate named Denzil and drop off some stuff at his house which had an extremely steep driveway, like a rocket launch pad. Jason was inside doing the deals and I was waiting in the car on the driveway, when Adrian, another friend of his, pulled up at the top of the drive, blocking me in. I made him aware I was leaving soon and asked him to reverse up so I could drive out before he parked.

Adrian was your cool black man, and known for being a bit of a fighter. He owned a brand-new VW Golf with all the trimmings. I asked him again to move back. I could see he did reverse a little, but I couldn't see clearly out of the windscreen. Like I said, I was having trouble with the clutch and this was a bit of a pressured moment as I was being observed. I gave the car some good acceleration, because I needed to hit the clutch's biting point to get me up the damn hill. It was the mightiest hill start of all hill starts. I found the biting point and slammed the accelerator to the floor and crunch, I drove straight into Adrian's shiny new car and ripped the bumper off.

"Oh shit!" I heard myself say. I pulled the handbrake up sharpish and got out the car. As soon as I was out the door I started apologising.

At this point, I saw him searching for something on his back seat. I walked closer, saying, "Sorry about that, don't worry I'll sort it, I'll pay for it." Then at that point I saw he had a metal bar in his hand. He looked angry, so I kept apologising.

"Hey, man, don't worry it's cool," I said, while his girlfriend, who was inside the car, was shouting, "Adrian, stop, leave it." That's when I decided not to hang around anymore, the fear and adrenalin hit me, boom. It was fight, flight or freeze time, and I decided to fly like an eagle, because that felt like the best option due to the circumstances. I ran up the road as fast as I could, but he was faster, and all I could feel was the metal pipe hitting the back of my head. I kept running traverse up the middle of the road, trying to dodge the hitting, while putting my hands up to protect the back of my head as the hits kept coming. One hit my finger and dislocated it, then one hit me on the ear and cut my ear open. By then I was screaming, I couldn't get away so I turned around and ran back while still being hit all the way back to the house.

I ran into the garden and fell on the floor. Everyone was out because Adrian's girlfriend had been screaming and calling everyone. Denzil was saying, "Alright, Adrian, that's enough, that's enough, he's done, he's done." And Adrian replied something like, "You best pay, you best pay. You iiiiiiiiiiiidiooooot," and I was laid on the floor shouting, "Yeah yeah yeah I said I'll pay, I said I'll pay." I thought he was the idiot because he clearly wasn't listening to me in the first place.

His girlfriend was screaming, telling him he was stupid and that I was just a boy. I just laid there on the floor, keeping my head down with blood on my face and a swollen head. Jason was dismayed. I was taken to the hospital with concussion. My mum was called to the hospital and the police were called too, they wanted me to report the person who had attacked me. But I didn't. Grassing on anyone in this world was not an option, especially if you wanted to stay in it.

Later, when I was released from hospital, we got stoned and was laughing about the whole scenario, especially Jason who said, "I leave you alone for five minutes and you smash a man's car and get battered while I'm just trying to earn us a buck. I had to pay something like £300 for that beating."

After that day I mastered clutch control and hill starts were my specialty.

5 1

BOG ROLL

Jason had many flash cars and he invested a lot of money into exceptional sound systems. He owned customised Capris, Golf GTIs, BMW 325i Convertibles, limited-edition Alpha Romeos and Escort XR3I Convertibles, to name a few. I was a young boy developing my ego identification, caught up in the ideas of image, status and objects identifying me. Shit like this had meaning, and I felt privileged to drive them.

It didn't take long for me to become a Boy Racer. I won't say this is my proudest title and I would probably have denied it if you'd asked me. However, I did enjoy racing friends and strangers at every opportunity. Flying around the roads like a maniac, thinking I was cool. I recall pulling up at traffic lights and revving the engine, looking out at people in their cars and then racing them off the traffic lights. Pure ego-boosting adrenalin hit. I was basically racing with myself which is an interesting concept. Always wanting to be first, wanting to be number one. I wanted to be the best. I wanted to have the loudest car stereo, the best car, the best girls, the best everything. Which is funny, because my cars were rubbish and my stereos weren't great either. But this was a way of declaring my identity and showing my status. I was making statements with the music I played, the cars I drove, the way I walked and talked, the people I hung out with, the girls I attracted, and the places I went to.

I aimlessly cruised around most days. I loved driving, listening to music and enjoying the freedom that driving offered. Meeting up with friends. Bumping randomly into others. No real agenda just going with the flow. Circling around the city centre numerous times, heading to other towns close by, living in the moment, seeking the unexpected.

Tooting the horn at hot girls and women as we passed on by, because I needed to let them know that I thought they were sexy and deserved to be tooted at. Obviously they understood this as I drove past at 40mph right? The horn was like a wolf whistle. I was horny, that's for sure. It was not uncommon to pick up girls who wanted to be driven around and entertained. It was part of the lifestyle. They seemed to love flirting too and the potential of sexual encounters was exciting. I loved having sex in cars.

I'd drive to familiar places around the town where many went to either smoke drugs, or if you were lucky, have sex *and* smoke drugs. It was a beautiful play of polarity. Moving through the motions. Smoking a few joints, talking the talk. Knowing where it was leading but playing the game of lustful seduction. And then when the time felt right, making that move and hoping it all worked out. If the car windows got all Tina Turnered (steamy windows) then of course shit got hot and spicy.

During that first year of driving illegally, I was pulled over numerous times and became known for my blagging (lying) techniques. Police were always patrolling the area and we were on their hit list as suspects to keep an eye on and stop and search at will. In my world, the police always seemed be watching and intimidating me, but looking back at past photos, you can clearly see I looked way too young to drive. I looked dodgy as fuck. I would have pulled myself over.

Back in those days, police didn't ask for driving details on the spot. Instead, you would be given a piece of paper which requested to view the tax, MOT and driving licence documents at the local police station. It was easy to lie because I would give a false name to the police, tick some boxes and sign the form and they would send me on my way. I was often shocked that I got away with it. I wouldn't be going to any police station to produce documents, would I? After a while, driving illegally and lying became the norm even though it didn't always work out well for us.

One time, a fuel station had reported us for doing a drive-off, which we didn't do, not in our own car and especially not for £10. Jason had paid for our petrol, but the attendant didn't ring it through on the right pump, so instead of rectifying his mistake he called 999 and reported us for driving off without paying. Later that night, I drove past a police car and they turned around sharpish with the blue lights flashing.

Ah, the blue lights. They bring back so many memories. I tried to get away, but the automatic BMW 316 I was driving was as slow as a snail. After a hot pursuit of about

300 metres, I pulled over. The police walked up to the car slowly, as they do, and asked if it was my car? To which I replied cheekily: "Indeeeeeeed Officer." Then they asked my name, to which I replied: "Robert Smith."

I knew his address details, and for some strange reason it was the first name that came to mind. Now, Robert Smith was no criminal, just a nice boy. The police said, "Robert Smith?" and I said, "Indeeeeeed!" I don't know where the elongated 'indeed's came from at the time, but on reflection I know this was cockiness derived from the fear I was feeling. Anyway, it didn't take long for them to arrest me, handcuffs on and off for a little ride in a police car.

The police said they wanted to check the car over to see if it was stolen and of course they clearly sensed I wasn't Robert anyway. At this time, Granville, the officer in charge, was one of the scariest coppers we had come across. Most British cops looked overweight and unfit, but not Granville. He was a fit black man, could run bloody fast and was known for catching criminals. (Obviously, nobody liked him!) Granville had been into my cell on numerous occasions, asking what my real name was and I kept saying, "Robert Smith" and he kept saying, "You're lying, I know you're lying, just tell us the truth."

The fear and anxiety which was flowing through me when I was in the cell was pretty intense. My mind was all over the place, with thoughts of what may or may not happen, what I had done and not done previously, what they might know or not know and so on. I started to convince myself that I was in fact Robert Smith. The crunch came when Granville came in and I was laying down, eyes closed, trying to take my mind away from the situation. He pulled me up from the bed, pushed me against the wall and said, "Listen, stop fucking around and wasting police time, we know you're not Robert, how many brothers have you got?"

And I said, "One." Because I knew Robert had a brother. As I spoke these words, I realised I didn't know his real name, only his nickname!

Granville replied, "Yes! Correct, what's his name?"

It was at this point I knew I was caught out and knew it would probably be best to tell the truth and get charged and move on. Of course, I chose not to be that sensible. Instead I replied, "BOG ROLL!"

He said, "BOG ROLL!? You taking the piss?"

I said, "No, BOG ROLL! We call him BOG ROLL!"

At this point he put me down and said, "You're a joker. We have just been up to Robert's house and funnily enough he was in bed. I knew you were lying but wanted to hear it from your mouth."

With that statement he slammed the cell door and I lay there on the plastic mattress, feeling cold and caught out, while awaiting the consequences of my actions. An hour later I was interviewed after calling our gang's solicitor. We all had the same solicitor because he represented the unemployed and we all got legal aid. He had successfully represented a lot of the gang and the Topman used him, so we did too.

I was questioned and Granville said, "If I wanted to disclose some information about anyone I could." (Meaning did I want to 'grass' anyone up, or 'snitch' on anybody) but I declined and got charged with driving illegally and giving a false name. One tag to my name and added to the police awareness scheme. One disappointed family woken up in the middle of the night and one step up the ladder of trust within the gang, because I never grassed on anybody, but instead messed the police around all night.

THE GOLD RUNS

Now I was a 'driver', I was invited to drive to London to take gold to The Garden. These trips were called a 'Gold Run', and we were the pirates, making a perilous journey to Hatton Garden to weigh-in and get paid for the treasures we had found at sea. To get a good deal it was essential to know the right people or you would get ripped off.

The gold runs were very scary because we could be carrying anything from £1000 to £10,000 worth of gold, watches and silver. It was never worth making the journey until there was a good amount to weigh in and of course it was worth waiting for the price of gold to be at its highest value to make the most money.

Bogey on the lip became the nickname of the person we dealt with most. I'm hoping you are aware by now that it helped to have nicknames in this line of work. As I said with Swamp Foot, nicknames created themselves from random life experience and then these nicknames became code names. Think about Tarantino's film *Reservoir Dogs* when they were all named after colours. Mr Pink was not very happy.

Bogey on the lip got his name because that is what he said once to Jason while he was looking at some gold. It was funny because he wasn't looking at either of us when he spoke, he must have seen Jason had something on his lip, like a bit of food or something, and just randomly said, "Bogey on the lip!" Neither of us knew if we'd heard him right at first; then he said it again, "Bogey on the lip." Then we looked at each other and Jason wiped his lips because he did have a bit of food on them. I couldn't contain myself, I tried to remain professional, but I was in stitches.

The thing is, I didn't want to laugh out loud because of the serious atmosphere of the event taking place. It's important to act professional when dealing with these kinds of people. When you're in unfamiliar territory and you don't know the dealers well or what they are capable of, it's not a good idea to laugh at them. Bogey was a middle-aged man who spoke under his breath and always said, "Is that it?" Even if there was a lot of gold. His other favourite saying was, "No big stones?" (meaning diamonds). Bogey had a little room with a big safe in it and a few old framed paintings on the walls.

On the safe doors, he had stuck a page from the newspaper with the European football tournament cup table. His jacket was hung up in the corner. On his wooden desk, there were gold testing tools, scales with a silver tray to put the gold in, acids to test the gold was real, an eyeglass, files, pens, bits of gold, and some old watch faces. He had a sidekick who sometimes popped in with bundles of cash in a money holster under his long jacket.

Sometimes, to get the money to pay us, they would send the gold off to be melted down and sold up the road. Then their assistant would come back with the cash.

It always felt risky to be in London because the police were often watching The Garden and there were private security guards on every corner due to all the drive by smash and grab robberies that occurred there. This made it a very hot place to enter. We had to hide the gold under the bonnet of the car all the way to London. Then we would stop somewhere safe, before the destination, and put the bags down our pants (if not too heavy) and off we'd trot. Everything used to go down our pants in those days. Amazing what a good set of Y-fronts could hold! London was the city of dreams. This was my life. I thought I was living the good life, having fun being somebody of importance. Living on the edge, breaking the system's rules and writing my own.

BRIGHT LIGHTS, BIG TITTIES

Throughout my career as a criminal, Amsterdam was one of the only places where I could take my mind off the day to day hustle and relax a little. I felt it gave all of us a sense of freedom to smoke weed legally all day in coffee shops. We would eat hash cake, get extremely drunk, play pool, and hang around doing very little other than laughing, eating, male bonding, clubbing and paying for sex.

On my first trip to Amsterdam, at the age of sixteen, it was scary for me to look at women dressed in sexy lingerie in neon-lit rooms. The idea of actually entering those rooms for sex was terrifying. But this was to be my sexual initiation, it was part of the male bonding, for my friends to jeer me on to sleep with prostitutes. Was I man enough?

Before we went on the trip, I was still worried I hadn't had sex and I had this feeling of shame that I couldn't lose my virginity by paying for it. Somehow it felt wrong. I had a belief that prostitutes were not as worthy because they slept with hundreds of men for money.

I told myself I would have to have sex before leaving for Amsterdam. Jason must have picked up on my anxiety because he made regular comments leading up to the trip like, "You lost your fucking virginity boy? Wait till you get in the Dam boy, plenty to choose from there. You can fuck Diana if you want, she'll teach you some tricks." And other statements along those lines.

Don't get me wrong, Jason's girlfriend Diana was very sexy. She was an older woman, dark brown hair, tanned skin, scrumptious body with a cheeky and mischievous personality. She wore sexy, provocative clothes and had a lot of sex appeal. She had three kids from a previous marriage and left them all for an affair with Jason. She loved the excitement and the fast life. She loved living on the edge, the naughtiness and the bad boy image Jason held. She was like his sex slave and they had a lot of lustful passionate fire between them.

Jason loved her in the best way he knew how. She was always by his side no matter how he treated her and at times it wasn't very nice, quite violent in fact. But she would do anything to please him, cooking, cleaning, washing and ironing his clothes, massaging and powdering his feet, driving him around. She was at his beck and call and waiting on his every word. He called her 'Gangster bitch' and would often say, "Harden up or pussy out!" which was his way of saying basically deal with the situation or if you can't, then you pussy out, which means you lack courage. He would shame her or anyone else with this term. It's like saying you don't have the balls.

Jason always said to me, "Get a girl to love you and they

will do anything you want them to." So maybe this helps you to understand why she was a little intimidating for me at this age. I think deep down everyone in our gang fantasized about her. I know I did at times. There were not so many women around, so she got all the attention and lapped it up. Of course, not everyone offered their women for friends to sleep with but Jason was far from normal.

I sheepishly avoided answering his suggestion numerous times and managed to hook up with another girl from the estate. A friend tipped me off saying she was easy and eager. He had already slept with her. I was keen to hook up with her quickly and do what I had to do.

While I'd like to say my first time was a beautiful experience of what it means to unite with another body in sexual union, and that we were swinging from the chandeliers all night in ecstatic states of bliss, it was actually over before it began, thanks to my slightly premature nature. I had experienced many wet dreams and never really masturbated before this time and the arousal was too much to handle. I'm not entirely sure you can call it losing my virginity, but I continued with the attempt of still inserting my limp penis with a floppy sperm filled condom attached into her vagina and just pumped a few times. She was extremely wet and aroused so I just hoped she didn't notice and carried on through the motions. This was not the result I had been anticipating. Little did I know that premature ejaculation was going to become an embarrassing theme for me, more times that I would care to imagine.

A few days later off we flew to Amsterdam.

The Red Light District was a whole new experience. Having sex with a stranger; paying upfront and having my penis wiped with a flannel before I left the room was a vulnerable affair, and 'wash and go' became the running joke. The smell of condoms and musty lust permeated the streets, and when mixed with weed, it made the air subtly hypnotising as we walked through the tight alleyways which were full of mostly men, viewing women like meat in a butcher's window; bartering at the doors while trying to make eye contact and get a nod of confirmation.

Now and then, the smell of piss would fill our nostrils, and there was one alley that just stunk of urine, where men would empty themselves of beer. Hence we named it 'Piss Alley'. There were drugs being sold on most street corners by what we called 'Mulukans' (don't ask me where that name came from). These were sly street dealers and thieves, either selling drugs or leading you to the dealers who had what you wanted, and at other times, pick pocketing or robbing gullible foreigners who were chasing the high. That was their profession, they were ready to pounce at any moment. The alleyways were dark and dingy, with just the dim streetlights and the pink and purple glare from the neon lit sex rooms illuminating our way.

The time had come, I could feel the pressure from my nervous energy building up, I was stoned and a little drunk, and I could hold it off no longer. It was my time to choose a woman. I walked around viewing many windows while the guys were pointing and saying, "That one? Or that one? She's alright. That one?" and "Come on, boy, don't take too long, they are all better than anything you've had." They were all laughing, me included.

I wanted to choose one I was attracted to. It was not easy and the anxiety in the stomach was all-consuming. It wasn't as scary as stealing from someone's house, but the feeling in my body was similar. Hundreds of butterflies rising from the pit of my stomach into my chest. Nothing could go wrong could it? It's just sex! At least, that's what I said to try to convince myself.

Anyway, I chose a woman I had seen a few times and this time she gave me a wink and called me towards her with her index finger. Shit this was it. I walked up to the door. The guys were jeering me on, "Go on, boy, you can do it, she's fucking fit." The woman opened her door ajar and I asked how much, she said her price and I agreed. I was going to agree no matter what she said, but this was the procedure, right? I walked in and she locked the door and closed the curtain behind me. Then she asked me what I wanted. Suck or fuck? I tell her fuck, so she ushers me to get undressed. I laid down on the bed and she put a condom on me in a very smooth and slick way. Clearly, she had done that before! I can't recall every detail, but the main thing is, she fucked me. All I remember was this beautiful woman riding me like a horse shouting, "Rooster, oh yeah, big boy, rooster, rooster yeahhh."

For me, this was really losing my virginity. I put it down to the alcohol and drugs, but I lasted for some time until ejaculation. The whole rooster thing was so funny and surreal that I definitely walked out of her room a different person. It felt like in that moment she initiated me in the way a woman wants to be fucked. She did all the leading, and it felt like she knew what she wanted or she knew what a man wanted. I wasn't sure at this stage, maybe she just knew how to act and at this point of my sexual exploration, I didn't care too much if it was an act or not. It felt real to me. I was extremely happy to be fucked in that way. I walked out feeling proud and of course the gang were celebrating too. 'Rooooster' became my nickname as Jason and a few others had heard her screaming it from outside as they awaited eagerly to see my face.

Getting up to no good was all part of the excitement. I would get a pat on the back whenever I had the courage to enter another red lit room and the positive reinforcements from my friends carried me through until it became just another part of the excursion. It was always a little nerve-wracking, but like anything, after a few times it just became another thing to do and was no biggie. I enjoyed the anticipation, and getting high in the knowing that at some point there would be guaranteed sex. It felt great to allow the process to build up slowly by visiting a peep show or sex show to get aroused before that moment of walking around the canals and alleys to choose the next hot woman to fuck. Sometimes, men would sneak off to sleep with a woman they had spotted but didn't want anyone else to judge them on their selection; especially if it was an oversized mampi (which was the nickname we used for an obese woman). There was a street we named 'Mampi Row' and everyone egged each other on to sleep with an obese black woman for the experience. I didn't explore that option, but I was curious.

Forget the Hollywood dream, this was the drug dealer's

dream. Amsterdam was our Hollywood, bright lights and big titties. It was the escape from our daily criminal life that we all craved. Payment for all the grief and stress the world of crime created. Stress is stress, it doesn't matter what profession or lifestyle creates it. Once stressed, there is the need for release and whether a criminal or not, it's become quite normal in our society to use stimulants or other means to relieve the emotional anxiety that stress creates.

Alcohol, drugs, sex, TV, gambling, video games, social media, food, exercise and a multitude of other activities are what we have at our disposal to distract, numb and help us cope with stress and addiction that surviving in a dysfunctional society creates.

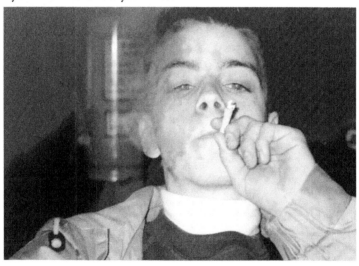

Smoking Dope in Amsterdam

Another reason for the Dutch excursion was that we could buy amazing sticky 'skunk' weed that wasn't available in the UK. If you had this quality of weed, for which there was great demand, it sold like hotcakes at home, hence the reason for going away so many times a year.

Of course, skunk is grown everywhere now and widely available, but at the time it was the new drug in town. Once this treasure was discovered, the question was, how to smuggle it back home? This was another way of gaining status and being named the Topman. 'Dam Skunk' (skunk from Amsterdam) would sell for £10 per gram in the UK, and twenty grams cost approximately £45, so there was around £150 or more profit to be made on one small smuggled ball. Add the exchange rate profit and it was a money-maker which made sense. Now that's a Dam-good profit.

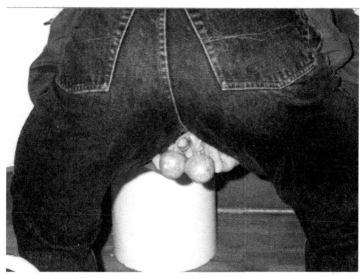

Skunk Balls

To get it into small balls the skunk needed to be compressed very tightly. The stickiness of the weed allowed it to be compacted into the size of a squash ball, and then the ball would be put into two condoms and tied off. That way, it could be pushed into our arseholes with ease. Men were able to carry approximately six balls or more (depending on how clear the passage was). It was quite possible to make around £900 for a weekend's work. Just another way to earn money and the bonus was, it paid for the trip as well. Eventually more of the drug was required, as the demand grew, so people started doing smuggling runs with girls too. A girl could obviously smuggle more because she could use her vagina too, maybe ten or more balls in total. Add this to the four or six balls a man could smuggle and it was a good earner. Take the girlfriend to Amsterdam for a romantic, dirty weekend and then ask her to smuggle drugs! It's what they call a 'win-win' in this business.

Unfortunately, the smuggling took away the relaxing holiday factor for me, because a few days before heading home, guess what arose? Stress and paranoia, the two best friends of fear. But those feelings soon transformed into relief and satisfaction when we arrived home safe, and then were literally smoking the good shit.

PISSING MY PANTS

I returned to Amsterdam many times after that first adventure. On one of the trips (trip being the operative word) I went with the Cellar Dwellers. Among the many things we got up to, was one of the most profound, yet frightening experiences of my life. Amsterdam has a reputation for people taking psychedelics and tripping to other dimensions within themselves, and you could say that my trip was an extreme example.

Though I had taken magic mushrooms a few times before, the results had always been fairly mild. I had experienced altered states of consciousness, in the form of entering a state of heightened presence and a lot of laughter. Which for someone like me who loves to laugh, was a lot of fun. I wasn't a big fan of psychedelics, I think I missed that era by a few years and the groups I grew up with didn't experiment too much with these so-called harder drugs. I was more attracted to weed and ecstasy.

On this particular trip to Amsterdam, I found myself

in a bar with the Cellar Dwellers, and everybody seemed a little low, tired and not sure what to do next. We had been stoned for days and the buzz was wearing thin, or just not hitting the spot. But buying class A drugs in Amsterdam was never really our intention. It would make us targets for the 'Mulekans' and you never know for certain what you could be buying.

Drinking in Amsterdam

Despite this, it was suggested we buy some magic mushrooms from a bar we knew, and everybody was up for it. The most stressful thing about taking class A drugs was the fact that the outcome was even more uncertain and less controlled than smoking weed or drinking alcohol, but we were willing to take the risk for a new buzz.

There were about fifteen tiny mushrooms in the small bag that was thrown across the table to me. I thought they were quite small, poured them all into the palm of my hand and washed them all down with a beer. I've never been one for reading instructions or manuals, but on this occasion after taking them, it was brought to my attention that the now empty bag had a piece of paper inside describing the type of mushrooms they were and the way they advise you to take them. It said something along the lines of: 'Very strong mushrooms to be taken one at a time'.

On seeing this and having just swallowed fifteen of them, we all thought this was hilarious. Nothing much happened for about 45 minutes, but then the laughter began, lots of laughter. I had experienced mushroom laughter before, so this stage was manageable. What happened next however was another story! I'm not sure if the course of events actually transpired in this particular order as parts are still quite clouded due to moving beyond the normal structures of time and space, but I'm pretty certain that I took a trip to another dimension or four.

Some of the others had experimented with psychedelics before and decided we should go back to the hotel to smoke weed and experience the trip in their room. I went back to the hotel with them, just as the mushrooms started kicking in, which meant I didn't really know where I was anymore having crossed a threshold into an alternate reality. I recall rolling around the room sideways, up the walls, across the ceilings and then back down the other side and across the floor continuously. Then every now and then I would stop to ask everybody if I should do it again.

Obviously, this wasn't actually possible, and I wasn't really rolling around the walls, but instead trying to climb them. Which apparently led to me attempting to climb out of the window, three stories up. When my friends asked me to calm down, I slipped and knocked over a pint of water. In normal circumstances this doesn't sound like too much of a problem does it? But when I tripped, I slipped, hit my head on the sink and thought the spilled water was blood. This caused me to freak out as I thought something bad had happened to me. In this moment my friends, who were still coherent, decided it was best to get me out of the room and calm me down.

Problem is, wherever you are, becomes your trip and I was still in this deeply altered state of consciousness. While I know my friends were only trying to take care of me, it was not the best idea to release me onto the streets of Amsterdam. It started when I got outside the room and was walking down the stairs. As I put my hand onto the stair rail my whole hand and half of my body disappeared into the wall! Which was extremely fascinating and I wanted to continue doing it. It stopped when I was asked by the manager to leave the hotel. In his reality, I kept crushing myself into the wall, which was disrupting other guests and the hotel owner wasn't too amused.

Outside, it got really freaky. The whole of Amsterdam became a trip in this altered state and it was an eye-opener into what the brain/mind was capable of. Something was wrong and the normal boundaries of reality were gone. I was totally lost. Everything seemed multi-dimensional. Kind of dream-like, but it's very hard to describe with words. It was like the past, present and future were all happening at once. It didn't feel real as I knew real to be. My senses were heightened to the point where my ears hurt, because I could hear everything all at once. I could hear people talking far away in buildings, I was hearing the sounds of rats and of car tyres and engines, loud and clear. Then every human being I saw had the same heads as TC and his side kick. They were haunting me and I didn't like it. They kept looking at me everywhere I went. It was mentally disturbing.

I was standing on the main street of Damrak, which is the main touristic shopping street. I don't know how long ago I had left my hotel, but I realised I had to get back in there for safety. I remember searching my pockets and found a glass weed pipe. For some reason I thought this was the cause of my situation. I smashed it on the floor and the sound was excruciating. In that moment it all hit me; I must reverse everything which had happened to me, in order to find my way back home. I decided the answer was to run backwards down the streets of Amsterdam. Yes, backwards. And I agree that this decision must have looked hilarious for anyone watching. I had just become one of the memories or funny stories people would share with their friends when trying to describe their trip to Amsterdam. I was the guy who had clearly taken a bad trip.

As I was running backwards, I got stopped by two strangers who wanted to help me and I remember saying to them I had to get to 'The Grasshopper Bar' to meet my friends. They were trying to help me, but I freaked out for a moment and thought they were conspiring against me and setting me up for more danger. As I looked around in panic I spotted a friend on the streets, and I endeavoured to follow this character, but I couldn't seem to track him down so he probably wasn't real. If only I could find the hotel again.

Then it happened, there it was, I could see it in the distance. I was as happy as a person who had just seen water for the first time after walking in the desert for months.

I went to ring the buzzer but every time I pressed the doorbell my finger went through the button and door frame. Yet in reality, I was ringing the bell continuously and nobody was answering. It looked from the outside that I was causing a commotion, so the owners of a restaurant next door came out and beat me away from the building with a broomstick handle. This little scenario took me on another journey deeper into the streets of Amsterdam. It was a nightmare. I thought I had died, or was having an out of body, near death experience while I was stuck in some feedback loop from hell. I lost time completely. Finally, I blacked out.

When I came back to this reality I woke to find I was laid in the corner of the entrance of a 'Bureau de Change'. It was the very early hours of the morning and I had urinated in my sleep. My jeans were soaked through.

I had been tripping for around six hours or more. I stood up and peered into the window of the 'Bureau de Change'. I distinctly saw Phileas Fogg, or at least an old man with the longest moustache I had ever seen. This freaked me out a little. Was I still tripping? I was disorientated to say the least. I could sense I was in another country but was feeling displaced as I had forgotten I was in Amsterdam.

Slowly, my memory was returning. I looked around and the place was quiet, cold and had that calm morning feel of a city waking up. There were very few people around. I walked back towards the hotel which surprisingly was only a few buildings away. I found myself buzzing the buzzer which I had buzzed so many times throughout the psychedelic trip and nobody ever came, but this time my friend Richard arrived at the door and it was wonderful just to see his face. He opened the door and then very casually asked how I was and wondered where I had been. Which I found extremely ironic.

I said, "What the fuck? Where have I been? Where have you all been? Look at me, I've pissed my pants." He was laughing as only Richard could, and slightly concerned as he could see I was looking dishevelled. I made my way straight up to the room to clean myself up. While I was showering, the water hit my head and pushed me through the floor. My body disappeared. I felt like sponge and I wasn't sure which dimension I was in. I felt the best thing I could do was call my mum. I had to hear her voice for some sort of safety and sanity. I know if I have to call my mum, things are bad.

Getting High in a Coffee Shop in Amsterdam

Throughout the day, these sensations slowly wore off and then like any trip, this became an experience, a funny story to share. I was told by my friends that they were actually watching over me and that they had to get me out of the room because I was literally going crazy and freaking out. They knew I was having a bad trip, but of course couldn't reverse it. I felt alone and abandoned at the time and thought they could have supported me better in that state, but in hindsight we were just a group of boys wild and free. And in that moment, they did the best they could.

What did this teach me? Reality as I knew it, was not all that it seemed to be, and reminded me that we don't always see things as they are, we see things as we are, oh and it may also benefit me to read the small print.

EVERY CHOICE YOU MAKE - MAKES YOU

Forget Park Life, I was getting hooked on nightlife. And that included cocaine, ecstasy and sex. Enticed into seedy venues by the loud music, you could find me womanizing and dancing till the early hours. Or smoking copious amounts of marijuana, snorting cocaine off the back of toilet seats and washing pills of ecstasy down with a swig of rum and coke. I was thoroughly enjoying myself in the underworld of hedonism.

How to describe the buzz of clubbing? First, there was the anticipation of what a great night out it could be. Standing in the queue, hoping we all get in. Spruced up and equipped with drugs. Then the thrill of the lights in the dark nights. Heightened senses, and the potential of experiencing freedom through ecstasy. Taking drugs was always a gamble, as I never knew what would happen. What it would be like? Who would I meet? It was all unexpected.

Connection. Excitement. Freedom. That's what clubbing was for me. I've stood in so many queues at the entrances of night clubs. I couldn't name them all if I tried. What was the pull? Addiction, desire and lust.

Drugs took me to that same place of fear. The fear of taking a pill that could kill. I've been on dance floors when people have passed out and been removed by the ambulance crew. Some had overdosed. Thankfully that didn't happen every weekend, but the point is, it's risky taking drugs. Though you could argue that it's also risky crossing a busy road. I had decided I couldn't let the fear win. I was a rebel. And that's the line I walked when I decided to ingest man-made substances designed to get me high.

It was no different to breaking into someone else's house. The fear was my buzz. I would lay in bed late at night listening to and feeling my heart beat erratically, full of fearful thoughts that the drugs I'd taken may just kill me. But they didn't. Sadly, they have contributed to killing a few of my friends along the way. One took an overdose of heroin and another supposedly freaked out and committed suicide by jumping off the top of a multi-story car park. It was extremely hard for me to accept this story as the full truth, but he was found dead, and drugs were involved, so that was the scenario they went with. But I wouldn't say it was just the drugs that do the killing. There are many factors at play. And who ever knows what is really going on inside another human being?

As I opened myself wider to experience this darker world of hedonism, Jason and I went on a quest to sleep with one hundred women. Jason thought it would be a fun challenge and I happily agreed. Of course, I thought sleeping with one hundred women would be a great achievement in life.

Especially if I didn't prematurely ejaculate every time! I loved meeting new girls and playing Casanova. The Alpha male, the cream of the crop. I was a stud. Rooster's my name! As Jim Carrey's character in *The Mask* would say, "Somebody stop me!"

IN THE DEEP END

All seemed to be going well, aside from being caught in the middle of a conflict between two strong opposing polarities. Jason and Topcat had been friends for some years since the day TC had welcomed both Jason and Steve under his wing and into his operation. However, the time had come for Jason to fly the nest. Although he had a lot of respect for what TC had taught and shared with him, Jason was ready to go it alone and in his own way. He wanted to be his own Topman. And while I had been getting closer to them both, I was now in a pickle. There was the pull towards Jason into the world of hedonism, drugs, nightlife, travelling to other countries and sex, and there was the pull towards the authority of TC with the power, status, drugs, and money. When I look back, I see how the choice was a bit crazy, because both role models were basically offering the same thing. I was a criminal, no matter which choice I made. To be with Jason felt more fun and freer, but there was no certainty, and as strange as it may sound, there felt like some weird sort of security and fatherly attachment to TC. Could I become his next TopBoy?

During this tense time there was a crisis playing out at home too. My mum was living with a man named Craig who she didn't want to be with anymore. He was not treating her with any respect, and was causing a whole heap of tension and stress in the house, and home life was disruptive. Thankfully, Lloyd's dad Roger was the only man that had ever used physical violence, but relationship abuse takes many forms and it could have become physical for all I knew, and I didn't want that. I felt guilty because I introduced Craig to my mum. He was a friend and someone I had looked up to. He was helping me to look for a good job and taught me how to brick lay and gave me work as a labourer. I always wanted my mum to have someone who would care for her and Craig had a very kind heart and was always generous to me. Their relationship started out lovely, as relationships often do, and mum seemed happy with the attention and connection. They were quite sweet together at first. He was a lot younger than her. A bit of a toyboy you could say.

After they had been seeing each other for a while, he moved in, brought a German shepherd dog into the family, and brought other life experiences and adventures. He was a professional craftsman earning good money, and one of his hobbies was training to be a pilot. He once took us up in the small training plane, and that was a very unique experience. But I witnessed how the environment of Castlefield soon gripped him and it wasn't so long until he was in the gang circles, buying his dope, running errands for TC and some of the other boys. After a while his dope addiction got him more active in the gang, and he even came on a few trips to Amsterdam with us which was weird because he was with my mum and I knew he slept with prostitutes, as we all did.

Craig was becoming complacent, his energy dramatically changed, he became paranoid and controlling and then he began checking out from Mum. It was as if Mum had become a mother figure for him. His mother had died of cancer not long before and I think this was part of the attraction to my mum in the first place. He loved his mum dearly and losing her was not easy for him cope with. But I didn't join these dots until later in life. Near the end of his relationship with my mum, it was becoming intense and his actions were not acceptable in my book. He was using the house, was lazy, smoking weed, and stopped caring for himself and his dog. I wanted him to leave but he kept lingering around. He was older and physically stronger than me; not someone I could easily throw around or I would have thrown him out months before.

After a number of disrespectful and dominating incidents, I said enough is enough. Craig wasn't listening to my mum's requests and I could feel her helplessness. It was a last straw when I found out he was watching porno movies late at night on the sofa and falling asleep stoned. The whole situation was pissing me off and I had to find a way to get him out of Mum's life. I felt responsible. I said to Mum, "You need to leave Castlefield because this guy's not going to leave the house until you leave. That way he will get the message."

I didn't know who to ask for help and was disappointed

in Steve because I felt he didn't do anything to support me at the time. He was caught up in his own life and had also become friends with Craig and it was all weird. I don't even recall all the details and timelines, but I just had this random idea that if she left Castlefield for a short while and took my brother Lloyd with her to live with her parents (which was in another part of England, a few hours' drive away), then it would force Craig to leave. It's crazy that measures like this even had to happen. I was planning on possibly going with them, but instead I said that Steve and I would look after the house until she returned. Reluctantly, she agreed.

This was happening in the same period that the police were clamping down on TC's actions. He'd been arrested a number of times and really needed to move his operation to get the heat off himself. He was considering his options, and I don't recall how it happened, whether he suggested it or Steve and I suggested it, but somehow it was agreed for him to start running his operation from mum's house. Perfect decision? Probably not.

Through this series of events I had chosen TC over Jason. TC was always looking for someone else to do his dirty work, and this time, that someone else was me.

Suddenly we found ourselves with a three-bedroom house, running the Topman's organisation. What the fuck just happened? It's mostly a blur, but in essence our house was the new dealers' den where we could all hang out, play cards, computer games and party. Craig left the building. I could invite women round to have sex and live it up as I wished. Plus it served its purpose of taking the heat off TC, so all seemed well. A win-win on all levels, except for my mum's house. What had I done?

We had all these clients coming by to buy drugs. I'm talking high quantities of marijuana, kilos of the stuff. We were weighing it out into manageable quantities and hustling daily. I became the main dealer on the estate. Seventeen years old and co-running this huge operation. Can you imagine? It was, in hindsight, you could say, very foolish.

My ego was loving it though. I was the man, right? I was running the show. Look at me, I'm TC's right hand man. Watch ya back, fools.

After some months, Steve and I could feel the strain and imbalance. There were highlights, but also many low moments too. I was on the edge and the paranoia was consuming me. I got a taste of what it must be like for Topmen. Selling drugs on that scale wasn't all it was cracked up to be, and not as great as I had projected. I was missing mum and my brother Lloyd and it felt wrong that people kept coming into her house all the time. I felt like I had deceived her, making her believe that I was taking care of the house, when I wasn't. She didn't know we were using her house in this way. I was lying to myself and her.

Steve was also not as I knew him to be, he was due to have a baby with his girlfriend and was also feeling like leaving the whole gang lifestyle. Jason was his closest friend and since he wasn't around much anymore, I now understand that Steve was feeling the grief of that relationship ending along with the stress of the many life adjustments of having an unplanned baby on the way. Steve didn't need to be going to jail in the near future, he had got away with enough close shaves. He had to change his ways to become a reliable parent for the son he would love deeply and who would change his life for the better, even if he couldn't see that at this time.

And then it all seemed to come to a head at once. Everyone was affected in one way or the other by the choices Jason, Steve and I had made. And of course we were all affected by previous choices made by others. The gang as I had known it to be was drifting apart and changing form. Everyone seemed to want to go their own way. It was all crumbling, or maybe that was just how I perceived it. I just wanted the whole operation to stop. It was too much for me to handle and I felt I made the wrong decision. I wanted out. I wanted to run towards Jason and the potential freedom and safe haven he represented. He became my light of opportunity. I had no other reference point.

I felt trapped by my agreement with TC and guilty too. I didn't want to hurt him either. He had also treated me with respect and trusted me with his money and business.

I know he was a manipulative man and he had his eye on everyone and everyone feared him. I feared him for multiple reasons too but he was also charismatic and kind, hence the pull to be like him. The past stories I had heard and from the direct experiences I had witnessed, I knew this man would not hesitate to hit friends with blunt instruments. He was unpredictable and that's fucking scary. Once he put a gun in a friend's mouth to threaten him and keep him in check because he felt he was getting too big for his boots.

He couldn't trust any of us fully. And you bet his paranoia contributed to our paranoia and our paranoia ironically made him trust us less. It was a vicious emotional circle. Fear was TC's greatest weapon and it was certainly an effective one.

I wished I could reverse the decision to use mum's house. I was absorbed by it and needed a way out. Though Steve felt the same way, this experience didn't necessarily bring us closer together, we were both feeling the pressure and I think deep down feared the worst outcome. But we are brothers and we loved each other to the core even if we struggled to communicate that love clearly. Steve backed me up on my decision as he always did, even if he didn't fully agree with my actions. We found ourselves in this messy scenario and we had to unite to free ourselves too. You could say he was in even deeper than me.

I just wanted to run away into the night and forget about it all. But life is not that easy is it? You could say this was a life lesson I couldn't avoid. When I make a choice, I must face the consequences of my actions. Rather than run away, I had to face it head on. So that's what I did. I made the decision to shut down the operation and leave Castlefield for a while. This final decision obviously didn't go down too well. It caused a lot of upheaval, and a lot more heated drama was about to kick off.

ESCAPING WASN'T EASY

I remember the weather on that day I chose to leave, it was gloomy and overcast. A friend of mine, Zak, came to help me move out. Jason said I could stay with him and Diana if I needed somewhere to crash. I instantly said yes, I just had to get away from Castlefield. It was getting way too much for me and I needed an escape plan.

TC had heard I was leaving. I knew for sure he was watching me from somewhere. Either from his front bedroom window or from a garden close by. It was not unusual for him to be hiding in people's gardens and listening through their windows. I kept having a lookout every now and then, to make sure the coast was clear. Zak and I loaded the car with some of my belongings and then just as I was about to drive off, Topman appeared out of nowhere with one of his sidekicks, brandishing a brick, saying "What the fuck you up to, you little cunt, where you off to?" before smashing the brick straight through the windscreen.

Zak and I jumped out fast, saying "What's up? What's

up?"

He replied "You know what's up, don't fucking talk to me you grass."

I replied, "Grass! What do you mean?" I wanted to defend myself, but I also knew not to back-chat him too much; so I said to Zak, "Let's leave."

Topman said "Yeah, you fucking well leave mate and if I see you again you'll get more than this." And some other explicit words. He then threw the brick at my car a few times. But the rage didn't stop there. They lifted my car onto its side by pushing and bouncing it up onto the curb. Then threw the brick a few more times at the car before walking off back to his lair. I waited a while before pushing the car back onto four wheels and kicking the windscreen out, then I drove to my new home. It was about ten miles away, and not having a windscreen was a nightmare because glass dust kept blowing into my eyes and I couldn't see clearly.

This event created more ripples of suffering, because a few nights later, we went to steal a windscreen from another car to replace mine. For every action, there is a reaction, either positive or negative.

I had finally got out of Castlefield. But I was on the run and worried what would happen next. I knew this decision meant losing friends and going back to Castlefield would be extremely dangerous. I went away for a while. I visited my mum. (As always, I know I'm in trouble when I need to call out to Mum.)

Then a few days later I got news that TC had sent his cronies in to do the job of vandalizing my mum's house. They graffitied the walls, literally smashed in the staircase, so it was almost impossible to get to the upstairs rooms. They ripped the whole place apart. They took whatever was worth taking and left the rest. It was a vicious thing to do. But it taught me some vital life lessons. The first one being that when you want to follow your truth, it's not guaranteed that everybody will be as happy as you about the change. Try to be aware of the unwritten agreements that are in place when you make decisions.

It didn't end there, of course. I still had to travel back into Castlefield now and then and just did my best to avoid encountering any violence, but I was still always on edge.

Despite wanting to escape the situation, I still considered TC to be a friend of sorts and my intentions were never to hurt him. I know I had let him down by changing my mind. I'm sure there was a part of him that liked me and didn't really want to harm me, I was just a little boy to him. He was more like a father pissed off with his son. He was fucked off, angry and wanted to teach me a lesson.

One day I was at Jason's mum's house and Jason said TC had summoned us up to his house as he knew we were in the area. That was the weird dynamic of the whole situation. We often visited and partly lived at Jason's mum's because Jason was also introverted and needed his own space away from Diana and anyone else at times. Whenever we visited the area we did our best to keep a low profile, but that wasn't so easy when his mum lived on the same street as TC. Of course, TC could see if our car was parked in the drive way or nearby. Deep down, we wanted to make peace, and thought it would be better for us all in the long run, so we decided to visit him.

As we approached TC's house, he was standing outside his gate waiting for us. I didn't see the Shillelagh (a wooden club) he had in his hand. Out of the blue he pulled it out and bang, hit me on the top of my head. "Ah fuck!" I said as I ran off down the road. Jason was surprised too and moved away quickly, but wasn't attacked. I can't remember clearly what happened next, but some aggressive words were shared as we fled. I could imagine he was proud of himself after that little surprise attack on an unarmed boy. He got to release his anger, made me feel small and warned off his supposed threat. It felt to me like a father smacking his boy for doing wrong.

Another time, Jason and I were ambushed while cleaning a car in his mum's driveway. TC and his sidekick came down the road looking aggressive, one holding an axe. His sidekick jumped on Jason and a tussle took place. More verbal abuse and shouting and then off again they went back to base. Random acts of violence were not unusual in those days. As they say, before it got better, it had to get worse.

I thought I was moving in the right direction. I had left Castlefield and my mum's house was no longer a drug dealer's den. I was living in a new area with Jason and Diana. New experiences and a new chapter were born. But it wasn't all rosy. I was still avoiding the destructive energy of what had happened. My world was disruptive and all over the place; I felt scared, unstable, confused, let down and sad. The savage violence and mental abuse that had come my way had taken its toll, and I was feeling the post-war waves of shock, the unsettling sense of trauma. Despite this, nothing much changed. I continued my crazy life of wheeling, dealing and stealing, attending the gym in the day, stealing at night, clubbing hard, and on the quest for sex at the weekends. I was still a rebel without a cause on the hedonistic path, unaware of the suffering I was enduring and of the pain I was causing along the way.

In a distorted way, I was free. It felt like I was doing new things, hanging around in new friend circles, and it seemed like a huge change was occurring. This change gave me hope. But there was a part of me which believed I would never really be able to leave Castlefield.

9OZ OF WEED & A CHEESE PLANT

BANG BANG BANG.

Ah, that familiar banging on the door.

I looked out of my window and saw police climbing the scaffolding which was up for maintenance repairs around the block of flats I was now living in with Jason and Diana. They surrounded the building, moving like spiders up the wall.

This was a BIG problem. I had an 8oz bag of weed in the flat. Silly, very silly. Nobody could have known I had the weed as I'd only stolen it a few nights before, so I needed to get rid of it. I ran to the toilet and contemplated flushing it away, but it was too big and wouldn't have flushed. I also resisted that choice as my greed was thinking about the money at stake. Then I thought of putting it down the air vent heating shaft. Which in hindsight, would have been the best idea, but I didn't. Instead, in my frenzy, I hid it underneath the cheese plant in the corner of my room.

Then simultaneously I remembered I had another 1oz

bag of weed in the pocket of a pair of trousers, not to mention a canister of CS gas close by. I frantically grabbed them both and put them in my pants pocket and tucked them in the dirty laundry bag. (I wasn't kidding when I told you, everything went down your pants in those days.)

It was a crazy thirty seconds. At the same time, I was telling Jason and Diana not to open the door. "Not yet," I said. A moment later, the door flew open and the police were in. When the police enter, they enter fast. They locked off all the rooms and told us to all get in the same room. There was shouting, noise and questioning. Immense fear and adrenalin were flowing through my body. The police enter with fear and force because they have no clue what they are entering into. For all they know, there could be guns, loads of people, or any other number of unexpected dangerous situations.

Diana asked them, "What's the problem? What is it now?"

The police said they had a warrant to search the premises. By then there were police officers in every room. I was just being quiet at this point. My mind was transfixed on the weed and wondering if they were going to find it. It was all going well, until Diana got really pissed off and started moaning about them messing her flat up and rummaging through everything. Kicking up a fuss and complaining can help to some extent, to stop the police from going too crazy. Then Diana walked into the room I had been living in and saw her cheese plant leaning slightly to one side. I had been subtly observing this situation, and yes, thanks to the weed underneath, it had been slowly leaning over, but I wasn't going to mention it, was I?

Diana was not happy, not happy at all, in fact, it would be better to say she was vexed. Fuming, she walked over to the plant in a huff and started moving it around, trying to straighten it, shouting "Who's been touching my cheese plant?"

I never knew she loved her plants so much. I was thinking 'I am fucked. What is she doing?'

Diana was transfixed with her plant, thinking the police had damaged it. The plant drama took all the focus in that moment, and of course the police became slightly concerned too. Well, it was clear what was coming next. Low and behold, one of the police officers said:

"I think there is something under it, restricting its balance, let me help you." And there it was, my 8oz bag of weed. Nice one, Diana! Though of course, I didn't blame her in the slightest. She didn't know I had hidden the weed there. Bad timing, shit happens.

The police made a subtle but clear point of letting us know they were tipped off. (That means we could have been grassed on.) The police knew the game and they knew what was going on in the area, and if they could stir things up to draw the rats out in conflict they would. That way, they had a chance of catching criminals in the process. The question is of course, could we trust them? They were very smug about it. Either way, not a good day for a police visit.

That little incident led to my first Crown Court case and the potential of being sent to jail. Thankfully, due to it being my first convicted crime of this kind and with a great character reference from my solicitor, I got sentenced with community service. I can't remember how many hours I was sentenced with, but I got allocated to a nursing home, cleaning up after old people. It wasn't a bad set up, it was a bit smelly in the building, but could have been worse. Friends I knew in the past had to dig holes in roads or paint houses, that sort of stuff. The worst part for me was washing the carpets clean of the faeces from the ones who couldn't get to the toilet in time. I used to think to myself, it's not easy getting old. Bless them.

On top of that, I got probation for one year. Probation is like monitoring. I had to report to a social worker weekly and they ask lots of questions and check that you are not participating in criminal activity.

You'd have thought that maybe this sentence would have stopped me, but I felt like I'd got away with it in criminal terms, so of course, I carried on as usual. I was addicted. It's not easy to stop habitual behaviour just like that. The world would be a very different place if it was.

There is no telling what the future could have held or what may or may not have happened if I stopped committing crime right there and then. Any number of scenarios could have played out. The point is, I didn't stop, but it wasn't long before the next offence that I got caught for took me past the tipping point. I was pulled over by the police some months later, and unlucky for me, I had stolen goods in the trunk of my car from a burglary.

This offence would be the one which sent me to jail. And as it says in the board game, Monopoly, "Go directly to jail. Do not pass go. Do not collect £200."

LOCKED UP
LOCKED DOWN

The road to jail is paved with bad intentions. It was 1995, and I was just eighteen years old. It seems it was time to get locked up. Prison was another surreal experience, another test of character. The moment I heard the judge say "four months" it didn't register at first, because I thought I would get a suspended sentence. My solicitor put forward a good case again, but it wasn't going to be. When I was convicted in the Crown Court for the 8oz of weed, it was more nerve wracking because you can get sentenced anywhere from twelve months to life. Whereas in a Magistrates Court, the maximum length of a sentence was twelve months.

Four months wasn't a long sentence in the grand scheme of things, but it felt a lot longer than it was. I was scared of spending any duration in a prison cell, and this time there was nowhere to run, it was time to be banged up. I think the judge thought, 'This guy isn't getting the message, so let's give him a sentence, which might teach him a lesson.' I remember looking at Jason and Diana at the back of the courtroom as I was handcuffed and taken downstairs. Real sadness came over me and all I could feel was this overwhelming sense of failure. I felt like I'd let my mum down and I'd also let myself down. I was riding on a wave of fear, status and ego-identification, unaware of my actions.

At the point when you go to jail, you say, "Right, this is it, it's happening, this is what criminals talk about and what everybody fears." It's one of the lowest points a thief can get to, being all alone while walking deeper into the unknown.

I had often wondered what jail would be like. I'd heard stories and watched films so I had some idea. But the minute I was locked in a cell at the Court, uncontrollable thoughts of fear started rushing through my head. What have I done? What will happen? I started to think about the trouble that might happen on the inside, along the lines of sexual abuse and getting beaten up.

Being in a confined space creates a lot of pressure, which heightens tension, stress, anxiety and paranoia. I cried when I was in the sweat box (the lorry that takes prisoners to jail) but not for long, because it just so happened that somebody I knew was in there too.

Knowing he was there gave me a feeling of support and I decided I couldn't cry. I had to step up. I had to be a man. I thought crying was for babies and men don't cry. They just got on with it. I had put myself in this position, now I was going to ride it. I'd always taken on board the motto: I'm here, I've created this, I've made these choices and now I've got to get on with it. I didn't want to show my pain, weakness and fear. It was all showmanship, ego and avoidance of my vulnerability, but it was necessary in that moment.

When I arrived at the jail I was taken through many gates. I remember the sound of those electronic gates, buzzers and keys. Then I got escorted to where I had to leave all my belongings, then strip-searched and after that I received a tracksuit. Horrible style, just wearing it made me feel vulnerable. In this jail, at the beginning of their sentence inmates had to wear the same thing at first, in either grey, red or blue. I think this was for the screws (officers) to identify who was who. We were allowed to wear our own clothes eventually, but not at the beginning. Once I was all checked over and briefed, I was allocated a cell on the wing. My new home for a while.

The first night was the worst. I was alone in an empty cell with just a bed. It was all very strange and unfamiliar. I was confused, scared and lonely. I just went to sleep as quickly as possible in the hope it was a bad dream and I'd wake up in the comfort of my home.

Not that easy is it? The next day I got woken up early and moved to another cell with a little guy from the South of England. He had ginger hair and wasn't very street wise. I thought he was a nice guy, but I knew I needed to find out who the 'in' crowd were, sharpish. I wasn't about to start getting bullied. I knew I had a good sense of humour and wasn't that stupid (depending on your perspective) and I felt a lot older due to the life I'd been living. It wasn't long before I knew who was who and how the system worked. I knew a few heads (people) on different wings, and some of the boys knew me from the estate. I would just hang out with them passing the time 'running' each other (taking the piss out of one another), fabricating stories from our adventures and fantasies in life. One guy told us all he had robbed a whole train on his own. He wasn't very happy when nobody believed him. I met random rebellious and crazy boys in that place. All thrown together through circumstance. There was one particular guy who had some serious bad BO (body odour) so I nicknamed him Bobby Orange. Then after a while, just Bobby for short. He accepted his new name and I'm sure he didn't know why. There were many other stories shared from young boys trying to establish their identity and survive in this harsh environment. It wasn't long until I managed to change cells and move in with Arnold. My ginger cell mate wouldn't take his pants off in the shower and he was getting a bit of grief from other boys; it felt like I should move on.

Arnold was the Daddy (Topman) of the wing; he was strong and loved a fight. He had been in jail many times before, so he knew the prison system well and what he could get away with. The thing about being the Daddy, is that you would attract fights and trouble. It was of no surprise to me that I gravitated towards the Topman.

One day, Arnold had a big fight in the corner cell with a guy who wanted to take him on. Arnold won this battle, but the fight went on for quite a while. This took place when we were on cleaning duty and I had to keep a 'lookout' on the wing and pretend I was cleaning the floor. Sound familiar? I was just repeating the same old crime cycles, just in a new environment.

I was surviving as an inmate and getting through prison life using the savvy I had picked up along the way, which isn't necessarily a bad human trait, but I knew if I wanted to create a different lifestyle, I needed to learn some new skills that would support the changes necessary.

Arnold also got a little more respect from the screws because they didn't need any extra trouble on the wings; they had enough to deal with. Often we would hear the fight alarm go off and if we were out of the cell we would be ushered into them quickly, while the guards investigated.

The cells we were in had a metal toilet, a little table and bunk beds. I had the bottom bunk with random bedding that consisted of a blue under sheet and then this weird green cotton cover. Every inmate had to clean their cells every three days, including polishing the metal sink and toilet and have them inspected by the guards. I got to use this big old electric buffer for the floors which was fun to try and handle. This was of course a way to create some sort of routine and order through cleanliness. We had to keep our cells and ourselves clean. It reminded me of the war movies I had seen where the soldiers had to polish their shoes for hours and if they were not clean and shiny enough, they would get reprimanded from the officer in charge. Our laundry would be sent off in see-through cotton bags which were tied up with a type of cable tie. Then they washed the whole bag and we'd get it back exactly as we'd sent it.

Arnold was a cheeky chap, he would often take people's food if he was hungry and beat boys up and steal whatever he wanted. He took a pair of new trainers from a boy who had just arrived on the wing. It was silly bringing in new trainers to jail. Clothing was definitely one way to create some sort of status and still is, but I wondered who was he hoping to impress? The screws or the inmates? Either way, you have to be careful what you bring into a hostile space like this, as you could just bring unnecessary attention to yourself, especially if you can't hold up the image you are trying to portray.

Our food supplies were stocked up when Arnold had stolen food or won food from playing card games. On tuck shop day, once a week, we could spend ten or fifteen pounds on sweets and extra food for the cell. Food, tobacco and of course drugs were our currency to barter with, and cookies were a big thing; especially the chocolate chip ones. (Everybody's sweet tooth wanted them.) Dinner was always an interesting experience too, because we all knew what food was going to be served on certain days, so I'd swap food with inmates as we walked back from the serving hatch. We'd swap ice cream and jelly for potatoes depending on what we liked most. We had to eat in our cells and had our own plastic bowl, cup and cutlery. At night we were allowed to get a cup of hot water from a big urn near the canteen before lights out, to have a night-time Rosie Lee (cup of tea).

Arnold liked having me as a cellmate; he liked teaching me what he knew and protecting me. It boosted his ego and he was actually a very caring person beyond the hard armour he wore for his identity and protection. I didn't mind, I was happy. I knew I was in with the main man.

He used to do this amazing trick with the little square plastic mirrors we got to shave with, which were pretty useless because we could barely see our reflection in them. Arnold would tie a piece of string from the bed blanket around the mirror and launch it under our cell door, across the wing and under the cell door opposite. Which was a good six metres away. The person in the other cell would then tie Rizla papers or tobacco or anything else that could fit under the doors and then we would pull it back. I was quite impressed with this technique. As I said before, it's amazing the things we learn to adapt and survive in different environments.

I often sat on the wide window ledge in my cell. I would sit up there looking down into the prison grounds and could just see over the big prison wall surrounding us. I sat up there for hours some days, just pondering reality and wondering what I was doing with my life.

This jail is called a remand centre, which is basically the stop gap before you go to an allocated jail for the longer sentences. On remand, your rights are different to other jails. For example, I was only out of my cell for about four hours a day; maybe a little longer if I could get on the education nights, which included cooking, English or Art. Most days, you were allowed exercise time, either in the gym or playing football. I did a lot of drawing, it was something I enjoyed doing and one of the only talents I got good grades for in school. I liked sending my drawings to my friends. I remember sending my mum a picture I drew her of a rose, because I knew how much she loved flowers.

It was always really good to receive post as well, in fact I would look forward to it, and when letters came, I would read them many times over. Most days I was wondering if I would get any visits from friends as this would break up my week while at the same time it was hard, because I got a taste of the outside when I saw visitors and then had to go back behind bars.

Mum came to visit me once, but I told her I'd rather she didn't come again. When I went to jail Mum was so upset. She didn't know how or why it was happening. Even when our house used to be raided, I don't think Mum ever knew how deeply we were involved in crime. She was a little naïve and in denial. I know she felt invaded, helpless and that she had failed as a parent. She was angry we didn't have good role models and blamed herself for creating that environment for us. She felt she had let me down, for not advising or giving me the right support. Mum was just scared, powerless and didn't know what to do. In her naivety she thought we were a good family and functional. I have told my mum in her older age that it was not her fault.

From my perspective, Mum has shown me unconditional love all my life. Whatever I have chosen, she has always accepted my choice and most of the time has been encouraging. I call her my 'Love Lamp'.

My Love Lamp

Before I went to jail, I was dating a girl named Natalie, and during my time inside she came to visit to let me know she was pregnant. We were only together for a few months, nothing serious, it was mostly casual sex. After we talked and I shared my perspective on parenting and how I was not ready to be a father, she decided to have an abortion, as she really didn't want to have a child either.

I was determined not to create the same cycle as my father. My father, David, left the family when I was nine months old. I grew up with a vague recollection of meeting him once when I was seven, and a random memory of him giving me pocket money to go to the shops. I only knew what he looked like from old photographs, and only got to know him through asking my mum questions and using my own experiences to understand what he must have been going through in those periods of his life. As the years went by, it got easier to accept, forgive and love him for co-creating me.

Even back then, I had a subtle feeling or knowing that this past blueprint of my father's actions would need to be rewired. And this wasn't the first time I was going to have to make this decision. I never saw Natalie after that day. I was told she was doing okay by a friend, and it was what she wanted deep down. I am aware it's not an easy decision or experience for any woman to endure. It's a potential life that is being let go of and this stirs up an array of emotions. I understood her moving on, as we had only been together for a couple of months and I was happy with the outcome.

Thankfully, nothing too drastic happened during my time in jail, yet I got to taste this tragic existence where I know many atrocities do happen daily.

One guy did attempt suicide, but didn't succeed. He had come back from court having been sentenced to life. I could hear him crying for a few days, then he tried to cut his wrists, so he was taken down to the medical wing to be monitored. Arnold had to be put in solitude a few times for fighting and robbing others, but he didn't mind much. I realised jail was not much different from how I viewed societies around the world. What goes on in jail, also happens on the outside. It's all about status. It's about who you are, who you know, what you've got on offer and what you possess. It's about the false masks we uphold.

Being in jail taught me how easy it is to become comfortable in any surroundings, even if they are not great. Not that I wanted to stay in jail, I was just aware how after some weeks of understanding the procedures, the place was more familiar and acceptable. I think therefore a lot of criminals choose to go back and forth to jail, as there's often more comfort and stability for them inside than on the outside.

I could relate; for some men it is easier to keep committing crimes than to break the conditioned habits of behaviour that got them into crime. It doesn't help that it's not easy to survive in a society that doesn't accept people with criminal records, making reintegration difficult. I read an article saying the Criminal Justice were trying to clamp down on certain privileges in jails, because prisoners had made comments saying, "Going back to jail was actually better than being on the outside, because they got more privileges, were fed regularly, could go to the gym, and have a routine."

Repetition, routine and stability were definitely lacking

from my life and in my opinion are key requirements to thrive. These institutions are supposed to uphold and give this support, but I questioned how much they really help criminals, because the after-programs are atrocious. The system supports punishment not rehabilitation. There was no program on the inside that really helped me. Okay, they let us study English and read some books, but when I came out, there was no psychological support for why I was in there in the first place. I got sent to more probation, but we criminals saw probation as another form of control. Probation felt like I was being manipulated and monitored by the system even more. I was only locked up for a short time but there was still no support to help me stop committing crimes.

CRIME WASN'T MY CALLING

I had to make a conscious choice to make my experience in jail a beneficial learning curve or I would be heading back sooner rather than later. While locked up, I thought to myself many times; it's time for a change in direction. But when I got released, I went straight back to the same circle of friends. In reality, nothing much changes in a few months does it? But for me, being locked up and taken away from my comfortable environment and friends, made it feel like so much had changed. Time takes on a different form when you are locked up all day, alone, and with fewer distractions.

It's extremely difficult to break free from destructive patterns when you're in the same environments that created them. And my life of dysfunction had become a habit and habits are hard to break, especially unconscious ones. My thinking and awareness had changed while I was inside, but implementing those changes with few options at hand was not easy.

On my release I needed to have a fixed address so that

probation services knew where I lived. Luckily was able to move into Jason's mum's. But unfortunately, I was back in Castlefield. Despite returning to this somewhat destructive environment, I was super grateful to have somewhere to live. Shelley was good to me and had a huge heart, she cared for me like a loving mother. She made up a room and fed me well. A short, resilient woman with white hair, she had lived through some challenges, and loved drinking tea and smoking a cigarette or two. I shared some long conversations with her about life and the dramas from people around the estate. She taught me a simple life lesson I remember to this day; clean up the dishes while you cook! Whenever I was cooking, she repeated 'clean as you go, clean as you go and then it's all tidy once you begin to eat'. I have fond memories of her and enjoyed helping her with little chores around the house. I think she enjoyed my company too.

Going back to jail wasn't an option, that much was clear. Crime wasn't my calling. I had more to learn and more to give. I knew I had to make some serious changes and I knew my environment was far from serving me. But what next? I thought I had escaped and now I was back in Castlefield. It felt like I was playing a game of snakes and ladders and had just slid down a slippery snake. One step forward two steps back. Maybe this was just the universe testing my willpower.

I also had to deal with the fact that serving time gave me higher status. I'd survived jail. I'd done time. I was given brownie points for that from gang members. TC and some of the gang had eased their hatred toward me too. I think they felt like I had served my sentence and clearly, I wasn't a grass. This fed my inflated ego. I was lured back in and continued to commit crime, dealing drugs and fencing stolen goods, all the while trying to work out how I could break these patterns. How was I going to stop this behaviour? I needed direction, something big to give me focus and energy to break free from these destructive habits and addictive behaviours.

I know now that if we don't find something that's more beneficial than what we're experiencing, then there's no incentive to change. There has to be a reason or purpose to pull us out of the mud. We need a motive to create motivation. It can be a small thing, but there must be something to inspire or else it's all talk and no action.

One day (not so long after my 19th birthday) I was sat on a sofa smoking a reefer (weed joint), watching daytime television. *Home and Away* was on and as I was observing in my stoned state of being, I thought, 'This acting is crap - I could do a lot better than that!' (Light bulb moment.) Then I thought, 'Yeah, why don't I become an actor? I could get on television and be a professional actor, star in films, become James Bond and make millions. This would solve everything!' The vision had purpose and real meaning, even if due to being mashed up on skunk, it seemed like a simple thing to do. Even though I had no clue how, I was ready to give it a go.

Miss Moneypenny, watch out, I'm coming for ya, baby.

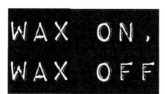

WAX ON, WAX OFF

I didn't wake up the very next day and just get on with it. I simply entertained the idea and let it linger in the back of my mind. I was allowing it to percolate, you could say. At school I had really enjoyed drama, it was one of my favourite classes, along with art. I always enjoyed entertaining and being centre stage, so maybe, just maybe, this idea was no coincidence. If they can do it, so can I, right?

This vision became my lifeline. The more I thought about it, the more it seemed possible. I started to drop the idea into some conversations with friends, to see how it landed. I was quite surprised that the responses were encouraging. It made some laugh and reply, "Yeah I imagine you as an actor." They meant more like a nice dream than a potential reality, but that was enough. If I wanted to get out of this life of crime, I would have to start turning down criminal invitations. I had to take control of my actions.

The first few times I said 'no', was not easy. So much fear of missing out and losing connection to Jason and other friends. What if I had made a mistake? But deep down I knew crime had to stop. I had made that decision in jail. Stealing was a quick fix that wasn't going to last. I had to find an honest job and change my ways.

It wasn't easy entering the normal job world, where I would work the whole month and get paid the same as I could earn in one night of crime. I was serious though, as I knew it was what I had to do.

After some searching, I found a job as a car valet, cleaning brand-new cars. A man named Mark Burton took me under his wing for a year. He trusted in me and we had a lot in common; he loved football and we shared a similar sense of humour, always winding each other up and sharing funny stories. He showed me a lot of love through his support and respect. He was a positive role model I could trust. There were about six employees in the valet team and they happened to be mostly guys I knew from around the local estates. Most of us were ex-offenders. We all had our own cleaning bay with a hoover, cleaning products, wax, cloths and sprays. I had so much banter with these boys.

Each day we had to clean as many cars as possible and we played friendly competitions to see who could clean the most. No cash reward or anything, just playful competitiveness to make the job more enjoyable. It was cool to drive all these flash new motors around the warehouse. There were hundreds of cars in the warehouse and you couldn't damage them when you parked them up so I learned how to park like a pro.

As Mr Miyagi would say in Karate Kid, "Wax on, wax off, Danielson, not everything is as seems."

Whatever this was teaching me, I was definitely becoming a master at cleaning cars, that's for sure.

During the spring of 1997, I saw an advert in the newspaper for a six-week evening improvisation class at an arts centre in town. I had no car at the time and was on a driving ban for drink driving. I rarely drove while drunk, but it was one of those rare moments when the police happened to be waiting outside the pub. Of course, they pulled me over and breathalysed me. I'd only had two beers but that was enough. That was a big kick in the stomach as I loved driving so much and cherished my driving licence. I could have continued driving illegally, like I did in the past, but I was doing my best to play by the rules now and I wanted my licence back.

My fear was coming up with multiple excuses why I couldn't attend and not being able to drive was one of them. Then I asked Jason if he could drop me off every week, and I guess I shouldn't have been surprised when he said yes without hesitation. No more excuses. These workshops were an awesome outlet for my creative expression. The teacher enjoyed my enthusiastic, lively energy and as we came close to the end of the course he suggested I take it further and enrol in a two-year theatre training in London, at a Theatre named Questors. This was a big thing. Was he serious, could I get into a theatre school? He and a few others in the group encouraged me. They said they were also going to apply and were happy to travel to the auditions in London together.

The improv teacher was another supportive figure guiding the way. I doubt he has any idea of the effect he had on my life. He saw in me what I believed was possible.

I don't remember his name but I would have loved to say a big thank you to him. As I write this, tears are flowing down my cheeks. I'm connecting to the realisation that these were hard times for me. Harder than I thought. I needed real guidance and I can see now that a number of people actually showed up to support me.

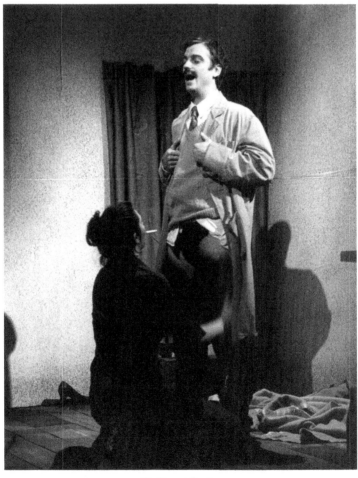

On Stage at Questors

To get accepted into the theatre training, I had to audition and perform two monologues. I had no idea how to audition, so I asked my old English teacher from secondary school. I remembered her because I had a crush on her. She was very receptive to my call and sounded happy with my direction. She suggested I learn a Shakespearean and a modern monologue. I wasn't told I should first read the whole play to understand the character arc and better grasp how that character maybe feeling at this stage of the story I was about to read. I just memorised the monologues in the way I thought best. Thankfully this got me through to the second group audition. Funnily enough, the tutor said my acting wasn't strong enough on the monologues alone, but he wanted to see me in a group improvisation. What are the chances? I was still in the running.

The day came, my heart was beating fast. The teacher was setting each of us scenarios and we would have to improvise them. And then some group exercises were set too. I gave my best, and once it was over, I waited nervously outside for the results.

When I was finally called in, Mr Emmett was sat at his desk, and asked me how I was feeling and after some small talk, and an explanation on the importance of commitment to the profession, he said he was willing to give me a place on the course. It was a 'yes'. Oh wow, this was such a great moment. So much relief within my body. Not only because my dream was getting closer, but because they thought I was good enough to begin training as an actor. It was actually happening. I was going to be a professional actor. I could feel it. My world was changing dramatically. I had found a positive interest to begin replacing my criminal activities.

Travelling to London by train and meeting new people was unfamiliar and I felt vulnerable. I was on the edge of my comfort zone again, but this time, the fear and excitement were present without the potential of getting into trouble.

On Stage at Questors

My focus had changed. I couldn't keep working full-time, so I handed in my notice to leave, I then got a few part-time jobs and borrowed £2000 from Jason to buy a van and start my own Mobile Car Valet business. I called it SUDZ. This gave me the freedom to earn cash and travel to London for the acting training. This was a big step, but I was supported by so many of my friends who invited me to clean their cars and some friends even got me connected to their workplaces where I could clean multiple cars at once.

Acting taught me a lot about the human psyche. One of the practices was to start observing my own and other people's body language, their actions, personality traits, behaviours and characteristics. People-watching became a favourite hobby of mine. We are an interesting species to observe. I saw it as watching live theatre everywhere I went. It continues to be most entertaining.

I met a lot of new friends at Questors, and many of them had a positive impact on my life. Jude was one of them. I class him as my first friend who didn't drink alcohol or take drugs. It was rare for me to meet people who didn't at least drink alcohol. He was ten years older than me and I enjoyed his wisdom and perspective of the world. We shared many stimulating conversations on all manner of topics. He welcomed me into his London life and represented a wise guide and mentor in many ways.

I was now training to be an actor and investing time reading plays and attending theatres to watch live performances. The training at Questors was developed from Stanislavski and was quite extensive, teaching us the ability 'to create the inner life of a human spirit and to express it in artistic form'. I learned how to read body language in others and began discovering the powerful possibilities of true emotional interplay.

We had classes working with voice and speech, helping us build an instrument that has power and stamina, flexibility and expression, so that we could understand our own voice and free ourselves of speech habits that could limit us in rehearsal or performance. Our group began rehearsing and performing scenes every week and I was inspired by the depth of the training. I really enjoyed the teachers too, they were very professional.

Acting at Questors

As an actor, the lights and eyes are on you. The stage was my new arena. As part of our training we performed the famous play *Trainspotting*. I got cast as Begbie who in the original movie was played by Robert Carlyle. Begbie was a charismatic yet violent character, but I had a few examples to base my character on! I began dreaming of the films I wanted to star in and the directors I would work with.

SHIT HAPPENS

As the two-year training was drawing to an end in 1999, a core group from the previous year's graduates planned to perform a play at the famous Edinburgh Fringe Festival. It's the largest arts festival in the world and takes place every August for three weeks in Scotland's capital city. The director John Horwood and Chris Storer chose a rendition of Alfred Jarry's play Ubu Roi. They called it UBU Rex and wanted to take it to Edinburgh. I was invited to join them. It was a play of crazy musical madness. It's even been described as an 'acknowledged masterpiece of absurdist theatre'. It was definitely absurd.

Regardless, I was happy for the adventure and the potential of being in the famous fringe festival. Who knew who I would meet or what opportunities might occur? Then something wonderful happened. During rehearsals in London we needed another cast member to fill one of the roles, when in walks Lucy Anne Holmes with her big smile and sassy sexy electric energy. It felt like I was watching myself as a woman enter the room. Intrigued indeed. Thus began a year-long random love affair with this beauty who happened to also love Marmite on toast and was as spontaneous and you could say, as free as me. Some may describe this freedom as all over the place, but I loved that. I liked to describe her as enchanting, sexy, magnetic, quirky and unpredictable, but also wild and free. I love how we are attracted to other human beings and then boom! Life is never the same again. Now I had even more reason to want to be in this play. Sexual attraction motivated me, and powerful women made me come alive. It's true.

As it turned out, Lucy was in and out of a longer relationship and I became her play mate on the side. I was cool with that. We cruised around in her little white Ford Fiesta, hung out in cool cafés, often the ones she worked at and drunk many bottles of red vino. We became great friends and laughter united us. It was quite uncanny how similar we were. Some often thought we were brother and sister. Lucy became a huge inspiration and support in my life, more than she would ever know.

After months of rehearsals, it was time to take the adventure to Scotland. I had suggested to the director that we could use my van to travel with all the props up to the festival, which was about a nine hour journey. A few weeks before, my van was making some funny noises, which seemed to be coming from the drive shaft. Not a great sign before I was about to embark on a trip across the whole of England, but I thought it would be fine. Then, on the day of departure while loading the van with all the props and equipment, the front wheel bearing and some other important part broke. Shit! We were stranded before we even got started.

Then Lucy had a nifty idea. She happened to have an AA card (Emergency Roadside Assistance) and part of the clause was if you have set off on your journey then the AA would take you to your destination in the event of breaking down on route. This was perfect! They would drop us at a garage in Edinburgh. Legends. Problem solved. Great teamwork, baby. So we loaded the van up and then I drove it a little way down the road away from the theatre and awaited our chauffeur driven lorry to drive us the nine hours to Scotland. Whoop, Whoop. Where there is a will there is a way. I must say, we were an awesome team, Lucy and me.

The van saga didn't stop there. After we paid to get it fixed at the garage in Scotland, I needed to park it somewhere for the duration of the festival. When I returned to pick it up, it was gone. Yep, it had been stolen. Can you Adam and Eve it? At first, I was sure I must have been on the wrong road. I walked to a few roads close by and nothing. I then knocked on a few doors to be sure I was looking in the right place and some of the residents confirmed they had seen a beige transit van outside on the street. Off I trotted to the police station to report it stolen.

It turns out that vans like mine were hot property for criminals in the area to steal and 'ring' them. (A 'ringer' is a stolen car that has had its identification numbers replaced by a set from another, usually written-off vehicle.) I know that game. Shit happens. I headed back to my friends and let them know we had no van. Then I ordered myself a brandy and coke and got on with the festival. You know what the icing on the cake was? In order to get home, we called the AA again and they drove us all the way back to London because we genuinely needed recovery.

Some of the group thought I had actually planned my van to be stolen by a friend who came to visit me. It's funny how events can be perceived. They said it felt like I had taken the loss too easily. Must have been an insurance scam. But they didn't know about my past. Many people didn't know about my life of crime. It wasn't something I would ever speak about. I was still holding too much guilt and shame for that to happen. For them it was a big loss. And yes, I lost my van, but for me the van getting stolen was more of a sign to move on. I was an actor now. And having stolen from others so many times, I was not so attached to material possessions. My way of thinking was, how could I justify being so angry and upset when something was stolen from me? Shit happens. Better to let it go than let it keep hold of me. It was taken away from me, maybe for a greater reason, who am I to decide? Some call this karma. Whatever your belief, it was a life lesson in acceptance. As one door closes, another opens, and I was really bored of cleaning people's cars.

The Festival was like a leaving celebration from the two-year theatre course. The beginning of a new chapter. It was a wonderful experience hanging with a bunch of misfits striving to be famous actors. We performed our show every night, sometimes drunk. The show itself was not the greatest in the Festival. Let's leave it like that shall we?

One of the highlights of the whole experience was taking ecstasy with everyone and walking to the top of Arthur's

Seat, an extinct volcano with panoramic views. You see ecstasy was still with me even in these different circles. The drink and drugs were part of a persona not quite ready to die (just yet).

If I were to become a professional actor, it required the three d's: dedication, discipline and determination. I needed an agent, photos and show reel. Let the games begin.

'Carpe Diem', 'Persistence beats Resistance' and 'Where focus goes, energy flows' became my daily affirmations.

Acting Headshot

DON'T LOSE SIGHT OF THE DREAM

The core of discipline is remembering what you want. It's not that discipline is hard, but rather that we forget what we want, or deviate and get distracted from our vision. Sound familiar? Although I had a dream, it wasn't as easy as I'd anticipated to get work as an actor.

I got myself a job in catering for film sets. I saw this as my way of breaking into the profession through the back door. I got a taste of where I wanted to be. I saw how big professional film units functioned. I was waking up in the early hours and driving to the different locations at 5am, then setting up in the back of a small van, my workstation/mini kitchen where I would make 150 sandwiches. From egg mayonnaise, ham and cheese, or ham and salad sandwiches, for the afternoon break for the cast and crew. Doesn't sound so glamourous does it? After the daily sandwich mission, I'd help serve breakfast from inside the catering lorry. A lot of banter with the crew was had during breakfast and lunch.

As I served the actors, I would think, 'This is getting me

closer to my dream.' I was keeping it cool, mingling with all the crew and cast, keeping them sweet with chocolate bars, teas and coffees. I catered the movie *Shiner* staring Sir Michael Caine, Matthew Marsden and Andy Serkis. I had to deliver food at times to their mobile dressing rooms, and always thought, 'One day that will be me.' I strolled through the film sets patiently harbouring my desire to be on the other side of the camera. Andy Serkis (Gollum from *Lord Of The Rings*) said something lovely to me one day when we

Acting Headshot

were passing time, he said, "Never give up, don't lose sight of the dream." Simple words, but super encouraging to have a reminder like that, from someone I aspired to be.

Castings were so sporadic. I didn't have a regular income and needed money. So many of us struggle to keep focused on our dreams while having to do things we don't actually want to do. I resisted this fact, but maybe that's just how life is. I didn't want to believe it. I wanted an enjoyable job that excited me enough to get out of bed in the morning. We give most of our living days to working at jobs in this society. We work forty, fifty or more hours a week in jobs we dislike while getting paid a pittance.

Who makes the rules anyway? I wanted to work for myself and be the one who decided my terms and how many hours I worked per week. I didn't care about labels, what I cared about was not having some boss tell me what I should and shouldn't do and when I should eat or take a shit. My response to systems like these was "Fuck this shit." This was a lingering common catchphrase in my vocabulary. I see this expression as a release of anger which helped my rebellious side keep the middle finger up to the subtle and not so subtle controls of Western society.

The catering job faded out and unfortunately provided no back-door entry into the movie industry. So I decided to study and qualify as a Personal Trainer and Sports Masseur. I loved the gym, it was like my second home. I had been training my body regularly since I was seventeen years old. Back with Jason when we were criminals, we would go to the gym almost daily to be fit for crime, and for aesthetic reasons of course. Having a six-pack washboard stomach and pumped chest was another way to be someone. To show off my pumped body, to feel strong and attractive. Women love pumped up pecs, right? That was my belief, because I loved my chest feeling hard and taut.

As we headed into the year 2000, Mum decided she wanted to live closer to Steve and I. She was fed up with living so far away. She found a house swap with an opportunity to move to a small village called Datchet. When she told me, I said what about I move in with you and Lloyd? They both agreed. This worked out perfectly as I didn't have enough regular income to move to London just yet. Many years had passed since we had all lived together and I missed them. This was our family reunion.

A time to build new friendships. Lloyd had been battling some serious health challenges, so it felt right for us to be together. I didn't really know him that well, he was only 11 years old when they left Castlefield. Back then he was just my younger brother and as you know, I had a greater desire to be with Steve and the older boys. Lloyd and I began sharing more time together and became great friends. We had more in common now and shared new experiences. He started helping me in so many ways and supported all my crazy ideas and ventures. He is a tech savvy master and was teaching me things I would rarely remember, which challenged him, but he has greater patience than me.

It was no surprise that a spontaneous conversation I had in the gym years before linked me to a Premier Training program based in Windsor which low and behold was now only a few miles away from Mum's new house. Synchronicity. I reached out to the company and excitably got myself enrolled with a scholarship and all seemed to be flowing smoothly.

I felt that if I could find a profession I enjoyed while pursuing my dream, all would be well. This new profession gave me insight into our beautiful bodies and how magnificently they function. It was rewarding being a Personal Trainer and Sports Therapist. I found great satisfaction in motivating others to reach their goals and feel good about themselves. Blood rushing through my veins, and my muscles being used in the ways they are designed to, is a wonderful feeling.

I do love it when my body feels strong and dynamic. It

My Beautiful Body

made sense to me to help others feel the same. I met great people, some of which became close friends. I massaged many bodies too. The day I started the massage training, I walked in the room and thought to myself, I better sit next to a woman as I'd prefer to massage a woman's body than a man's. Then after the intro talk the teacher said you will all get to massage everyone in the class.

I realised then that I had a fear of touching men or being touched by a man. It was an inbuilt program from my past. That men touching men is wrong. There was a gay phobia that had been instilled in me growing up, a cultural belief upheld throughout my youth by damaging jokes and innuendos about boys being gay if they acted in certain ways. It was okay for girls to be touchy feely and sensitive but if men were, they were gay or a sissy. It was so interesting noticing how these indoctrinated beliefs had shaped my life. And after facing my fears I found I actually preferred the stronger touch I received from men.

Massage is such a great tool for healing. The training made me realise how much we humans are starved of touch. I enjoyed using my hands for therapeutic healing and physiological repair. I saw this intensive training as part of a tool kit for life, giving me self-awareness of how I can control and enhance the body for the roles I would be playing. It was all part of the master plan. Or at least that's what I made myself believe.

I received my graduation diplomas a few months after the twin towers collapsed in September 2001. I remember watching the news on the TV in the gym. I did not know the magnitude of the effect that this day would have on all our lives. And as I write this now, it also had not dawned on me at the time how interconnected we all are. I did not know how that one event would impact the many people I would later meet in life.

At this point, I was just interested in myself and wanted to get out there in the world and begin generating money from my newly obtained skills.

Personal training and massage ran alongside pursuing my acting career. I took part in some improvisation theatre and small unpaid performances. But with my high expectations, it all felt rather drab. The dream was active in my mind, but the results were not showing any significant progress. I knew deep down I wasn't actually giving it one hundred percent. I was distracted. I was blagging it. I was still clubbing and still had one foot deeply grounded in the hedonistic drug scene.

London to Brighton Bike Ride

OLD HABITS DIE HARD

Yes, I was a health and fitness professional and fitter than ever before, but I still had demons in the closet when it came to addiction. I knew these addictions were blocking my progress. I was hooked on ecstasy and weed, even cocaine at times. I still loved getting high. I loved the whole buzz of it. Preparing for the weekend, choosing what clothes to wear, ordering, collecting and weighing the drugs, excitable conversations with those who would be joining me – it was a ritual. I was addicted to the sensation of the anticipation. I was a social animal.

This spoken word poem from my friend Christian de Sousa sums up the deeper essence to my addiction with hedonism and the buzz of the nightclub dance floors.

"Since I was a kid, music has been a playground and a refuge, bringing joy to the everyday and offering emotional and spiritual solace in times of difficulty. Navigating the London streets, drum &

bass and other genres of electronic music provide a soundtrack and a resource. The beats give us something to ride on while moving through the matrix...Electronic music describes, in audio, the nature of the way we're living.

"To the uninitiated, it may seem like just a noisy barrage of catchy breakbeats, but on the dance floor it's the heavy artillery in the fight for soul survival. Shaped by concrete and infused with smoke, the musical healing is rough and rude... This is the assault of the capitalist system, alchemised into a chink of funky liberation.

"There is nothing like those peak moments of dance floor communion, that rush when everyone is coming up on their drugs and the DJ drops a killer bass line followed by a soaring vocal. There is nothing like those journeys dancing for hours in total abandon to rhythm and the perfection of the moment. There is nothing like the feeling of being there with a friend or even a complete stranger just feeling love so strong and speaking freely from the heart.

"It was House music that was the root of the dance floor revolution. In alliance with a pharmaceutical compound called MDMA, it changed the world... The experience of taking ecstasy and dancing to house music gets urban youth opening their hearts and minds, even across racial and class divides. It creates a window in the spiritual brick wall of modern life and makes authentic connection and unity readily available on a Saturday night. It's a freedom thing: suddenly the whole rat race seems less overwhelming, less inevitable even, and for a few precious hours, life becomes about joy and unlimited possibility.

"In these moments we remember who we are, and even if it all dissolves by Tuesday, something has changed."

This spoken word describes the whole experience and deeper psychology of night clubbing and my experience.

Clubbing on Ecstasy

One of my closest friends was a DJ so we often got invited into clubs as VIPs. The ego was still getting its fuel from long nights of overindulgence. I was slightly hooked on having sex while on ecstasy too. Seeking sexual encounters was a huge driving factor for me. Like a vampire hunting for blood. That doesn't mean I always got what I wanted. I recall many times being drunk, hanging around like a leech at the end of the night, hoping to be invited back to someone's house for the potential fuck. Crazy when I think back, how at the beginning of the night I would be looking for women who I thought were super sexy and my type and after a night of alcohol and drugs, the 'beer goggles' would be on and then everyone looked fuckable. No wonder so much sexual abuse occurs from these unconscious states of being. I'm not saying this was the norm for all, but I definitely went through this stage during those early years of sexual exploration and that quest to sleep with 100 women. It took some time for that drive to calm down.

It became easier when I found myself in a long-term relationship with a girl named Julia. We met through our friends of friends who were together. It started off very casual as we both didn't think we wanted a real relationship. But this little energetic beauty became my clubbing partner and lover for several years. I could write a whole other book on our crazy time together. She was studying to become a lawyer at a university in Bournemouth, so we shared a long-distance affair for large parts of our time together. I really enjoyed leaving High Wycombe and losing myself in a cocoon with her. Our relationship was fuelled by clubbing, drinking copious amounts of alcohol and carefree fun. You could also say I was hopping onto the student lifestyle vibe. Her love grounded me, and I recall a magical moment which I later abused, which would become a catalyst for my desire to speak truth and never lie again.

I think I've always had a seed within me that believed

in telling the truth and not lying. One evening, we were taking a walk down the seafront as we often did, with a cheap bottle of wine in a paper bag. We were like two little hobos. It was windy and we were wrapped up warm in many items of clothing. We loved our quirky desire to dress up in random clothes and go walking around town without a care in the world, so this wasn't unfamiliar to us, especially on hangover days. I'm sure I recall a time when we went out in white bath robes.

Anyway, we were sat there, a little drunk, soft and loved up, closely embraced as we shared the bottle of wine together, listening to the crashing waves and feeling the taste of saltwater from the sea spray. We were having one of our long talks about life, the mystery and whatnot. We would talk for hours. And that night we made a pact, we shared that we would never cheat on each other. Always speak our truth and be honest about whatever we have going on inside us. It was a very clear moment in our relationship as we both respected our love and friendship. My mum had always been cheated on and I didn't want to repeat the patterns of my father figures. There was a part of me that genuinely wanted this and another part of me that would find this extremely difficult. The next years ahead morphed into an epic adventure of me striving to be an actor and Julia striving to be a lawyer as we tried our best to focus on weekdays and get high as kites on the weekends with all our friends.

Later, as the years went on, I began complaining about how I felt on the come down from taking drugs and alcohol and yet be back on it most weekends. I knew I had to quit them at some point. I even remember Julia saying to me,

"You are always complaining, why don't you just stop?" Just stop? I wished it were that easy. I was my own worst enemy. But I couldn't ask for help, because I didn't fully know how much I was subtly addicted to recreational drug use and how much I craved the hedonistic scene.

I was running towards an idea, a dream I had projected into the future, when in reality, I was being run by old habits I couldn't control. It is said that one of the hardest things in life to change is the behaviour of another person. That makes sense because it's hard enough to change my own behaviour, let alone trying to change another. Change is a constant in life but we all instinctively avoid it. It's easier to sabotage our dreams and convince ourselves that it couldn't happen, than to actually do what it takes to make it happen.

Constantly changing jobs and learning new professions was a clear sign to me that I doubted my ability to make this dream come true. Acting was a job, why couldn't it support me? Doubt is a killer, it's an enemy on the path to success. I could have responded to this idea with, "It's not good to put all your eggs in one basket," or "I'm doing the best I can." Or my favourite, "Variety is the spice of life." But though there are some truths in these sayings, it was hard to decipher if they were supporting my greater vision or just plain procrastination and avoidance. I had to get real with myself.

I heard George Clooney say, "If you have a fall-back plan, you will fall back." This made me stop, look at my actions and seriously rethink my plan. Not long after, I made the decision to refocus on acting again and base myself in London and guess who showed up? Lucy. We hadn't spoken for years and I reached out to let her know my plans, because maybe she knew some contacts who could help me. As it turned out, her parents had just bought her a flat in Camden Town so she could get on with her acting career. More synchronicity. She said I could crash in her front room on the sofa bed while I landed on my feet. I heard the words of Andy Serkis keeping my flame alive, "Don't give up."

It was around 2005 when I made the move. I really needed to leave High Wycombe for good. My relationship with Julia had been rocky for a few years, ever since I broke our pact because my desire for spontaneous sexual encounters was too strong and Julia had lost trust in me. Often it was just a case of checking out by flirting with other girls. This behaviour came to a head on a promenade in Ibiza. I had gone away with friends to experience the famous nightlife of Ibiza. I knew Julia would be meeting us at some point of the holiday. And before she arrived, I was out partying for a few days in the bubble of ecstasy. The night before I ended up having sex with another woman. In the heat of the night it led where it led. The irony is, it was nothing special. As I walked away from her house, a sense of sexual gratification and disappointment struck me. I said to myself, not again, this must stop now. As much as it felt gratifying on some level, the exciting build up, the fun with friends and the anticipation of what could be, when the sexual act was over and the guilt of cheating seeped in, my expectations and desires could never be met. Not from this foundation of lying.

This time I felt really deflated, I had a girlfriend who I'd said I loved so many times, and she was arriving soon to meet me, why couldn't I just wait another day? I knew I had to own up this time and come clean and deal with the consequences. Julia already knew on some level. A woman's intuition is way sharper than a man's. In the last few years together, we shared numerous conversations about what it may be like to have other partners. We were young lovers who knew it was over but couldn't face it. I couldn't speak truthfully and share that it was over for me. I had already broken our pact just by the way I was seeking other sexual encounters. I had cheated in my mind way before any physical act ever happened.

I hesitantly planned to meet Julia and as I walked towards her I knew she knew, I was guilt walking. She could read it all over my face. I can't recall now if I told her first or she just walked straight up to me and slapped me in the face and said 'you cunt' among other words that I cannot recollect. The thing is, the slap and the words were totally valid and welcomed, but didn't change anything.

What did change me in that moment was what I saw on Julia's face. I saw and felt her pain. In that moment, our life together crumbled, it all flashed through my mind, the amazing times we shared, the love and laughter, the adventures, the great support, the family connections, and friendship, all now dissolving. It was heart wrenching.

It was then that I realised I hadn't just cheated on her, I had ultimately cheated on myself. The course of events were a blur after that point. Out of almost seven years of being in one another's life, this moment was one that would stick the most. One that would also need forgiveness later along my path.

We did stay together for a while after this event, as Julia tried to forgive me. Her career also had her move to London for a new job with a reputable company, and so we stayed connected for a while and as always, she showed up in the best way she could. We were friends and loved each other, no question but this wound was not going to heal so quickly. At the core, her trust was gone and it was mostly unfulfilled dreams of what could have been lingering and holding us together in the hope things might change. But again my focus was elsewhere.

I wanted to follow my dreams to be famous and this chapter had to end.

PERSISTENCE BEATS RESISTANCE

After making the move to London, I landed a few paid acting jobs and one was to play alongside Sir David Jason. He was the main actor who played Del Boy in the hugely successful series *Only Fools and Horses*. I got the opportunity to be in his new TV programme *Diamond Geezer*. I'm sure my hands started sweating when I got the call. The audition was a serious test of speaking my truth because the part I was to play, was a criminal in jail. They asked me in the audition if I had ever been to jail, and in a split second I was confronted with the question – could I speak my truth? If I said yes, they could have judged me and not cast me, but if I'd said no, they might have already known, and branded me a liar. I had a criminal record which I guessed they could have researched if they wanted to. I figured many actors are known to be ex-criminals. I chose honesty and said, "Yes, I had served a short time in jail and was a criminal once." I still got the part! Yes!

It was my first real paid professional acting job, or at least, the first one worth talking about. Being on the professional set with David Jason and having a scene where I had to beat him up, blew my mind. There I was, kicking Del Boy in the belly while he lay on the floor in front of me (he wasn't Del Boy in this program, but he would always be Del Boy to me). It might not seem like a big thing, but this was like a dream within a dream and confirmation I was on the right track. There's a quote by Napoleon Hill, "Whatever the mind can conceive and believe, it can achieve." I was indeed achieving what I had been conceiving. Miss Moneypenny's soft voice was calling me.

Acting Headshot

On Set

I was consuming self-development books in order to understand my mind and how to rewire my subconscious. I wanted to master myself. I was ingesting all manner of theories, ideas and concepts on how to be successful in this game of life. What I found was that so much of success in our society is measured by money alone. I collected two affirmations that defined success for me very well: 'Success is measured by what you have overcome in life, not how much money you have in your bank account'. And 'Wealth is what you have left when all the money is gone'. These two truer perspectives helped with my limited money flow and lack of acting work.

The book *Born to Succeed* by Colin Turner asked the question, "Are you willing to become the person you need to be to achieve what you want to achieve?" Was I? I was proud of myself for getting this far, but I was struggling. Was I able to make this dream a reality? Or was I just running to some future outcome which was not obtainable? Was money and fame going to meet all my needs? One thing was for sure, I was determined. I started filming my own short films rather than waiting for some professional job to come to me, and I created my own opportunities to act. Then I got an audition with a man named Lajuane (who I called Laj for short). He had written a script for a feature film and wanted to cast me in it. After a number of conversations, we began filming some scenes but unfortunately the movie never got completed. This happens a lot with independent movie making. This meeting with Laj however connected me to a friend of his, Sav, a Turkish director and two Armenian friends, Paul and Ludwig, who were also directors. These four became pivotal in my acting quest. They would often use me as their guinea pig. Sav had a short film idea called *SPUDS TOO*. It was an interesting visual concept of a dive into the warped mind of a criminal, moments before he committed a violent crime. It ended up with me in a cage in just my Y-front pants being prodded by midgets who wanted to experiment on my brain. Maybe it was the midget drug dealers I had offended when I was drunk that day, come back to get me? You know what they say in acting? Play to your strengths. I thoroughly enjoyed making this short movie because of their passion and professionalism. In the end, we didn't cast any small people to prod me, it was just me in a cage.

What was clear is that these guys were serious about making movies, it was their passion, and this is exactly what I needed. Paul later introduced me to a writer named Geoff Thompson, which was a great connection. Geoff is a BAFTA-winning writer, filmmaker, teacher, and self-defence instructor. He has written several books on self-help, self-defence and martial arts, and has written many screenplays for short and feature films. One of his well-known books is called *Watch My Back,* and is his story of being a former British bouncer and the dangers he faced working at bars and night clubs in Coventry. It's a great book and boy, did he have to deal with some violence. Many of his books became a great resource. One of my favourites was *Fear the Friend of Exceptional People.* It was all about making fear a friend, which was a completely new perspective for me on fear and how to manage it. My interest in his work was heightened when I got to meet him in person. Geoff's story is one of overcoming extreme adversity and he showed me what was possible. He also made movies with professional actors like Ray Winstone and Paddy Considine and was in talks with Paul and Ludwig to direct and co-produce a short movie he wrote called *Romans 12:20.* They asked if I wanted to help co-produce.

Filming Romans 12:20

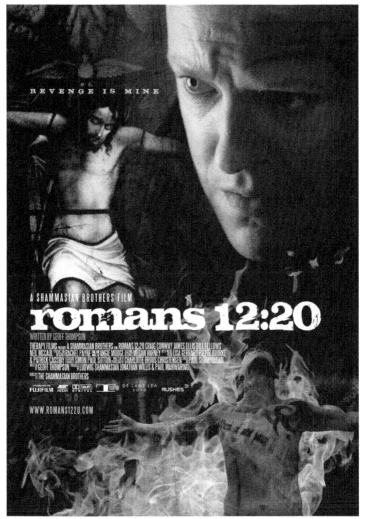

Romans 12:20 Movie Poster

This was an epic opportunity. The movie touched on the raw topics of loneliness, sexual abuse and the power of forgiveness. One of the protagonists was a priest who had committed sexual abuse and later burns himself to death

Fidget the Drug Dealer

due to an encounter with the boy he had abused. We set up the whole scene with a stunt man who was actually lit up on set. It was quite a feat to capture that scene. The film had meaning, and I was proud to be a part of it.

Not long later, Geoff's book *Watch My Back* was optioned to be made into a movie called *Clubbed*, and the shooting date was planned. I heard they were casting small roles and I managed to get the part of the character named 'Fidget'.

I'm not sure if the universe is always laughing with me or this just confirms you attract what you are, because Fidget was a drug dealer in a night club dealing ecstasy tablets and that's exactly what I was still doing.

I had one line and got beat up by a bouncer and chucked out of the nightclub. Talk about parallel universes. The director commented on how realistic I had made the performance look. No shit, Sherlock. Here I was, just playing myself again.

As an actor you must follow the crumbs until you find the loaf. I had read that becoming an overnight success takes fifteen years, so I still had some distance to go, if success was what I was seeking.

COCKOLADA

To know and not to do is not yet to know. The cost of living in London was a challenge and my hustler mentality was in overdrive. Lack of money was side-tracking me again. Which is how I got into business with a man named Dan. I met him through the club scene. He was a breakdancer, singer, designer, entrepreneur, and was super talented and creative. We had a similar sense of humour and a lot in common.

You could say I've always been an entrepreneur, but I hadn't given myself this title until Dan became my new business partner. He had lots of ideas, and together we had big dreams that would make us rich. Money, as always, was the driving factor. I enjoyed having a friend to co-create with, but like any business, there was no quick fix and we had to build our business up slowly. I justified this distraction by saying that once I had loads of money, I'd be able to make even more of my own films. I can see now that I was not clear with my intentions and actually quite delusional. We called our business AP4 – A Project for anything that creatively inspired us. We started off with a few random projects that didn't really mature into anything. Then while away at a breakdancing event on Tour in Germany, he found these little unique drinks. He sent me a picture and said, "What do you think, Si, could we sell them?"

Cockolada

Don't ask me what I was thinking when I said: "Yes, awesome, we could sell those, no problem!"

And that was how we started distributing Cockolada.

What is 'Cockolada' I hear you ask? Oh, just a Pina Colada alcoholic cocktail drink in a (mustard style) Cocktube with a bellend (penis head) drinking cap. I called it Penis-colada.

Despite my desire to get out of drinking alcohol and going nightclubbing, I had somehow made a decision to start a business selling alcoholic drinks in cock-shaped tubes to night club owners. We made a few trips to Austria to meet with the millionaire who was producing Cockolada and Go Wodka, and found he also produced Hello Pussy and Dark Knight sexual lubricants, which were also sold in mustard tubes with bell end caps. His father had passed on and left him the famous mustard company, but Gustav was too cool for mustard, so he decided to change the contents and fill them with his own branded vodka and edible sex lubes. Sounds crazy, right? By now you must be aware that I'm not your average Joe. After that initial meeting with the stylish Gustav in Austria, we made a decision to be the sole UK distributor of these products.

This was it. Dan and I had done the math: Cockolada was going to make us millions. (Talk about *Only Fools and Horses*, I was Del Boy for real and Dan was Rodney.)

It took us six months of meetings and planning to get the Cockolada into Ann Summers, the largest store for sex toys in the UK. This was great news. In the meantime, I had been dressing up as a Mexican with a sombrero and fake moustache to sell this cock drink in gay bars and nightclubs across England. Genius.

I was definitely the star in my own movie, as Paul had even recorded some marketing videos of me as the Mexican. This was my new role and I had to get into character. As crazy as it all sounds, it was never boring. One of the events we were invited to sell the drinks at was a sex party in Brighton.

We arrived at this sort of warehouse area, and there was a small sign with the name of the club. Dan dropped me off and I walked in dressed as the Mexican with my boxes of Cockolada tasters.

The idea was that we would show up and give tasters to the punters in any club who wanted to potentially purchase the drink. As I walked in the doors, I began seeing the crowd of eclectic men and women of all ages, many dressed up erotically, some in pure rubber, others half-naked with chains hanging from their skimpy attire, and then against the wall there was a man strapped to a board as someone was arousing his nipples with electrodes.

Had I just walked into a sadomasochist sex dungeon dressed as a Mexican with a sombrero about to sell alcoholic cocks? I think I had... Only you, Simon. I am sure that anyone at that party was likely just as bemused at seeing a man selling cock drinks dressed as a Mexican. This was just one night of tasters, but definitely the best one of a few more random nights of attempting to introduce this unusual drink to the LGBT party scene.

All was obviously going well and on track, until the first big shipment of Cockolada leaked and the Ann Summers stores declined any more orders. Sometimes in life you only get one chance. The Hello Pussy and Dark Knight sex lube didn't work out either. It was a slippery business and it didn't make us a penny.

Can you feel the resistance I had to my becoming what I truly wanted to be? Yes, I was having a laugh and entertaining myself, and my friends enjoyed their free cock drinks, but waking up to see them in the fridge every morning, along with some edible sex lube, was becoming a bore. I was lost, distracted and procrastinating. Worst of all, instead of having the money to make more films, I was just getting into more debt and it felt like my dream was slipping away with the lube.

ALL THE WORLD'S A STAGE

Life is an act. Shakespeare was onto something when he said, 'All the world's a stage'. I was acting in all of these roles. Put on the sombrero and moustache and I'm a Mexican; put on a suit and some shiny shoes and I am an entrepreneur; get a little bit of cash and invest in some properties and I am a landlord; pass an exam, put on a tracksuit and hold a stopwatch and I'm a personal trainer; grab some oil, towels, a white vest and couch and I'm a Swedish masseur. Pop on a uniform and I'm a parking attendant, a policeman or batman. I had performed all of these roles (apart from the last three).

Amidst all this madness, I asked myself – Who am I? What am I? Why am I here? What am I doing?

These deeper questions needed answering because I was drifting further out to sea without a paddle. I was running around chasing my tail. Wasn't I on my dream path which gave me purpose? Doubt had crept in and hid my dream under a little rock where I could hardly see it. I was going to be James Bond by the time I was forty; Miss Moneypenny was calling me, wasn't she? Had my path lost meaning? I wanted to act, didn't I? I was sick of hearing the old cliché that 90% of actors were out of work. I was disheartened when I saw other people my age or younger making it as famous actors. I was comparing myself left right and centre. My agent said the same old catch-22 story, "You need to act more to get the better roles and you can't get the better roles until you act more" and "Nobody will see you until you have done more work", blah blah blah. The bullshit industry talk was winding me up and making me angry.

I phoned Sav and said, 'Look, I have a HD Camcorder and we need to make a feature film, because I need to show I can hold a film together as a lead actor. Are you in?' He agreed and set up some meetings with Laj. They had been writing a feature film with a working title *London Thing* which later changed to *Other Side Of The Game*.

Shooting Other Side of the Game

153

It seemed to be perfect timing. It was June 2007, and my mantra 'persistence beats resistance' was very much alive. At this time, Dan and I had quite a few commitments, but I was ready to focus on my acting career. I told him I wanted out of the business. He was disappointed and felt let down. I felt guilt for changing my mind but I knew I had to say no. It didn't feel right in my gut.

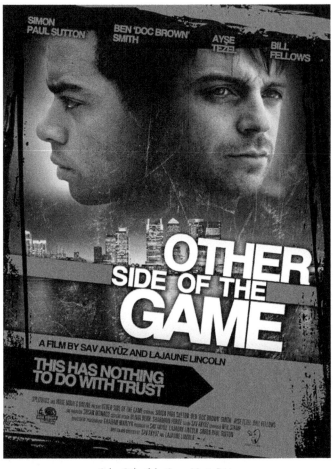

Other Side of the Game Movie Poster

Our friendship slowly deteriorated after this decision and I was sad as I really appreciated Dan and the time we shared together. I was learning that every time I followed my truth it affected all those involved and that's something I had to learn to deal with.

Sav, Laj and I went into pre-production and planned to shoot our first feature-length movie in the summer 2008. Time to find the crew, cast our actors and raise the budget to make the film. Yes! I was back on track. This goal energised me to get things rolling and step up as a lead actor.

But my life, as you have read so far, rarely goes to plan…

CAN I HAVE A BITE OF YOUR MUFFIN?

On December 9th, 2007, I attended a seminar called 'Your Best Year Yet'. Yes, this sounds great, I thought. I need next year to be better than this one. Plus, it was free, which is great for an out-of-work actor. I took my brother Lloyd, and friend Scott, along for support.

On the morning of the event, I walked into the foyer of the hotel and as I walked among the hustle and bustle of the attendees, I spotted a beautiful woman and BOOM! In that moment I experienced love at first sight. I was mesmerised by this young woman wearing a purple beanie hat, and knee-high purple socks and black boots. I was so taken by her that I said to my friend,

"Hey! Hey! Scott! Did you see the woman who was standing next to you?"

"What woman? Do you mean the one who left her coffee cup on the floor?"

He didn't like people who littered, so of course that's all he noticed.

I said, "She was there, she was there right next to you. Beanie, socks, hair, eyes, body, beauty…"

I looked around and couldn't see her. That was it, I was on an uncontrollable quest to find her. As I walked into the busy conference room, I scanned the room left and right, while people walked by me, blocking my view as they found seats. I waited as the room calmed, and there she was, I spotted her to my right. With super sly tactics, I managed to move myself through the line of seating and passed her to sit three chairs away. Then I spent the next few hours sending telepathic loving vibrations.

I am here, to your right. Hello?! Surely, she must have seen me. Apparently not. My telepathic skills were rusty it seemed. I hadn't felt attraction this intense in my life. Not much else happened for me at the event. I have no clue what the key speakers said, other than make lists and set intentions about what you wanted to achieve in the year ahead. Which didn't impress me much, I'd been writing lists for years anyway.

I wanted one thing and one thing only: to connect with purple beanie girl. All my intentions were directed in attracting her attention.

Just before the lunch break, I found the perfect opportunity to make my move, just when she was about to eat the cake she had unwrapped. I walked up casually and said, "Hey, can I have a bite of your muffin?"

Yes, that's what I said! Not bad hey, considering I had fallen in love with a complete stranger who happened to be eating a blueberry muffin, which I might add, were also my favourite muffins. It was hard enough to even speak. And if it's hard for me to speak, you know something's up!

Thankfully, Alice enjoyed my introduction and agreed to have lunch with me and the boys. I was elated. I eagerly led them all off down the street to a local English pub. I can't remember much of lunch other than nervously talking way too much. When we returned to the event, we sat next to each other. I was donning a constant smile, slightly hypnotized. At one point we were asked to split into groups for an exercise. I tried my best to get into her group but to no avail. Patience, Simon, Patience. When the event finally came to an end, I moved in slowly to complete the next part of the quest by obtaining Alice's number. Cha-ching! I was over the moon.

The seminar had worked. I had a feeling my next year was definitely going to be the best one yet.

Little did I know what this explosive chemistry had in store for me. During the first month of knowing Alice, I experienced overwhelming feelings and many realisations. Before meeting her I wasn't aware of feeling unconditional love for another person. These feelings had opened me up to something unfamiliar. I could describe it like a nut being cracked open, or my hard shell, armour (which I was not even aware of having) was softening. Maybe this was what being mushy felt like. What followed, was a state of joy and expansion as my worldview changed immensely. I had experienced relationships before, with wonderful women that I had loved and shared great times with, but these intense feelings were unfamiliar to me. I was having an epiphany.

Many people have epiphanies or realisations throughout

their lives. Some small and some huge. You know the moment where suddenly you understand something? An 'aha' moment. Epiphanies shift our perspectives, they awaken us to new realms of possibility. They allow us to see what we were unaware of before. I definitely became more aware, present and in awe of everything. Of simple, ordinary and so-called mundane things, like the trees, the sky, the clouds, the wind, the sun, the rain, insects, birds, animals, humans and even my own breath. My senses became heightened. I felt interconnected to everything. I felt ecstatic and could only compare it to past experiences of altered states of consciousness while on MDMA. But it was different this time, it had a different flavour, a purer one. Elation, yes this was a taste of pure ecstasy and not the short-lived high from taking a man-made pill.

I had fallen in love. However, it seemed that Alice wasn't having the exact same experience as me. I was definitely entertaining her though. I recorded myself singing a song to her. 'I gotcha gotcha gotcha gotcha in my sooooul.' You had to see it to believe it and let's just say I was slightly crazy and possessed by love.

These feelings of love lasted way past six months, which is apparently the duration of the honeymoon period. It was as though many cogs had clicked together. Aspects of what I had been reading and intellectualising were falling into place experientially. Nothing I was striving for in this man-made society really mattered. I didn't need to be a successful actor, famous or rich. I didn't need to be anything other than what I was in the present moment.

With this new realisation, a big energetic release flowed

through my whole body. I felt weightless and at peace with the present moment. I felt a deep feeling of self-love and an overwhelming appreciation for being alive. I had indeed fallen in love, not just with another amazing beautiful human being, but with my unique magnificence and the whole of this phenomenal existence.

I phoned my mum, because as you know, I always phone my mum when something dramatic happens. I told her I was sorry for not loving her as she had loved me. I thanked her for co-creating me. I cried because of the connection to this true source of creation. I was vulnerable. The magnitude of what I was feeling was quite overwhelming. Tears of truth appeared. That's what I called them, cleansing tears of truth. It was like the tears were washing away false beliefs I had identified with. I was high on truth. I knew I had been asking important life questions, but was this the answer I was looking for? The void and emptiness I had been feeling was no longer there in those heightened moments. Was it love I was seeking all along? Not fame and fortune? Wow. Was I seeking to love, to be loved and to truly belong?

I had always enjoyed writing a diary and had been writing Morning Pages for some time as a recommendation from Lucy. She had read Julia Cameron's book *The Artist's Way*, in which the reader is invited to write three A4 pages of longhand, stream of consciousness, first thing in the morning. Julia says, "There is no wrong way to do Morning Pages – they are not high art. They are not even "writing." They are about anything and everything that crosses your mind – she also calls them 'mourning pages' because you have to literally die on the page, puke it all out, your thoughts, feelings, and mental chatter. She goes on to say, "They are for your eyes only. Do not over-think Morning Pages, just write three pages of thoughts, feelings or anything that comes to mind down on the page... and then do three more pages tomorrow."

These new experiences compelled me to write even more than I had previously. It was flowing through me like a river. This process took self-discovery to another level as I unravelled my life through my own words. I was writing about everything; the present and what was happening with me and Alice and the world, my past experiences, intimate relationships, and whatever else was arising in the moment, from feelings, thoughts, philosophical views and creative new ideas. Some great wisdom and insights would emerge after I had released all the surface noise of my mind. I had tapped into a well of knowledge I wasn't previously aware of. This practice enabled me to bring peace and understanding into my life. I gathered great insight into my past and present actions. The process took me into a deep catharsis and after some time inspired me to write my life story which amounted to hundreds of pages. I initially named that writing *Purging Castlefield* and some of those original outpourings have made their way into this book.

My body was tingling all over and felt charged with subtle electrical pulses. It was like I had a few extra thousand volts pumping through me. I felt a release happening through my entire being. I have been known to be hyperactive, but this was something else. My whole perception of self and reality was changing. An internal cleansing was in process. Many bigger questions were arising, which I wanted answers to.

Was the universe kicking me into gear? Was I shedding skin like a snake? Had I entered a new dimension? It was a huge transition, that much was certain.

This is taken from my journal one month after these feelings arose:

Tuesday Jan 8th 2008 - Love realisation

I was just listening to a beautiful song called *Stop the world* by Elcho. I have a very powerful urge to log this whole experience I am going through at the moment, this realisation and feeling of unconditional love elevation. It has been one month. I cannot describe fully what I am going through but I will try: I feel content, peaceful, aware and fearless. The deep truthful communication I am having with myself and everybody else is enhancing me as a person. Thoughts come into my head like, 'If this is so amazing, how can it get any better?' But I abolish that thought with a positive reply that it doesn't need to be any better, it doesn't need to be anything other than what it is. It feels easy to love without expectation, is this because I have found myself? It's true that everything I am, I love. I admire myself, I trust myself, I adore myself, and I am my every thought. I have taken responsibility for my actions and I have forgiven everything I have blamed myself for.

We all think about ourselves more than any other thing on this planet, but those thoughts can create separation. We see in others what we do not see in ourselves. We may think of ourselves more than any other thing, but we very rarely take responsibility or ownership of our thoughts. As we look out, we find ourselves blaming others for our current situation and that outward looking blocks the inner vision we crave, which is the path to inner love. This elevated feeling I am having feels strong and boundless. I have a heightened sense of sight, taste and feeling. The stillness that I have been longing for has arrived along with an immense excitement of all possibilities. It's like a weight has been lifted from my mind and I have a freedom that has made me fly above this man-made reality of greed, competitiveness, money, violence and negativity. This connection has given me the strength and confidence to shine freely. I am beaming inside and through beaming inside and using this energy I can now see how I can help others to shine their light. It's like the missing piece of the puzzle. Right now, I am looking forward to the adventure ahead. I have fallen freely into love and trust what is to come.

I became so present in those initial months with Alice that this connection opened me to the sacredness of life. This experience brought a depth of meaning, love, respect and gratitude for myself and all life forms. How could I have any real consideration for others when I have no consideration for myself?

You know what they say about getting really high? What goes up must come down.

SHIFT HAD HIT THE FAN

It wasn't as if everything was fixed overnight, because transformation doesn't happen in an instant. If it did, it wouldn't be called a hero's journey. Some of you may know the classic story structure that is shared worldwide called the Hero's Journey. It was coined by Joseph Campbell in 1949, and is outlined in more detail in his book *The Hero with a Thousand Faces*. It's a universal pattern of adventure and transformation that runs through all kinds of mythic traditions across the world.

When I made the decision to never lie again, little did I know that I was in fact asking to be shown the truth, and in order to see the truth I had to face all the lies within myself and thus the lies that were manifested in our societies. This was going to be a lot harder than merely making the decision. I was about to embark on a journey and perceive reality like I had never known before.

Firstly, I had a lot of entanglements in my current state of affairs which included £60k in credit card debt. I had invested in buy-to-let properties with friends, a business with Dan, and was co-producing *Romans 12:20* and also *Otherside of the Game*. Then I got offered the lead role in a big budget UGC film production called *AO The Last Neanderthal*. This would mean filming in France, Bulgaria and Ukraine for nine months of 2009. My ultimate dream was finally arising, just at the point I was being pulled in a different direction. Why does everything happen all at once? I felt tied up in the life I had been wishing into existence, but at this point, it had lost its meaning. This was hard to fathom. I had invested so much energy into this dream of being a professional actor, that this was not the best time for an awakening.

I don't even remember how information was coming to me or from whom, it was as if just by asking for the truth, I began receiving links to books, articles or documentaries on themes I had never heard of before. Topics like secret societies, government control, the military, the food and the pharmaceutical industry, monetary systems, education, law and big corporations. I was digesting videos on Codex Alimentarius and the control on food legislation, 9/11 and the July 7th London bombings and information on UFO disclosures and what's supposedly happening on other planets. I was consuming mainstream movies like *Network 1976, Soylent Green, The Matrix, Revolutionary Rd, The Truman Show, The Celestine Prophecy, The Shift, Into the Wild* and many more. I was no longer watching films for entertainment. They were transmitting a message to me about what was actually happening in the world, what was going on in society and the extremely imbalanced and dysfunctional way humans were behaving. What were we doing to ourselves?

Multiple documentaries shared facts about big corporations and what they ruthlessly do to make their money. Big water companies were polluting our water supply so that bottled water would become the next commodity to invest in. Check out *Blue Gold*. There are landfills full of plastic bottles and huge rivers and streams which are drying out. I was watching in detail, the violent abuse humans were doing to themselves and the planet. Mass killing of so many animals, including endangered species, for no sensible reasons. And the ignorant evil butchering of dolphins, whales, tuna and sharks for food distribution and expensive elite soups. Dolphin meat got sold as whale meat and caused an overdose of mercury in those who ate it. Watch *The Cove* to see for yourself.

The sheer belligerent, unconscious abuse that these actions were causing to nature and our ecosystems was shocking to me. Negligently spilling oil and other toxic chemicals, contaminating our oceans. So many unconscious actions that damaged and killed coral reefs, from coastal development, dredging, quarrying, destructive fishing practices, boat anchors and recreational misuse from the touching and removing of corals plus the devastation from pollution that originates on land, but finds its way into coastal waters.

I read that an estimated 35,000 children as young as nine risk their lives to feed the world's growing hunger for cobalt. They work in perilous conditions to extract cobalt from the ground in the Democratic Republic of Congo, one of the poorest, most violent and corrupt places on earth.

I was even more shocked to read that there are more than 4 million victims of sex trafficking globally. A study from the United Nations' International Labour Organization estimated 3.8 million adults and 1 million children were victims of forced sexual exploitation in 2016 around the world, with the vast majority (99%) being women and girls, though men, boys, trans, intersex and non-binary individuals can be victims as well. I was becoming aware through documentaries of the disturbing information about the extent of manipulation and violence that large multi -national corporations go to in order to maximise profit. Of course, a statement like this raises controversy, but the story of Ken Saro-Wiwa and MOSOPs (Movement for Survival of the Ogoni People) fighting against a big oil company comes to mind as just one horrific story of how power and corruption affects innocent people. It seemed to me some companies would do whatever was necessary to fulfil their agendas.

There were people sharing evidence that we have had the cure for cancer since 1928 and it is being kept under cover because cancer is big business. Cancer is a biocode gone wrong. In 1928, Dr Max Gerson documented that diet can cure cancer. Robert C. Atkins M.D said "There have been many cancer cures, and all have been ruthlessly and systematically suppressed with a Gestapo-like thoroughness by the cancer establishment." To see for yourself, watch the documentary *A Beautiful Truth* by Steve Kroschel.

I read that it was common knowledge and clearly documented that AIDS was man-made and therefore another big business. Dr William Campbell Douglass wrote in WHO MURDERED AFRICA that HIV was genetically engineered in 1974, by the World Health Organization (WHO). African AIDS is the result of the smallpox eradication vaccine program conducted by the WHO during the 1970s. Wow, could this be true? I didn't know at this point what was 100% true or not but either way, all this information was coming into my awareness and destabilising my perception of reality. I had definitely entered a rabbit hole or two!

All these stories and more were rocking my world and bursting my bubble of ignorance. They evoked many more questions like: if all this is really happening, why doesn't everyone know, and what is being done to change it? And how are these organisations and business tycoons allowed to orchestrate and get away with what I can only perceive as crimes against humanity? It felt like I was uncovering the real-life examples of what I'd seen in movies, when corrupt warlords and Mafia cartels do whatever they want to make money.

I delved into the monetary system, debt and credit card scams, and read about the Magna Carta, Black's Law dictionary and how our society and Law really functions. People who had studied Law were stepping forward saying we are always guilty, regardless of what we have done in the eyes of the Law, because our parents signed over our names as a company when we were born. Our birth certificate, driving licences, National Insurance cards, and passports are just ID cards that tie us into the game of commerce. We are just numbers on a computer screen, born into a society with a capital letter name and number. That capital letter name isn't actually you or I as a person. The person is a corporate legal fiction created with the birth certificate. The birth certificate is an enslavement document. It just labels and registers us as a corporation in the eyes of the financial world.

I found further information that The Bank of England monetary system and the Federal Reserve is all a farce, there is no gold or silver to back up what our promissory notes are supposed to give us. Every country is bankrupt and any money there is, is actually ours because the only currency the country has is our labour! Was my mind fried or what?

This led me into a web of information from whistle blowers (I prefer messengers), from the likes of Edward Snowden, Julian Assange, David Icke, Michael Tsarion and Peter Joseph. I watched video testimonials from the military, health sectors and government organisations, sharing the atrocities they had witnessed or directly committed. I read about Economic Hit Men who give other countries three chances to hand over power to America and if they didn't play ball, they get bombed and taken over regardless.

According to his book, *Confessions of an Economic Hit Man*, John Perkins wrote that Economic Hit Men (EHMs) are highly-paid professionals who would cheat countries around the globe out of trillions of dollars and convince the political and financial leadership of underdeveloped countries to accept enormous development loans from institutions like the World Bank, the U.S. Agency for International Development (USAID), other foreign "aid" organizations, huge corporations and the pockets of a few wealthy families who control the planet's natural resources. Their tools included fraudulent financial reports, rigged elections, payoffs, extortion, sex, and murder. They play a game as old as empire, but one that has taken on new and terrifying dimensions during this time of globalisation. I was experiencing the information age.

Shift had definitely hit the fan, and I wondered what was going to blow my way next.

THE LAST NEANDERTHAL

Alongside all this researching, I accepted the lead acting role in the major motion picture called *AO The Last Neanderthal*. It was a phenomenal opportunity that I couldn't pass up. I loved the script and the courageous vision of the director and, for once, the project had nothing to do with being a criminal. I'm not going to say the money wasn't a pull either, especially after struggling for money all my life. I was being offered a nice wedge (£80k to be precise) to do what I loved and had been wanting for years. It was a 'hell yes'. I later found out the budget for the main role was much higher, but I wasn't a well-known actor, and my agent wasn't the greatest negotiator. But I wasn't complaining, the money was a godsend and supported Alice and I so we could focus on our art and the greater mission of love that was bubbling in my veins. This money would enable us to live for the next few years and maybe even longer, as I was quickly becoming a minimalist.

All the information I had been absorbing was making me

adapt certain habits. For example, the idea of pumping my muscles in front a mirror at the gym lost its appeal and I was drawn more towards the practice and philosophy of yoga, which I'd read was 'a journey of the self, to the Self, through the self.' Yoga was more than just physical exercise which it has often become in the western world. I understood it more as a technology through the different postures and breathing to awaken me to the greater truths within. The word 'self' written with a small 's', refers to us in this physical form, our ego, and who we consider ourselves to be on a daily basis. The word 'Self' with a capital 'S', refers to the true self, Atman, or the divine within us.

It was of no surprise then that the feature film Sav, Laj and I produced, *Otherside of the Game*, was all about a drug dealer wanting to break free from his dysfunctional lifestyle which I had pretty much now accomplished and then just as I was in the midst of this huge awakening and asking who am I and where are we from, I'm cast in *AO The Last Neanderthal*, a movie about the origin of our species, a

Photo by Patrick Glaize

On Location for AO

172

Photo by Patrick Glaize

Being Transformed into AO

prehistoric love story based around 35,000 years ago.

I dreamt of being James Bond before I was forty but instead got the prehistoric version, called AO.

This movie was an actor's dream, a life-changing experience. I needed three hours of make-up every day to become AO. Often, I would fall asleep as the make-up artists did their magic and I'd wake up transformed into AO. They didn't seem to mind my head nodding.

The locations we filmed on were breath-taking. From peaks of mountains to ancient caves, chasing wild boar through forests, interacting with eagles, bison, wild horses and even fighting a polar bear named Agi.

I had never seen a real polar bear up close before. She was magnificent. I know what you are thinking, I obviously couldn't fight a polar bear, she would have killed me with one slap. Instead, I had to fight a man dressed in a polar bear suit against the green screen. I had to pinch myself at times. The owner of the polar bear then wore my costume and rolled around with Agi. Making her act and supposedly roar because in the movie my whole tribe is almost wiped out by the big ferocious bear. When in fact, she was just opening her mouth for biscuits. She was a softy, bless her.

Photo by Patrick Glaize

Agi the Polar Bear

I will never forget when Agi came on set one morning and elegantly walked into the area which had been fenced off and set up for filming her. She laid down on the snow and spread herself out flat like a pancake. Made herself comfortable and didn't get up for the rest of the day. A true prima donna. This really challenged the production team because it cost a lot of money to have one hundred people on set for a day of filming nothing. They had flown her in from Canada for the shoot, and she had her own trailer too, which looked better than mine.

I thought the fact she never got up all day was beautiful. Yes, she has been trained to some degree, but at the core she was still raw nature, not some human puppet to be controlled.

On top of these unique experiences, the adventurous script had me hanging from cliffs, making love naked in the rain and drinking from wild rivers, which almost killed me with dysentery. I had been building up my body for the character and during a test shoot the director wanted me to drink from a river, at first I just pretended to and then he said "The camera can see you're not drinking, Simon, get the water in your mouth."

For some reason my body knew not to drink this water, but I took a little in and didn't swallow, but what did go in was clearly toxic and wiped me out for almost two weeks. I had to visit some freaky hospital to get tested and there was talk of quarantining the whole cast and crew as they didn't know exactly what was wrong with me. It was a disaster because I lost so much weight. All that hard work puked and shit away with diarrhoea. The shooting had to be postponed and eventually when we could shoot, I felt like a

Photo by Patrick Glaize

The Fake Agi

weak and frail Neanderthal. I just accepted that AO was the last Neanderthal, and in the script, he nearly died numerous times so it sort of worked.

The other spectacular challenge of this movie was that the cast learned a whole new prehistoric language made up by the team. I was acting with Bulgarian gypsies who couldn't speak English, so our conversations were mostly through body language and the use of this prehistoric language we had learned together.

Photo by Patrick Glaize

AO and the Bison

I did experience quite a sad moment during filming when I had to pull a spear out of a dead bison. It was said this beast was old and due to be killed. Apparently, farmers sell animals for films in this way. I was not convinced. I had watched this particular old wise bison the day before. The way the other bison were all moving around him, it seemed to me he was the leader of the pack. It didn't look like he was dying. The next day he was dead on the floor and I had to film a scene where my character AO pulls the spear out of his belly and then lays down head to head and speaks to him with reverence. Like a prayer of respect and gratitude before eating it. Research somehow found out that 35,000 years ago, hunters practiced sacred ritual, and maybe some still do. It wasn't easy for me to accept we had to kill this beautiful alive creature. To make things worse, this scene didn't even make it into the final cut.

Photo by Patrick Glaize

AO the Prehistoric Bond

Despite everything, I did have respect for the director's vision because it had great potential to become a cult classic. Unfortunately, though, the movie was a flop. Due to dramas with the production team and fear that the movie wouldn't be understood, they decided to cut many of the scenes to make it a PG movie and add a voiceover in the first person. Not a wise move.

Photo by Patrick Glaize

AO on Top of the World

I may not have been James Bond, but I was a lead actor in a high production movie with all the trimmings, and starring in this film taught me so much about the industry I had desperately been trying to break into. But my motivation for this profession was waning. There was a greater force motivating me now. Attending the Cannes Film Festival and taking a trip down the famous red carpet clarified this. The insight those few moments brought to me were simply profound.

RED CARPET INSANITY

I was walking on the red carpet that I had observed for so many years on a TV screen, watching the famous actors and actresses in awe and admiration and wishing one day that it would be me. The film festival was not an award ceremony but had the same taste. The likes of Quentin Tarantino and other A-listers were all arriving at the premiere of Terry Gilliam's new film.

I was suited and booted and slightly nervous as I got closer to the entrance. Then the red carpet touched my shoes: I had arrived. I took a moment to soak it up and noticed cigarette butts and rubbish on the carpet. For some reason, I felt a sense of disappointment about that. I mean this is the famous red carpet that stars walk on. Who the hell dropped their cigarette butts here, of all places?

It was another one of those surreal occasions, and I was getting flashbacks of where I had come from, as my name was called out on the speakers (all part of PR for films in production). The paparazzi were going wild as they do.

Cannes Film Festival

Taking photos of me and others arriving. It was all very glamourous.

As the press lights constantly flashed, my gaze was drawn behind them to the partitions fencing off the stars from the film fans and public spectators. Life moved in slow motion as I saw these desperate people, fans who wanted to see these amazing actors, producers and directors. Wow, these people are so amazing right? The fans, the onlookers and the wannabes were on ladders to see over the partitions and take photos. Even more disturbing, were those who didn't have ladders or a way to see over the partitions. They were jumping up, extending their arms and snapping the camera randomly, hoping to get a picture of one of these amazing human beings.

Unique human beings, phenomenal manifestations of supreme life, jumping up and down, to maybe catch a picture of other unique beings walking on a red carpet. And just because they created a film. And to top it off, they couldn't even see who they were snapping.

The magnitude of this unconscious behaviour hit me in my chest. I became aware of what the craving, idolising, and desire to be a part of this 'puppet show' really felt like. It's show business. It is what it is. What did I expect? Sympathy as my illusion revealed itself?

I have no regrets. I needed to witness my delusion for the façade it was. I had made assumptions and false projections and do not want to judge anything that happened as right or wrong. But for me, the whole experience of *AO The Last Neanderthal* gave me great introspection which helped me reframe my reality. I realised that idolising the 'famous' and making them more worthy than myself was of no benefit. If I had become famous like the individuals I idolised, I wouldn't suddenly have everything worked out. The world of success and fame was just another act within an act. Jim Carrey's words from his speech to graduates at Maharishi University summed this up nicely.

"I've often said I wish everybody could realise all their

dreams, find their wealth and fame so they could see it's not where we are going to find our sense of completion."

In *I AM*, a documentary produced by Tom Shadyac, one of Hollywood's most successful writer/director/producers who made Jim famous, Tom asks some of today's most profound thinkers, two questions: What's wrong with our world? And what can we do about it? After an accident and shift in perception, Tom shares his story and how the world of fame and fortune was not giving him what he thought it could. Don't take my word for it though, because I had to have experiences and spend many years seeking them in order for me to also have this perception. It's always easier said than done. I heard many stories telling me I didn't need to be famous in life, but that didn't lessen the drive I had to realise my dream. I knew crime and taking drugs were not the healthiest, most honest or beneficial actions for my life either, but that didn't stop me needing to experience them for myself.

Life is all about perspective, and I am aware some of you reading this may think that who I am being now is just another façade. Even personal development coaches, spiritual gurus, yogis, peace activists, saints and noble ones who are supposedly serving humanity, can be found caught up in subtle ego traps, spiritual bypassing and experiencing conflicts and abuse driven from unresolved trauma and the messiah complex. It's not dissimilar to the craving for fame and fortune. Humans have needs to be met; we all want to belong, to be seen, acknowledged, held and heard. Ultimately, we all want to be loved. We are seeking the love we were unable to receive from our parents and care givers.

This was why fame and fortune was so hypnotising to me. But now I realised, I had been looking for love in all the wrong places. As an actor, I was a product for sale. Films are products, this book is a product. I am a product of society in a materialistic world. Everything I had been seeking previously in that unconscious state felt hollow. As I went through the motions of finishing the film, the more my real eyes were opening. I was realising (real-eyes-ing) how out of alignment I was with the bigger picture playing out in the world. I didn't know where I was heading and I wasn't prepared for what this new light of awareness would bring up on all levels. I soon found out that the shadows were not too far behind.

One thing became apparent, the movie we call life was in need of some real-life superheroes, conscious directors and new vision scriptwriters. Some motivated ambassadors of LOVE, daring leaders and enthusiastic co-leaders of a new world. I felt connected, engaged, and a little overwhelmed.

I had a new dream and it was bigger than ever before…

DARK NIGHT OF THE SOUL

You must first go out of your mind, in order to come to your senses. Weaving all this information and my experiences together was all-consuming, and anxiety, depression and fear were present throughout. I made the decision to renounce all that I thought was causing problems in my life. I even withdrew lovemaking with Alice, the woman I thought I wanted to share my life with. This beautiful human being who catalysed this transformation in so many ways was the one I was resisting. Is that what love would do?

This resistance was my response to the realisation of the abuse that women have endured for centuries from the dominating dysfunctional men who unconsciously let their hungry cocks lead them on a quest for friction at all costs. I was deeply impacted by the images and stories I had read about acid attacks (also called acid throwing). This is a violent assault involving the act of throwing acid or a similarly corrosive substance onto the body, usually the face, of another with the intention to disfigure, maim, torture, or kill. These attacks can often expose and sometimes dissolve the bones and, in many cases, lead to permanent blindness in the victims. And guess what? These violent attacks often occur as revenge against women who reject proposals of marriage or sexual advances, sexually related jealousy and lust or because of the woman's position in society. Other motivations for these disturbing violent acts are gender inequality, racial or religious conflicts and gang violence. These attacks can happen to men but 80% that are reported involve women.

I was touched deeply and angered as I read stories of the futile suffering caused from what I can only describe as ignorance. I would say a lack of conscious sex education is the root cause of this extensive mental, physical and sexual violence that is evident all across the planet. All violence is a tragic expression of our unmet needs, unhealthy sexual desires and fearfully craving connection with distorted intentions. The dense emotions I was feeling throughout these months were a strain on my health and wellbeing. My nervous system was in shock. Although I may have had some theory as to why this occurs, I was still asking why. Why anyone would want to cause so much harm to another human being or to any species? It wasn't making sense at all. I couldn't wrap my head around it all.

Within this breakthrough, I was having a breakdown. I was absorbed by the process. I called it 'a glitch in the Matrix'. I had seen the film *The Matrix* and thought it was an interesting movie, but now I was interpreting it as a documentary highlighting what is actually happening in my world. Talk about red pill/blue pill. I was looking for the white rabbit when all along I was in the never-ending rabbit hole. Everything I thought I knew became a mystery and within this mystery, my identity was dissolving within and without. What did I really know? I was anxiously questioning everything and suffering from information overload. The more I knew, the less I understood.

If what I am describing has already started happening to you, don't panic. (Easier said than done.) Breathe deeply and observe. This is called an identity crisis or existential breakdown. I found that when I allowed what was happening, it was easier, but whenever I resisted or reacted, it often felt more intense and more challenging. If it starts happening then it's going to happen either way, so it's better to practice surrendering to what is. Resistance caused more stress. It's hard to accurately describe an existential breakdown as they are all uniquely personal. Depending on who I spoke to, they would diagnose or assume they knew what I was feeling when they didn't really. They could only assume to know.

For example, feelings of depression, anxiety, confusion and fatigue can be part of the process. And those same feelings, from my experience, pop up now and then as part of day to day life. Especially when I question the nature of reality. If I tried to explain my existential breakdown to some doctors, I'm pretty certain many of them would diagnose me with Depression, Schizophrenia, Epstein-Barr (EBV), Chronic Fatigue Syndrome, Hypothyroid, Low serotonin or maybe ADD, ADHD, Oppositional Defiant Disorder (ODD) or any other number of so called problems which can be apparently treated with drugs.

I resonate with Charles Eisenstein's perspective on this;

'Doctors in our current system have no time to sit with patients and ask real questions to get to the bottom of momentary dis-eases - The notion of a cure starts with the question, "What has gone wrong?" But there is another, radically different way of seeing fatigue and depression that starts by asking, "What is the body, in its perfect wisdom, responding to?" When would it be the wisest choice for someone to be unable to summon the energy to fully participate in life? The answer is staring us in the face. When our body is saying 'no' to life, through fatigue or depression, the first thing to ask is, "Is life as I am living it the right life for me right now?" When the body is saying 'no' to participation in the world, the first thing to ask is, "Does the world as it is presented to me merit my full participation? What if there is something so fundamentally wrong with the world, the lives, and the way of life being offered us, that withdrawal is the only sane response?'

The movie *I Heart Huckabees* encapsulates these existential breakdowns in a humorous way. It depicts the pain and confusion life often incurs when we seek the meaning of life. It has a great cast of actors too, Dustin Hoffman being one of them. I also really appreciated Jeff Foster's approach to depression, he named it 'deep-rest' and pointed towards surrendering to the moment and allowing the depression to be an opportunity to pause and rest rather than fight what was happening. From his own experience of depression, he suggests this is a great moment to reflect and realign to the truth of who we are.

Thankfully for me, my brother Lloyd was having parallel experiences, exploring similar information in his own way.

This brought us closer together. I needed somebody who I could share and connect with on this level and Lloyd was that grounded friend I could crack up with, in the true sense of the word.

GROUNDHOG DAY

Late one afternoon I was walking along the High Street in Hove, a seaside town in the south of England. As I walked along I looked into each shop as I passed and kept perceiving human beings sat inside looking bored, some of them selling things which from my perspective, were pointless. What I was viewing all seemed mundane. As if I had entered a different dimension. I continued observing through the windows of every shop, sometimes pausing for a moment to observe with more presence. I asked in disdain: 'What are we doing to ourselves? Spending our precious days stood in shops, cubical rooms, no bigger than 5sqm just waiting to sell merchandise to potential buyers. Is that it?'

I had this knowing that deep at their core, they didn't truly want to be there. It was like I could see lifeless souls. It reminded me of the movie *Groundhog Day* with Bill Murray. Of course, I thought I knew how society functioned, it wasn't as if I had never seen, visited or benefitted from shops, it's a consumer industry, and we all need money to survive, I get it. But my awareness was showing me the depths of the consumer trap, the hooks and lures that keep us in the cages of society. Everything I was observing seemed fake just like the red carpet. Another theatre stage. I had never seen it this vividly before. I had even worked in shops selling products myself but now I was seeing the illusion beyond what I was seeing. I was seeing through it all as if wearing x-ray goggles. Accessing the deeper layers of control playing out. I saw life force dying in front of me. Dead living beings. All just waiting. Waiting for what?

I made my way to the seafront on that wet and windy evening. As the night sky drew in, I stood under a streetlight watching the raindrops pour down through the glow of the yellow beam. Just watching the water dancing with the wind. Feeling into it all, witnessing the mystery. Feeling confused, upset and lonely. I switched on my camcorder and began speaking about what I was witnessing. That night I shouted and screamed my anger out to sea, "What the fuck is happening? Aaaaarrrrrghhhh!"

I often recorded my breakdowns. The dark night is not just one night. I can only speak for myself, but I experienced many more moments similar to this as my nervous system adapted to this new way of seeing reality. Some were less intense than others. Many happened at home, when my mind would be racing, seeing the depth of the madness and insanity but not knowing how to fix it or what to do next. Paralysed.

Some days the mountain seemed too steep to climb. I'd just stay in bed for a while, observing the visual dynamics of thoughts, and the mental constructs of information all whizzing around my awareness. I would flip out for a while, make some strange random noises, realise how it must be to crack up, try to rationalise what was happening and then get up and get going with day-to-day mundane tasks.

The psychosis was close. I envisioned it like walking on a tightrope of insanity. I read that during an awakening process the madness must become heightened in order to rise above it. It all has to come into awareness before we can truly see it for what it is. Great, so I had to go mad to realise I wasn't mad. What a dichotomy. Was I starring in my own version of the movie *One Flew Over the Cuckoo's Nest*?

YOU GONE CHURCH?

Along the way, many friends distanced themselves from me. It's all part of the journey, and it probably didn't help when I began overloading some of them with the information I was finding. I wanted the whole world to see what I was seeing. 'Come and hang out with me in the dark nights, go on, I promise it's fun!' I thought it would help end the mass dysfunction and destruction. This need for others to get it, was in fact a call for help. People thought I had lost the plot. A girl friend invited me out for dinner, saying softly while eating pizza:

"People are talking, Si, what happened to you?" She asked if I was having fun. From the outside looking in, it must have looked serious in the morphic mess of chaotic change, and that's because it was.

In hindsight, it wasn't the best idea to attend a family wedding in 2011 and meet past friends and acquaintances while moving through the process of a psychological meltdown. Paul, (Swamp foot) who I have fond memories of, was one of Steve's friends in the bedroom that memorable day where I smoked my first joint. In my younger years he became a good friend, always looking out for me. We had shared many experiences together. He pulled me to one side at the reception to have a serious chat.

"Si, you gone Church?" he asked.

"Gone Church?" I said. "What does that mean?"

"You know, you found Jesus?"

"How can I find Jesus? I don't know what he looked like or where he was buried!"

"You know what I fucking mean."

Of course, I knew what he was asking, I was just playing the game, I'm a joker. He was asking if I had found God. Had I become religious and was I singing hallelujah praise the Lord every Sunday at mass?

To some extent, depending on your personal definition, I had found God. But the word 'God' has many connotations and unless somebody shares their interpretation of what God is to them, many assumptions can be made so I found it best not to use that word. Any talk of Jesus or God when I was growing up, and you would have got laughed at or received some serious mental, if not physical harassment.

It baffled me that people were concerned I might have turned religious, yet most of them celebrated Christmas, got married in churches and baptised their children. Now if that isn't contradictory, what is?

People will always hear what they choose to hear based on their own indoctrinated beliefs. I was definitely seeing reality in a new light and how I was speaking was not dissimilar to prophets and holy saints. I hadn't been sucked in by the Jehovah witnesses or attended any churches, but I was aware it could seem like I had. We can make anything our God, from Hooliganism to Spiritualism to any other ism, from criminals, to sport heroes to fictitious heroes. We aspire to be our idols.

There are many words that define the essence of what many point to when they use the word God, such as source, consciousness, divine, grand creator, quantum field, master, the father, Allah, Krishna, Ram, great spirit, the sun, the light, Aztec, Greek or Mayan gods and the list goes on. So many different names all pointing towards that which cannot be fully explained, hence why millions of humans argue over whose God is the real God. I've mentioned it before and I'll mention it again, in the name of God and religion, violent and vicious conflicts sweep across the globe creating absurd amounts of futile pain and suffering. I find it incomprehensible when I truly ponder it, this need for humanity to segregate and insulate themselves.

It makes sense that my behaviours were strange to many who had known me before this shift in awareness. The information I was researching had and still has the ability to shatter cultural and conditioned beliefs as it did mine. When we ask the big open questions, we must be ready to challenge our identity and all that we believe to be true. This will induce states of fear, aversion and depression. That's why the phrase *ignorance is bliss* serves the masses. Taking responsibility and facing our shadows is a vulnerable path, travelled by the few.

Once the truth is evoked, there is no turning back. If I had turned back now, I would have been in denial. I didn't know all of what was happening in this great mystery, it would be naïve to think I even could. If anything, I knew very little in my limited awareness. But the beauty was that I now knew that I knew very little. Which made it clear that there was a lot more to uncover. My glitch in the Matrix said: look at the world in all its glory and then look at what we humans are doing to its beauty from ignorance and unconscious actions. Images began playing out like a film roll in my mind's eye, highlighting how my thoughts, words and actions were upholding many collective cultural stories from beliefs I now saw as delusional. My false beliefs had to be rewired.

Whose beliefs was I upholding? Were they solely mine? Or inherited from past ancestors, friends, parents, collective myths and religion? I continued silently asking: Who am I? And who or what is asking the question?

It was as if I had this anxious hum in the background of my being. Apparently, time was running out as 2012 approached. It was receiving a lot of press in terms of it being the end of the world. The media was causing a frenzy among people all over the world, and it was hard not to get sucked into the apocalypse drama. The story of the great floods and devastation for all mankind was about to arise. Noah was building his ark and nobody had a ticket. Mass confusion spoon fed to the blind by misinformation and unfound claims. I didn't know what was going to happen, how could I? It reminded me of the doomsday event in the year 2000 called the Millennium bug or Y2K. The end had been said to be nigh. But it hadn't ended then either, so my bets were against the planet suddenly imploding in on itself or being blown up by a huge meteor or Planet X.

But these themes brought up a lot for me around these apocalypse stories and religious narratives that just seem to be woven into the fabric of our societies without question. Why do humans constantly fear the end of the world? Maybe something big was dying, but what was it? So many conflicting stories I read felt untrue. Some seemed to hold strands of truth from the evidence being shared, but a lot was just New Age poppycock.

The Mayan prophecies were maybe the most probable. A range of eschatological beliefs that cataclysmic or transformative events would occur around 21st December 2012. This date was regarded as the end-date of a 5,126-year-long cycle predicted by the Mayans.

Big directors of mainstream Hollywood movies even cashed in on the end of the world sagas, as this made for great moviemaking. People were said to be building underground shelters and stocking up on food for the potential floods and impending global meltdown.

Paradigms were shifting that's for sure. Veils were lifting and false beliefs peeling away like onion skins.

With the help of the internet, the truth was being called out like never before, but it wasn't one sided, the internet has also highlighted humanity's polarisation. So many conflicting beliefs and opinions. It's easy to get lost in invisible prisons.

THE INVISIBLE PRISON

On one side of the coin there was boundless potential, loving awareness and blinding clarity, on the other there was darkness, extreme limitations and confusion from within the constructs of this dual society. I felt caged in and caught up in a number of catch 22s. I named this dichotomy 'The Invisible Prison' which represented the cage of invisible walls created by our fears and indoctrinated psychological beliefs.

It's the lies we tell ourselves and others that creates those walls. Why do we lie? I can only tell you why I lied and that's because I was scared. I lied because I didn't even know I was lying, I was frightened of being humiliated, rejected, and losing control, even though I was never in control. Lying helped me to uphold my identity and vanity. And on some subtle levels I was frightened of uncertainty. Lying is much easier than searching for the truth and accepting it, no matter how inconvenient it is. Of course, when I lie to myself, I lie to others.

Another term I use for this aspect of our human experience,

is the 'hamster wheel of dysfunction'. Highlighting the repetitive daily cycles we perpetuate without questioning why we're doing what we're doing. And if we do pose the question, it's rarely followed through with a deep inquiry into the root of the issue. When we're in these invisible prisons or on these hamster wheels, we are not aware there's anything outside of them, until somebody breaks the hypnotic cycle and makes us see the invisible walls (the illusions). It's like the old saying, when you're in the shit, you can't smell it.

Breaking Out of My Invisible Prison

When we're in the invisible prison we have no other option than to numb ourselves in a multitude of ways, with food, drugs, dysfunctional relationships, lies, hobbies, and sex. This is exactly what I had been doing most of my life.

I know how easy it is to avoid and distract ourselves especially when we believe what is fed to us through mainstream media. If we have limited beliefs and they can be justified by the people and environments around us, then it's much harder to see what is real or not. In our invisible prisons we all become ignorant and detached from reality. We enter a deep state of psychosis without realising. As I was having this discovery it made me aware of what the term 'sheep mentality' was describing. When we follow the herd (gang peer pressure was one example in my case) without taking a moment to stop and ask 'Where am I going? Who am I following?' We become sheeple.

A great example of this cultural conditioning was found in the book *Where Do We Begin* by Nicholas Eldridge. It's a book which challenges our truths and asks us to look at our core beliefs. This monkey experiment was shared to highlight a theory on how we function in group dynamics and very simply how we get conditioned within our society without realising.

"Five monkeys are placed into a cage with a banana attached to a rope directly above them. A ladder is placed in the middle of the room to enable the monkeys to get to the banana. However, as soon as one monkey climbs the ladder to retrieve the banana, he and the four other monkeys are sprayed with cold water, forcing the monkey back down. After a while, a second monkey goes to climb the ladder and again they are all sprayed with water. Lesson learned. Now, no other monkey attempts to climb the ladder. One of the monkeys is then removed from the cage and replaced by a new monkey. This new monkey sees the banana and goes to climb the ladder. Not wanting to be sprayed again, the four other monkeys turn hostile to the new monkey and stop him from climbing the ladder. And so another original monkey is replaced by a new monkey who also goes to climb the ladder. The three remaining original monkeys again attack the new one joined by the first replacement. This changing of monkeys is carried on until there are no original monkeys left, yet, when a new monkey is introduced and goes to climb the ladder, the four remaining monkeys attack him. Why? None of the monkeys in the cage now have ever been sprayed with water, so what is the problem? None of the monkeys know the reason for not going up the ladder yet they all carry on in the same conditioned way."

The invisible prison is an amazing self-perpetuating design, meaning the suffering we witness in our societies is held up by our collective acquiescence because we so often keep doing and reinforcing the same behaviours over and over again without questioning why. We accept many situations as the norm because that is the way it's always been. These unconscious actions and repetitive cycles form our habits, behaviours and beliefs and from here we form consensus realities. A consensus reality is that which is generally agreed to be the accepted reality based on a consensus view. This means that humans agree upon certain concepts of reality that other people in the world, culture or group also believe are real or treat as real and then this is just how it is. But if someone disagrees then they are often referred to as 'living in a different world or dimension' or breaking the rules. Some may even say statements like 'she's off in the clouds again' or 'he's in la la land' and in some cases we see people being cast out of these consensus views because of broken agreements or the individuals now have nothing in common. These consensus views that form our realities also arise from the fact that humans do not fully agree or understand the nature of knowledge or ontology. I don't know about you, but I had never considered the reality I had grown up in, to be my definition of real. I thought everyone was experiencing the same reality as me.

I was now able to see beyond these invisible prison walls that are created through consensus and engage with the collective realities or what I would call collective prisons of mass consciousness (that we humans have agreed to) in a whole new way. I realised why my choices are so powerful because they literally co-create reality. What I agree with and give focus to contributes to forming the fabric of the society and cultures I grow up in.

I pat myself on the back for making it through these dark nights even when I couldn't see the light around the bends in the tunnel. As I witnessed the illusions which were making me ill, I found myself in a deep metamorphosis from a lost caterpillar hoping to find my wings to fly free as a beautiful butterfly. I could hear Richard Bach's words from his book *Illusions*: "What the caterpillar calls the end of the world, the master calls a butterfly." I wouldn't call myself a master, but maybe I was on a path that would require mastery to navigate my ship through the storms ahead.

BLACK RUBBER CLOWN SUIT

Gandhi once said, "The enemy is fear. We think it is hate, but it is fear." And I read that 'Fear is the thief of humanity's light' which is a pretty big statement, but the more aware I was becoming of these invisible prisons, the more I witnessed humans keeping themselves in situations and lifestyles that did not serve them.

For some years I had been reading text from spiritual teachers from the likes of Eckhart Tolle, Neale Donald Walsh, Craig Hamilton, Wayne Dyer, Byron Katie, and Ram Dass to name a few. All of them in various ways referenced the ego identification and the path of self-actualization in their teachings. Highlighting the ego as a necessary part of the psyche to understand and become aware of.

Tolle's teachings invited me to look closely at the repetitive cycles that occur in our lives and why. He was the one who introduced me to the term pain-body which is an aspect of ourselves that dictates many of the choices we make in life. He described how our egos are addicted to suffering. He opened my mind to the concept, 'I am not my mind, but the observer of my mind'.

This was hard to grasp at first. He helped me make the connection between my pain and the fear I experienced from living in the past and the future, while missing what was happening in the present moment. It's a term he calls *The Power of Now*. He says we all have a pain-body. Some may be more dormant or active than others, but we all have one. The pain-body is the shadow aspect of our being, the emotional part of the ego. In Tolle's book *A New Earth*, he describes the pain-body as a 'psychic parasite' that possesses us and causes us suffering. It derives its energy from pain. Pain is its food.

Tolle goes on to say, "The pain-body wants to survive, just like every other entity in existence, and it can only survive if it gets you to unconsciously identify with it. It can take you over, become you, and live through you. It needs to get its 'food' through you. It will feed on any experience that resonates with its own kind of energy, anything that creates further pain in whatever form: anger, destructiveness, hatred, emotional drama, violence, and even illness. So, the pain-body, when it has taken you over, will create a situation in your life that reflects back its own energy frequency for it to feed on." Pain can only feed on pain. Pain cannot feed on joy, it finds it quite indigestible.

Learning about the pain-body gave me clarity on how my destructive behaviours and actions had been staying alive longer than I would have anticipated. When I first read this it allowed me to bring more focus to the components of my ego and this pain-body character who now had a spotlight on it.

Over time I found out that my cunning little pain-body had many pseudonyms too. The shadow, the unconscious, inner child, the wound, freak, mental patient, the wounded tenderness, the devil, energy vampire, the psychic parasite or the black rubber clown suit as coined by filmmaker David Lynch. I am sure there are other terms, depending on the person describing this part of our wounded selves.

The pain-body is so extremely sly it can also masquerade as love in all forms. It will take on my intellect and use my wisdom to give intelligent reasons to justify its behaviours, which at times can feel very plausible. I needed to be alert. The many different teachers I listened to were all pointing to the same place within. To uncover and face the emotional pain and trauma experienced in one form or another during the early stages of my life.

Just being born is traumatic enough, let alone trying to survive in hostile environments from the get-go. I needed help to catch this deceptive part of myself! It's a stubborn little fucker that is pissed off with the pain it had to endure in the past.

I enjoyed how physical therapist Val Zajicek defined 'PAIN' as 'Pay Attention Inside Now'. Ah! So I could allow my pain to communicate with me. It has a voice I can hear if I silence myself enough to listen to it. My body speaks to me and my pain is alerting me to where I need to bring focus, what needs to be addressed. But with all the distractions of everyday life, it's hard to know what the pain wants to communicate.

Exploring of the ego was a little confusing at times because there were multiple perspectives from different cultures and some of it felt very intellectual and heady. Sigmund Freud's theory (one of the originators in psychoanalysis) describes the personality as having three parts: id, ego, super-ego.

Some just say kill the ego with no real solutions of how to deal with this part of ourselves. Killing anything didn't feel true for me but understanding this part of myself felt less harmful and very important. When I understand something, it can no longer control me and I preferred to keep it simple because I'm simple Simon after all.

Our ego is the unobserved mind, it's that part of us that functions from our unconscious conditioning. I enjoyed the movie *The Shift*, starring Wayne Dyer because it showed how the unconscious ego shows up in our day to day lives.

There is a part where Wayne is being interviewed and he explains the ego as having four components and that we build identification and attachment around what we have, what we do, what people think of us, and from the belief that we are separate from everything else. This really rang true for me and I appreciated having a clearer reference point so that I could distinguish when I was acting from my egoic identification.

The first component of the ego makes us believe that, 'Who we are is what we have'. When I identify myself with my possessions and beliefs associated to them then I adopt the belief that the more that I own means I think I am more valuable as a person. And the attachment to these possessions causes addictive behaviours.

The second component of the ego is that, 'Who I am is what I do'. Wayne Dyer explains that this whole world of

'I am what I do' means we strive for constant achievement and become consumed by success, value, and our worth is based on how much we accomplish, which makes us want more. More money, promotions, status, labels, which fuels the competitive mentality that makes everything about me, me, me, and that births a belief that we need to be better than everybody else in order to get more, more, more. This craving for more is insatiable. This aspect of the ego pretty much summed up my competitive nature and desire for fame and fortune. Shit. So, I was just on some big ego trip all along?

The third component of the ego is that, 'I am what other people think of me'. Therefore, 'I am my reputation'. This one is dangerous because we can end up trying to be someone different every day in order to people please. We can never just be ourselves because of the fear of being judged by others. I associated this with my multiple personas. From a wannabe gangster, to the stylish dude in designer gear who thinks he's sexy and cool, to the geezer who thinks he knows everything, to the actor, the list goes on.

And then we move onto the fourth component of the ego, which Wayne Dyer says develops later on, which is, 'Who I am is separate from everybody else'. This suggests that I am separate from everything that is missing in my life, which means the things I want and crave for. It points to the false belief that I am never enough or complete and always fragmented in some way.

These components supported my expanded awareness and highlighted the traits of my egoic identification which was attached to false beliefs. So what happened when I was able to feed my intellectual mind with this understanding? I was able to shift my focus and experience more of what Wayne calls the 'meaning phase' of our lives. This stage is where we realise that we come from a source of energy, whatever we want to call it. The same source that is everywhere. We are always connected to this energy at all times. There is no place that it is not. Which means I am already connected to everything.

I can let go of these mental constructs that separate me and make me live and uphold false beliefs. I can question my beliefs and ask which ones are driving my actions. I can surrender and be lived by that which is living me. These realisations assisted me greatly in my personal practice of accepting, allowing and being patient with how life presented itself in any given moment.

This last component was pointing more towards the idea of oneness, and that we are all connected in some way by the same life force energy. When it came to 'all being connected', it is easier for me to think of it as the trees breathe in the same life force as I breathe out and I breathe in what the trees expel. Which gave me an example of the intricate interconnectedness of everything.

John Muir said, "When we try to pick out anything by itself, we find that it is bound fast by a thousand invisible cords that cannot be broken, to everything in the universe."

TRIGGERED

The term 'triggered' became a new word in my vocabulary. To be 'triggered' is when the pain-body is activated by an emotional reaction to someone's words or actions that trigger the past emotional pain within us. And though it's useful, it's extremely irritating when someone else asks 'are you triggered?' I got to know my pain-body and this part of my ego very well with the help of Lloyd. When we lived together, we would say the word 'ego' to each other whenever we felt the false ego was present in the way we were acting. This didn't always go down very well because it would piss me (my pain-body) off when I was caught out in my unconscious actions and behaving in an unloving way. And Lloyd wasn't always happy either.

We never fell out for too long, but you could say we did have some quite heated debates, which would end in not wanting to look at each other in the eyes or talk to each other for a while, even while knowing that we would come back together at some point. I saw it as our inner wounded stubborn children battling one another, when really, both of them just wanted to be held. When our pain-body is activated, we really do not want eye contact. It reminded me of when I was a criminal and liar. The truth is in the eyes and we don't want to be seen in our pain. And lying is definitely a trait of an activated pain-body.

Unconscious actions are called 'unconscious' because we cannot see them. So it's helpful to have someone else point out these actions and behaviours, and I really needed Lloyd to help me during those times. Triggers cause unsatisfying emotional and physical sensations in my body. Most commonly, I feel the unpleasant sensations in my throat, chest, solar plexus, or belly regions. My pain-body can be vicious, destructive and extremely annoying. It would often mentally beat me up for being triggered, and it would do anything in its power to stay activated and justify the pain. As Tolle said, "It feeds on pain and wants to stay alive by upholding old resentful and often negative stories and memories from weeks, months or decades ago."

In the beginning I demonised my pain-body, telling myself I shouldn't have one and really battling with myself intellectually. This behaviour just fed the pain even more and kept me locked in vicious circles. The dichotomy at the core, is that the pain-body wants to be loved while simultaneously it fears its own death. But it has to die, dissolve, be felt in order to feel and access the love that it yearns for. That's the funky paradox right there and causes a lot of confusion. Empathy was required, and I couldn't just disregard my pain or kill this aspect of myself off. Love was absent in those past emotional, often traumatic moments, and I wanted to welcome love back in, and do my best to not create more suffering. This was why I needed reflections from others to bring this part of me into sight. The trigger is actually a gift when viewed from this perspective because it is actually highlighting where I didn't receive the love I wanted or needed at the time.

I realised I didn't need to overreact and retaliate, instead I could feel the pain as it arose and then passed and love the part of me that needed to be seen, held and heard.

**FACE IT,
FEEL IT,
HEAL IT**

Remember when I was training as an actor, I told you I began to 'people watch'? That habit happily continued, but now after all this inner observation, I began witnessing the behaviours of pain-bodies everywhere. I was like 'Shit! Our societies are run by activated pain-bodies'. The way people talked to each other, the shouting, the ignorance, rarely any eye contact, the road rage and aggression, the shaming, the subtle or often not so subtle bullying and hate speech on social media platforms, the fearful news reports and our collective dysfunctional actions that swept across this planet.

I was observing it all as the result and outcome of being unconscious of our unconsciousness. If we as a species have not been taught about the behaviours that occur from our unresolved trauma and pain, then how can we understand what's actually happening to us? Instead we just make up some rational surface reasons why we acted like we did without doing any deeper inquiry. Most of the time we blame other people for how we feel. And I don't recall the pain-body on the school curriculum, do you? Many more dots were linking together, and I was getting a broader understanding of the outer world being a projection of our inner worlds. Whenever I function from my unresolved wounds I keep unconsciously repeating them over and over again without realising. Depending on where I focused, I could witness drama, gossip and hatred on the menu 24/7 and violent communication was the default way we had learned to communicate. The result of these behaviours is the manifestation of hostile and brutal environments. How did this happen? How did the human species become addicted to drama, gossip and so identified with their pain?

I was shocked at how extremely seductive pain and drama is and how it has so many of us hooked. This addiction to fear and acting from our pain-bodies for me is the root cause of why there are so many wars, lies and conflicts taking place between our species. When I was growing up I believed it was me against the world. My path was driven by unsatisfied feelings that fall under the umbrella of fear. Frightened of not being somebody, panicked of living in lack, wary of becoming a success, worried about not being a success, afraid of failure, ashamed of rejection, and disappointed with not being seen or loved. I was scared, and I lacked the emotional intelligence to communicate what I was feeling. I'm not sure I would have known what I was truly feeling. I'm certain I had never asked myself the question: how do I truly feel? If I were asked, I'm pretty certain I would have replied, okay, not bad, fine, alright, but none of these responses are actual feelings. They tell me nothing about what is going on inside. I wasn't able to say I feel sad, I feel lonely, I need to be held, because I wasn't aware of it myself. I just wanted a better life and was running to the future trying the best I could to create it from my limited state. I was never told to look inside, to explore what I was feeling. Instead, I focused on the outside, projecting onto the world my unconscious wounds.

Many humans, and some of you reading this, literally live whole lives in the pain-body activation. Reacting to everything from fear and fighting what is. Fighting what is, is like teaching a cat to bark, highly unlikely to be successful. It's not easy to uncover these shadow aspects, that's why they are called 'the shadow' because we cannot see them very well. Awareness is the greatest tool.

St Paul said, "Everything is shown up by being exposed to the light, and whatever is exposed to the light itself becomes light." My eyes are the lights of loving awareness and I know now that my pain always wants to dissolve into love and the more I can welcome these shadow aspects of myself into the light, the more fun it is to see what I can learn from their arrival.

And so that idea from Geoff, that fear is our friend, was no longer a concept from a book I read but actually a lived experience. Fear is my guide. When I face my fears, and move towards them, they dissolve.

I got some great practice with this from spending time on mountains. I enjoy snowboarding, and am blessed to say I got to experience a few excursions to the beauty of the Austrian mountains. The fear I'd feel when I was about to fly down a mountain on a thin plastic board was quite intense. There were the mixed feelings of excitement and nervousness. As the courage built up, I could feel reservation and resistance in my body, and my nervous system would be in the amber/red zone. If I let fear control my movements, I'd often fall over and hurt myself. And most of the time, I'd fall right on my coccyx, which is super painful. However, if I wanted to control the snowboard, I had to lean forward into my fears and when I did, I had more control and could direct myself with more awareness down the huge mountain peak I was now surfing. Then I would get to feel the exhilaration that the sport had to offer. It's as if something within says okay, you are now ready to face this challenge, and with that inner awareness, the fear resides. With fear as a friend who is helping me, I can have a different conversation with what is arising. I can act consciously rather than react unconsciously. When I am scared and unaware, I react to the fear and run away in flight, freeze in shock or stay and

Snowboarding in Austria

fight. But I uncovered another way. I can listen to what the fear is showing me and move towards it courageously.

When I feel fear rising in my body, I stop, take a deep breath or three and say, "Hey friend, come in, what do you want? What do you need? What are you showing me today? I know you're my guide and friend, you must be checking in with me to see if I am serious about what I want or am about to do. You're dropping by to ask if I am willing to confront my fears to receive or obtain that which I want, aren't you? Thank you for your consideration. I hear that you feel it may be scary, and that I may need some discernment here. Great, thank you. I feel we can do this; I am going ahead anyway. And I love you."

Or something to that effect. The important part is that I pause and take a moment to connect with my body's sensations to see what it is trying to communicate. The body knows if we are willing to stop long enough to hear its gentle voice. My new wordplay for FEAR became a choice, I can either 'fuck everything and run' or 'face everything and rise' When we let in the feelings, we can let them go. When I 'face it and feel it, I can surely heal it'.

SIMON
ON THE SOFA

Sav gifted me the book *The Last Hours of Ancient Sunlight* by Thom Hartmann. It's quite a bleak read of gruelling facts and insights about the state of the world and the velocity of depleting resources. There was a question posed which has stuck in my head ever since. The question was: With the knowledge you now have, you have a choice, and the choice is: "Do you want to be part of the cure or the cause of humanity's extinction?"

This question hit me hard. The fact all species eventually go extinct, is almost as reliable a rule throughout history as all humans eventually die. The question wasn't whether I was going to die, but how did I want to live and what did I want to create for the next generations.

Thus began the rise of Simon on the Sofa, a series of transparent conversations with people from all walks of life, to educate, awaken, inspire and support the shift in humanity's global awareness. I knew that Transparent Communication (which is the ability to speak our truth vulnerably and wholeheartedly) was the deciding factor as to whether our species would thrive or become extinct. We are wiping ourselves and the planet out, due to the lies and incongruency we continue to live by. I wanted these conversations to empower people to communicate their truth thus having an impact on their lives and enabling them to take responsibility for their actions.

Promo Shot for Simon on the Sofa

This was my first active response to becoming part of the cure. I had to lead by example and love knew the way. I had to speak my truth courageously, so together we could create a ripple of loving awareness across the planet. Only truth sets us free and in order to experience the truth, I had to find it within myself and speak it. I was willing to sniff out the bullshit and shine a light of awareness on all the active pain-bodies. I had nothing to lose and everything to gain.

Simon on the Sofa became an online channel capturing transparent conversations with real people from various walks of life. Supporting humanity as it awakens from fear into love. These dialogues would show that we are the same at the core and we are not alone. We are all experiencing the confines of fear, we are all struggling emotionally and often feel lost and confused, and we want to know how this thing called life works. We are all striving for survival through the swamp of lack, competition and scarcity. We all have to deal with personal trauma, core unworthiness and harsh self-judgements. And we all do our best at facing death, uncertainty and the unexpectedness of this experience we call life. Each of us seeking freedom and peace from all the conflict we endure through the false stories of separation. Craving so badly to be loved, held and healed.

I had this beautiful vision as each human awakens to their pure essence through loving themselves wholeheartedly, through realising they are already whole and complete, that the race is over. You and I made it, out of the millions of sperm cells that were released into the female reproductive tract, we were accepted, only a few of the strongest sperm cells make it to the womb. As a sperm cell we undergo a phenomenal series of biochemical changes that prepared us for fertilization. We made it through, penetrated the egg, grew in the womb for nine months and then rose into a new life form and then even after that we still had to survive the challenges of the next several years where we are fully surrendered, vulnerable and dependent on our carers for the ingredients we need to sustain ourselves and survive. WOW. What a miraculous journey. And we think we have something to prove? To become, to have to achieve? The intelligence and miraculous nature of our being is done, it's over, we are here, we made it, I repeat, the race is over. Literally we are the chosen ones, chosen by the womb. Chosen by the gift of LIFE. We exist, we are alive. It is enough.

As this realisation sinks into every cell and becomes embodied, our light switches on and together we shall light up the world like never before. We shine bright as beacons of truth. An interconnected web of loving awareness that pierces through the darkness of false beliefs.

Sounds great right? I'm totally excited now!

Promo Shot for Simon on the Sofa

I dove in the deep end as always and sent emails out to see who wanted to record a transparent conversation with me. I got one response from a friend who connected me to an interesting woman named Tiffany Crosara. She was a psychic mystic who read tarot cards and had a passion for transparency. Perfect candidate. We shared a beautiful conversation as she educated me in the tarot which is called 'The Book Of Life'. The only time I saw tarot cards was on James Bond movies when one of the bad guys pulled the hangman and said "You are dead, Mr Bond."

Now I was getting briefed on the 22 Major Arcana cards (which means major box of secrets) beginning with The Fool and ending with The World. Each of these cards shares the steps in life we take. The Fool represents the archetype of our soul being birthed into existence and then 22 archetypes that lead to The World which represents evolution.

The Major Arcana represents the gods or puppeteers while the Minor Arcana has 56 cards and represents the puppets and what's happening here and now. I felt like a fool listening to her. I had no clue about these cards of great wisdom. But I wanted to learn their secrets and how the cards supported people in healing their suffering and accessing their truth. Tiffany explained how the cards can get misunderstood and are often used to make predictions by those who have been called fortune tellers. These predictions can at times disempower the receiver and keep them in repetitive cycles. Whereas in fact the tarot is a hall of mirrors that can highlight the destructive patterns we have to face and give us awareness to see how we can change.

Since that day I've had a few readings from her. She was spot on in knowing what was happening for me in that moment without me having given her any clues. During our Sofa conversation, Tiffany spoke about Reiki healing which I had some interest in after reading *Dream Healer* by Adam. Transparently, she shared her challenges with IBS (Irritable Bowel Syndrome) and having to spend £80 on prescription drugs every month, while feeling hopeless with the pain and discomfort that was affecting her whole life. She described a Reiki attunement, and her scepticism about paying £40 to be Reiki attuned after four hours. "Surely, we must have special talents or train for many years to access this healing energy?" She said the attunement helped her connect to the tap of energy and abilities we all have. Reiki enabled her to heal herself and stop taking prescription drugs for good. I was surprised and intrigued at the same time.

Near the end of this expansive conversation she went on to tell me about 5Rhythms dance, created by Gabrielle Roth. My ears pricked up as Tiffany described how in a 5Rhythms, there's no drugs, alcohol, or speaking on the dance floor, everybody's just dancing for joy. After I quit drugs and alcohol, I lost my dance. I had been out to a few clubs sober, but it wasn't the same vibe because often many people were still intoxicated with drugs or alcohol and had that energy of seeking sex or holding up egoic identities. I now felt out of place in these environments, they were not a frequency match.

A few weeks later I headed down to this old church called St Peter's in Vauxhall, London to an event called 'Sweaty Thursdays' lead by Christian De Sousa. Anticipation was rising as I walked in through the big wooden doors. It felt no different to standing outside the nightclubs. Curiosity and excitement bubbling. Many people were in the main area warming up, some in yoga poses, some rolling around, and some sitting in silence. Others were adorning the altar that was being set up. I was taking it all in. I was beckoned by the dance once more.

As Plato said, "Music and rhythm find their way into the secret places of the soul." Let the 5Rhythms journey begin. I was energized by the freedom of expression and nobody was on drugs or drinking alcohol. Was this possible?

Everybody was enjoying themselves, happy, smiling and connecting through movement and sheer joy. I was taken on a transcendental journey and tapped into this ecstatic state without the need of any stimulants. This was a revelation for sure; a whole new way of expressing and exploring myself through movement, music, and dance. I had found my tribe. I danced a dance of gratitude for Tiffany and heard a song in my head, "Dance, dance, wherever you may be, I am the Lord of the Dance, said he, And I'll lead you all, wherever you may be, And I'll lead you all in the Dance, said he."

I couldn't remember where I'd heard that song before. Maybe from singing hymns at school, I don't know!

Anyway I was singing with joy and ecstatically pumped up and enlivened by this gift that Tiffany had shared with me. Who knew what treasures and opportunities this dance would bring? We were definitely going to meet again, that much felt certain.

I had already booked in the second Simon on the Sofa with a very interesting woman named Bridget Finklaire. She was a Harley Street Psychotherapist who had also studied many spiritual, metaphysical and esoteric teachings plus practiced different techniques from meditation to yoga, chanting and prayer. I first met with her in a random café in London.

Over tea, Bridget spoke to me about sacred geometry and often quoted a Book of Knowledge called *The Keys of Enoch* by Dr JJ Hurtak. She was a Reiki master and mixed this with a whole heap of other healing techniques from Hypnotherapy, Psych-K and EFT (Emotional Freedom

Technique). She told me some far-out stories experienced with some of her clients from taking them back into past lives.

My mind was opening, that's for sure. I was like a kid in a candy store. Bridget also spoke of Reiki and offered me a one to one session. Was it coincidence that Reiki popped up again in my second conversation? Or was it a sign? Either way I gladly agreed. The power of Reiki energy coming through Bridget's hands was hot. I had received massages before but never any form of energy healing without touch. I laid down on the couch, closed my eyes and relaxed. She started moving her hands across my body, without touching me, but doing some energy work and making sounds. I began feeling tingling sensations. Something was moving in my body. At one point I opened my eyes slightly to see what was happening because I didn't know if she was actually touching me or not. Then I saw her in the corner of the room stood up on a chair with her hands in front of her stretched out sending me energy from across the room! I laid there thinking, you can't write this stuff, this is far out, and I love that.

At the end of the session she asked how it was, I shyly replied, yeah, I could feel some energy moving but didn't know what else to say. She said she pulled out a big black chain from around my neck and removed a load of energetic blockages in my body. Really? Wow! Amazing! She said the chain was restricting my ability to speak clearly. Whether there was a chain there or not I could never know, but I trusted her and I left feeling uplifted and open to the invisible potential of what working with energy was all about. If I was going to continue this quest to speak my truth, then I needed all chains released from my throat chakra. It made sense.

On the Sofa with Samjhana Moon

Not long after Bridget came Stewart Pearce, another great example of how the Sofa connected me to all walks of life. Before we met in real life, this man had offered me great counsel while on the acting path, through one of his books *The Alchemy of Voice* which profoundly uncovered what he called our 'signature note'. Stewart says each one of us has his or her own 'signature note', which is the very song of our soul, an ancient concept made palatable for modern daily life. This note, which is unique to each individual, lies at the very heart of our physicality. If we are unable to sound the fullness of this note we become imbalanced: physically, mentally, emotionally and spiritually.

Stewart uses sound for transformation, he guides people

through a process of using sound to support their healing by restoring their vocal power. He told me one day over tea and cake that, "Our voices tell our stories, they are the very blueprint of our psyche and how we use our voice can utterly change our lives." I was totally captivated by the sound, depth and eloquence of his voice. Whatever he said sounded beautiful, whether I understood everything or not was not the point. He was expanding my perspective and I loved hearing that our 'voice and sound connect us all to the rest of the Universe'.

Stewart was Head of Voice at the Webber Douglas Academy and assisted the pioneering of Shakespeare's Globe Theatre. He had coached world acclaimed Oscar winning actors and prime ministers and royalty. He was a highly influential man, and there I was sitting in a plush hotel foyer laughing over tea and cake with this intriguing magnetic being as he shared how he changed his whole life to follow the call of his psychic abilities to channel the angels of Atlantis. This was next level!

On the Sofa with Peppi Gauci

I wanted to know more about the power of sound and invited my friend Scott to attend one of his chanting evenings with me. Stewart really knew how to conduct a space. It was a powerful group sound experience through chanting 'Aum'. This was my first experience of dissolving into sound vibrations. What do I mean by that? I mean I felt like there was no body for a moment, I was submersed into the sound chamber within the room. You could say I moved into a trance. I was reminded of the words of Hazrat Khan, "He who knows the secret of sound, knows the mystery of the whole universe." I could feel the aliveness in the joy of opening my voice. You'd have to meet this amazing being to get a feel of his unique charismatic presence. I thoroughly enjoyed his flamboyance. Being with him was quite something.

PROJECT SOS

I allowed the flow of synchronicities to lead me to the next person who would share their story and truth about themselves and the worlds they were experiencing. Susie Pearl, a magical and inspiring woman who sat with me, called it 'Project SOS'. SOS stands for 'Save Our Souls' and is Morse code used by ships in extreme distress, and I believe that the Sofa was becoming an oasis of support for those souls who were distressed or lost in the sea of confusion.

On the Sofa with Susie Pearl

It's also true that I am a natural supporter. This desire to help others has been with me since I was very young, helping my mum tidy up around the house. Then helping those who needed an ear to listen or a shoulder to cry on. When I was a personal trainer, I helped people to get fit while counselling them at the same time. It was all driven by the desire to help. I did have to learn though that helping others can also become detrimental if those I am trying to help do not help themselves. You can lead a horse to water but you can't make it drink. I could fall into the shadow side of the helper which is termed the wounded healer. I questioned many times if my help was actually making any difference. There is this little story that always stuck with me from one of Geoff Thompson's books, especially supportive in moments when my faith was faltering, and I thought who am I to make a difference in this world? It's called 'The Girl and the Starfish'.

Once upon a time, there was an old man who used to go to the ocean to do his writing. He had a habit of walking on the beach every morning before he began his work. Early one morning, he was walking along the shore after a big storm had passed and found the vast beach littered with starfish as far as the eye could see, stretching in both directions. Off in the distance, the old man noticed a small girl approaching. As the girl walked, she paused every so often and as he grew closer, the man could see that she was occasionally bending down to pick up an object and throw it into the sea. The girl came closer still and the man called out, 'Good morning! May I ask what it is that you are doing?'

The young girl paused, looked up, and replied 'Throwing starfish into the ocean. The tide has washed them up onto the beach and they can't return to the sea by themselves. When the sun gets high, they will die, unless I throw them back into the water.'

The old man replied, 'But there must be tens of thousands of starfish on this beach. I'm afraid you won't really be able to make much of a difference.'

The girl bent down, picked up yet another starfish and threw it as far as she could into the ocean. Then turned, smiled and said, 'It made a difference to that one!'

I just love it every time I read it, such sweet innocence.

As more and more conversations were being booked in, I needed help to edit them. Again, I sent an email out and just one reply comes back from a Portuguese man, Pedro, who was travelling the UK to broaden his skills in film-making. I had met him as a lighting assistant on *Other Side of The Game*.

We met up and I explained my mission of love. He looked at me curiously, not fully resonating at first. If you'd met him, you would see he was the complete opposite of me; tall dark, handsome and very quiet. Whereas I'm short, light, handsome and very loud. He'd been researching the state of society and had an interest in Mayan prophecy, science, healthy eating and multi-dimensions. There was common ground. He agreed to give it a trial and edit the conversations in between his day job as a nanny. He kindly offered to edit the videos as a gift to begin with to help me out, as he would be learning too. Our friendship grew through each conversation. It was fun having a new friend to travel around and share the experience with. I mean I couldn't save the world on my own, could I? Batman needed his Robin.

My or should I now say our quest continued as we travelled all over London meeting fascinating people on their unique paths, who trusted in us to share some of their deepest feelings and vulnerable experiences. From conscious musicians singing to me live, psychologists, lawyers, spiritual teachers, scientists, shamans, psychics, meditators, yogis, tantricas, sound healers, permaculturists, activists, mentors, coaches, to everyday people, young or old. People would share their books, knowledge, practices, online courses, and invite me to their events. A global community became apparent which brought me new friendships, opportunities and gifts of all kinds. I honoured them all and each of their stories expanded my mind and the human potential.

One of the first conversations Pedro and I filmed together was with the extremely unique young shaman yogi called Blue Man (because he was painted completely blue). He painted his body regularly as a personal ritual. He felt otherworldly to me. Like I was meeting a real Avatar.

He introduced me to Rapé (pronounced Hapee) a sacred and powerful plant medicine with deep healing, purifying qualities which have been used for centuries by Brazilian indigenous tribes.

On the day of our conversation, we were invited to film

him in his garden as he painted his naked body and proceeded to demonstrate the potential of yoga and the mastery he had obtained. His technique was exquisite. I guess you would expect that from someone who paints themselves blue and walks the streets as a living Avatar. He conducted a whole meditative ceremony for us to witness and document on film. The Rapé did exactly what it said, it was a cleansing for me, my tear ducts watered, my whole head/brain felt like it exploded for a moment, then I began crying and sneezing profusely which made Pedro quite amused. It was an intense but deeply gratifying experience.

After this we moved into the house to record our conversation while drinking herbal tea, I felt so much wisdom pouring from this dedicated young truth barer who had direct experiences with tribes and shamans. I could feel his apprehension of sharing his experiences with these sacred plant medicines. I felt blessed to document his intimate transmission and share with the world his wisdom and message from the elders. I named the talk 'I'm loving you with the passion of heaven' which were the words he shared in closing. Pedro and I left him that day feeling enthused and bonded through the shared experience. Unfortunately though, after some time Blue Man asked me to take his talk down. I felt it was due to him not feeling so confident on camera, and also not wanting to reveal so much information about himself and the plant medicines. He was very humble and respected the traditions which I feel played a big part too. Out of the 200+ conversations over the years that followed, this has only happened a handful of times. People change as the years go by and the camera crystallises a moment in space which for some they do not want to relive.

Another guest, some years after the conversation, wanted to get a serious job in politics but the problem was, every time people searched his name on Google, our Simon on the Sofa conversation popped up on all searches, and within that talk he shared openly about his spiritual values, UFOs and connection to other dimensions. This video was clearly not the best support for his new career move into politics! Of course, I took it down for him.

Another guest, a spiritual teacher and guru for many, also wanted his talk taken down. I felt reluctant to delete this one as his reasons were that he was becoming more known. I was sceptical and felt it was more likely because he didn't enjoy me getting him jumping up and down on the sofa we spoke on. For me and Pedro, it was a peak moment in the Sofa conversation series, that a somewhat serious guru with a wise message was allowing himself the freedom of jumping up and down on a sofa alongside me. I must say he did look quite awkward, bless him. I think Pedro and I were surprised he agreed in the first place. I mean we were out on the edge, two men jumping up and down on a sofa being filmed for the world to see. It made me chuckle, I must say, and I'm happy we shared that little moment of unexpectedness together.

The few others that I deleted along the way just didn't enjoy how the camera represented them. The camera never lies and shows us often what we cannot or do not want to see about ourselves. If I go back and look at myself, I could also cringe, but that's transparency right there. I am constantly changing and evolving, and you can witness that through each conversation.

Anyway, there were more souls to save, momentum was picking up and now I had a sidekick which made it much more fun and professional.

"Holy ravioli! To the Batcave, Robin, we may need the batmobile for this next chapter."

(Just be clear we didn't have a batmobile, but we did have a Vauxhall Astra which was donated to the cause from Lloyd. The previous owner was disabled and had no legs, so it had a hand accelerator which meant I could drive it and have my feet up on the dashboard at the same time. This often freaked people out as we cruised by. We named her The Blue Dragon. And she would be our trusty companion from now on.

THE TRUTH WILL OUT

Speaking truth was not, let's say, the norm. Transparency was not common and even more so when the camera was on. It's very vulnerable to show up in our truth. Self-doubt and judgements would creep in. Many who sat with me were happy to talk about concepts, but nitty gritty personal truths were still being censored. Often, more truth arose from the guests once the camera had been switched off, I could feel their relief and this allowed more of their natural selves to rise from their relaxation. There is much fear associated with speaking truthfully. Fear that we could harm somebody or get harmed for speaking out. Ancestors throughout history have been killed for speaking their truth, hence why truth is such a big taboo of our times. The irony is, the only time we harm somebody else or ourselves is when we withhold the truth. I'd often say, "Ah, I wish we'd kept the camera rolling." Or, "Wow, we must record another conversation to capture what was now shared." But it rarely happened. That's not to say the recorded conversations were never rich of truth and wisdom, because they were, I just noticed this pattern of concern about how they may be perceived. In order to speak our truth we really have to let go of any outcome. This showed me the importance of people needing to feel safe to communicate truthfully, and this only happens once we build a bond of trust.

Every conversation was also a reflection that helped uncover aspects of myself, like how often I easily accepted and agreed with what people were saying without really questioning their point of view. I noticed my own fears in challenging dogma and beliefs and how I was programmed to agree, even when I didn't. This was a test in whether I was able to be honest and share my truth and what I was feeling in the present moment. All these conversations became my training ground to practice authenticity.

A new saying emerged, 'Opinions are like arseholes, everybody has one'. Everybody I spoke to believed what they chose to believe, and this project SOS was helping me to question everything and assume nothing while noticing the judgements and expectations I was projecting onto people. I had to be discerning of what people were sharing.

I found there to be a hierarchical class state floating around within the spiritual circles too. Over-inflated spiritual egos and the need for recognition was just as rife as anywhere else in life. The messiah complex, superiority and guruism were new terms I was starting to understand with more depth. The ego does love to be somebody. It was understandable that the false façades would show up in this spiritual self-help world just as much as anywhere else, especially when it's a multi-billion-pound industry. But I wasn't happy about it. I thought I was entering a new realm of truth, but I needed to keep my eyes open for charlatans wearing masks of deception. I was here to sniff out the bullshit and uncover the lies and there was more than I may had imagined.

Money was another factor that really clouds people's ability to speak the truth. Our natural need and desire to make money in this western society means we have to be somebody, have status, or proclaim to be an authority or a person of influence in any given field. It makes sense from a sales perspective because when we are selling something, we have to create a persona, an identity to sell the product, idea or concept. We ourselves become the product on sale. I feel this creates spiritual dramas and galactic soap operas, and plenty of competitiveness, comparison, and one-upmanship, a 'my way is better than yours' mentality. Personalising, assuming, judging and gossiping were all still very present.

This disheartened me for a while and reminded me of the world of crime and fame that I had been distancing myself from. The same behaviours with a different front. I started saying it was like 'people were wearing the same jumper in a different colour'. This made me question this new world I was now involved in. I had high expectations and definitions of how an awakened person should act. I began 'guru bashing' as Lloyd and I called it.

This was a great lesson for me to see how I was putting people onto pedestals and deep down this was my own competitive nature wanting to be like them and feeling envious. I wanted to pull them down from the throne so to speak. I didn't believe in all this false adoration. Something felt out of alignment.

I was invited by a friend to a talk by quite a well-known commercial guru working his way up in the world. He gave a talk and welcomed people onto stage to answer their inquires or struggles. He was a sweet being and although I did not resonate with all he was sharing, I felt his intentions were pure and he was speaking some truths. But after the event, I wanted to record a short interview and I saw everyone idolising him and some were bowing down and kissing his feet.

At the time this felt unnecessary and I asked why he didn't stop them and say 'hey no need to kiss my feet, you are a divine being, no need to revere me in this way'. It reminded me of the divine beings jumping up to get pictures of actors on the red carpet. My judgement went to the guru, like he should let them know. I was impacted by those who I interpreted as having blind faith and placing their salvation within these demigods. But like any judgment, I was disconnecting myself from them. Who was I to judge what they needed? If they chose to bow down to him as a way to show their love and respect for this person, that was their decision.

They were mirrors for me and I could identify my own limited beliefs around status, money and envy. I judged there to be incongruences with what people were saying and how they were showing up in the world, but whenever I judge another, I cannot love them, and instead I create a big barrier between us.

It was an Indian Swami on a YouTube video that taught me a great way to practice non-judgment. When I point a finger at another, I point three back at myself and my thumb is the witness. Simple and true. Seeing judgement from this perspective allowed me to 'own my own shit'. When I catch myself judging now, I say three magic words, Just Like Me! It works both ways whether it's a judgement that condemns or elevates. This helped me to allow everybody to have and believe their stories without me needing to believe them or judge them as being right or wrong. I can choose to listen to understand or just let go because everyone is entitled to their own perspectives. Who am I to say otherwise? I can choose what feels true within me and allow everybody the freedom to explore themselves and the multiple dimensions of creation.

Don't get me wrong, this hasn't rewired easily and still shows up. Judging is a default state of my conditioning. Even the fact that I could feel the struggle of humanity all around me and how our ways of communicating were causing so much confusion and conflict can still be seen as just my perspective and judgment on what I am interpreting. It was Jiddu Krishnamurti who said, "The ability to observe without evaluating is the highest form of intelligence." I agree and my response to that is, practice makes progress.

I kept feeling how much could change for the better if everyone would just love themselves and speak their truth. The world would be a very different place. It was said that in 1949 George Orwell said, "In a time of universal deceit, telling the truth is a revolutionary act." And I would add that speaking our truth is a self-loving act and when we truly love ourselves, we express ourselves truthfully. Love and truth are not separate. I know this is difficult to grasp when our societies teach and profit from us competing with, judging and criticising ourselves. There is no road map and this makes it more challenging but also exciting. Would we really want to know the way? Isn't there more adventure in uncovering these truths through experience? Each of us have our unique path to walk and that's why I would just trust in the next step and be guided to where I needed to be and who I needed to meet.

I was kindly invited to be a speaker for an after-panel discussion of the beautiful documentary film *Road to Peace* directed by Leon Stuparich. The film provided a rare insider view into the life of the Dalai Lama and his powerful message of peace and universal responsibility. I was greatly encouraged by the Dalai Lama, not just by the tenacity, determination, humour and his dedication to peace but also when he said during the film that 'this is the century of dialogue and authentic courageous conversations are required as humanity navigates through these extremely challenging transitions.'

Yes that was it, universal responsibility is key and peace is possible and comes from the people. I must create brave spaces for people to be able to express themselves freely so we can then truly understand and listen attentively to the truths being revealed. Transformation happens most easily in the presence of another person. It is in the space of transparent heart to heart conversations that we come to see our own light reflected in the light of another. I appreciated how Mark Matousek said it, 'It is in encountering someone else's truth, even if we disagree with it, that we come to know the authority of our own inner truth directly, authentically and vibrantly'.

This new world I was imagining required a new language, a universal language that we all somehow know at the deepest core of our being, and that language is what I call Transparent Communication. It is the language of love communicating clearly. In order for all the lies and deccit to dissolve we must become translucent like water flowing freely, nothing to hold onto, nothing to fear. The real revolution is love and the battle, if there is one, is against the FEAR (false evidence that appears real), and these wars, conflicts, and turmoil we experience all originate inside each and every one of us.

WARRIORS OF LOVE

After a search online to find more events I could attend and meet new people on this path, I came across a Meetup group called 'London College of Spirituality'. I attended one evening to get a feel of the community. I saw a man who looked busy and engaging with a lot of people. It was Vaz, the founder and organizer, he seemed like the Topman! I wasn't able to have a conversation but managed to connect briefly and arrange a time when we could meet on the Sofa. I wanted to know more about this London College of Spirituality. Were they a crazy cult or another form of religion?

After a few meetings it was clear he was not running an organised religion and his intentions felt similar to mine. He wanted to help and support others to come alive to their full potential, whatever that may be. It felt like we had work to do, some lessons to learn with each other. Vaz had been writing about love and holding group events for himself and creating a platform for others to share their voice with the world. He would invite influential speakers from all across the globe to present on stage to his spiritual community. Naturally I invited him on the Sofa to share his transformative story from fifteen years of depression in the corporate world to founding the largest spiritual Meetup in the UK, he had some great experiences to share. After some months of collaborating we nicknamed ourselves 'Warriors of Love'. On a mission to awaken humanity. We recorded a few conversations and I was welcomed more into his core team and the wider community.

One day during lunch at our regular café hang out on London's Southbank, he shared his vision to return to Mount Shasta. I had never heard of the place. He wanted to take a large group of people on retreat to this huge energy centre of the planet. He asked if I wanted to join, I felt acknowledged and excited to be part of his vision. I trusted in him and his intentions. Vaz has a huge heart and is dedicated to serving love. We set the date, September 11th-17th 2011, and named the retreat 'The Heart's Calling'. It was an invitation to open to the vast love within and then share that love into the world at this time of mass destruction and global awakening.

Vaz had visited this mountain before and spoke highly of the surrounding areas recognised by Native Americans as places of sacred and spiritual sites. Shasta is a place of pilgrimage, meditation, ceremony and retreat for people from all over the world. The place is also known for multidimensional experiences and UFO sightings. Some say there is a city inside the dormant volcano and that's why it's a huge vortex, but I have no evidence of that.

This was nothing but an epic adventure into the unknown. Vaz agreed for me to bring Pedro along to film the excursion and create a mini documentary to share with the world. This excited us, especially as we had never been to America before. In the end, the team brought together a total of 44 unique courageous souls from around the globe to connect, meditate, face their shadows and open our hearts to the greater potentials of love. Many other souls all across the globe were meditating for peace and non-violence and this was our contribution. It linked in with the anniversary of the Harmonic Convergence back in 1987. It was our offering to all of humanity to awaken as love and plug into higher consciousness. An invitation to tune into the higher frequencies of our electromagnetic nature and rise up in truth beyond the dense matter of society's false beliefs.

The Mount Shasta Group

I had entered into an altered reality or dimension, it all felt like a kind of time warp. Or at least that was how I was perceiving it.

I found myself in this random little town in America meeting very quirky characters. Every time I met somebody, there was some sort of connection or far out story to try and wrap my head around. I likened it being in a Star Wars movie, when Han Solo enters a bar and there's loads of different galactic beings. That doesn't mean I was hanging out with ewoks, although I wouldn't have been surprised if they had showed up.

I also met a beautiful woman with high vibes. Anaiya Sophia, she called herself. She was a divine feminine goddess on the streets of California. We randomly (or not) bumped into each other as she heard my dulcet English tones when Pedro and I were crossing a road. Within five minutes we set up the camera and was recording a Simon on the Sofa conversation on the side of the road, sat in camping chairs. This location setting was a first.

I wanted her to speak about her Pilgrimage of Love across America, in relation to a book she was launching which shared wisdom and tools to awaken the creative powers of the womb. This was a whole new perspective for me. I was absorbing her words.

As I've said previously, I have been impacted by the vast amount of women who have been subtly and blatantly suppressed through violent abuse on all levels, and Anaiya was on a mission to support women to heal past traumatic wounds and access their sexual life force energy to ignite their true voices for the healing of humanity.

This felt perfectly aligned with my greater vision and intentions for being there. Sexuality was one of those big taboos that I was not hearing much about, even in these more alternative communities.

She talked about letting go of past conditioning and shared the deeper love that Rumi and many others had spoken of. A union with the divine. I was drawn to her in more ways than one and physically attracted to her of course. She was very sexy, so I'm not going to lie am I? Maybe she had something to teach me? I know what you are thinking, but it wasn't just sexual attraction, honestly. I was attracted to her passion and the sparkle in her eyes. I was becoming familiar with this magical twinkle in the eyes. It was like a new language, a new way of meeting people. It communicated that somebody was more alert, present, awakened, and aware. The eyes show everything.

I did have a thought at one point, that she may be the tantric goddess who could initiate me into the tantric god within. No expectations of course.

These constant synchronistic meetings reminded me of the profound book by James Redfield called *The Celestine Prophecy*. The protagonist sets off to search for an ancient Peruvian manuscript, long suppressed by the government, that is said to contain nine insights that mankind is prophesied to grasp upon entering a new era of spiritual awareness and understanding.

These series of insights start with the experience of synchronicity, and the realisation that there's more to these events than mere coincidence, for these synchronistic events actually lead us toward our true, and greater, destiny, fulfilment and passion. In subsequent chapters he shares how in these transitioning times we would connect more to, and have a new relationship with, the matter of energy. And that the idea of communicating intuitively and telepathically would become more the norm. I was definitely attracting more like minded ambassadors who were spreading the profundity of love in a quest to awaken humanity.

HANUMAN THE DANCING MONKEY

After our fun short talk, Anaiya said she was holding a goddess circle later that evening and we could go if we were free. Who turns down an invitation to a goddess circle? Not me! It sounded too interesting an opportunity to miss. I kept following the signs and gifts from those who sat on the Sofa.

Later that night I asked one of my friends to accompany me, and off we went to meet a group of divine goddesses. Not your average night out. We found the house and entered sheepishly. I had no clue what I was walking into. We entered the room to find the sweet aroma of sage and incense, and beautifully dressed women, many in white. It seemed the ceremony was almost ready to begin. I can't remember much of what was shared in the opening but a brief description of a guided meditation.

Anaiya led us into a transmission and on a journey into what she termed the gateways of the womb. We were laying down with knees in the air and feet flat on the floor. After a while I could feel a lot of energy moving and sounds began to come out of my mouth. I could hear another woman in the circle seemingly moving through some emotional release, screaming and moaning, it sounded like she was being harmed or raped or something, and my sounds linked in with hers. I was having this vision of healing her pain. Like our sounds were harmonizing.

All I know is, I was a YES to it all and surrendered into this energetic experience. It was like a full body orgasm without ejaculation. Orgasm is life force energy and my whole body was activated. It was pulsating and vibrating, then at one point uncontrollably flipped me over onto the front of my body, my spine bending and hips gyrating. I could feel Anaiya who was sat close by, put a comforting hand on my back. I stayed laying face down and slowly rested into stillness. Catharsis took place. It was a trip, let me tell you. With no mushrooms this time.

After I came back into the space, I felt extremely vulnerable. I recall some words from Anaiya closing the circle and I slowly sat up, not knowing what had exactly happened. Many of the people had left. Anaiya said 'well you took to that like a fish to water'. And that was that. Another profound unexplainable experience to add to the list. Let the initiation continue, why not?

As if this wasn't mind-expanding enough, it got a little too hard to handle when one of the facilitators on our retreat began channelling beings from other planets. I was curious about this fascinating being, Yantara, and his light language. We had already sat on the Sofa and recorded a conversation before leaving for Mount Shasta. Such an interesting talent he has with sound and its capacity to heal the body. In his event he opened a beautiful space and spoke a little about different dimensions and planetary beings. And then at some point he spoke in tongues to call in these different beings from other planets. He called it light language.

Don't ask me which aliens were being called in, I have no idea. I was like, what the hell man? Calling in different beings from different planets? I looked at Pedro and he looked at me and we looked shocked as each other. They proceeded with the ritual.

This moment was very challenging. It really pushed the boundary of what I could accept. It's one thing to hear voices and speak to the invisible beings, many people do this. Many speak to relatives who have died and I had seen people on video adopt the voice of those they channelled. Speaking in tongues is another term for this, and I had done something similar when speaking gibberish in an Osho meditation technique.

But this was calling in other beings from other planets or dimensions who could not be seen, into a room and then inviting those in the room to touch and connect to these beings. Something was happening because people were crying and breaking down. Some were elated. I think others actually either thought they were connecting or in their world maybe they really were. If they did, they didn't know how big these alien beings were because they were all touching them in different places. It didn't feel very consensual, either.

It seemed to me like gullible, lost humans simply touching empty space at different heights to connect to light beings that weren't there. Can you picture that?

On some level, I could accept that humans could believe anything. And as I said before, I was aware that people do talk to plants, animals and even ghosts or lost ancestors, but what was hard to grasp, was that some intelligent beings from distant galaxies would travel from their planet because they were summoned into a room and then just allow themselves to be touched up randomly by humans. It was too much. My rational, analytical mind was freaking out. It flipped me over the edge.

I walked outside and said to Pedro, "What the hell is happening?" He was smiling at me with an expression like 'what the fuck' and we began laughing together. I was thinking 'what the hell am I involved in? This is crazy, what's going on? Is this for real? Is this like some sort of alternative planetary fondling cult?'

That night, while laying under the stars by a beautiful lake, I sat down with Vaz, and I said, 'It's really hard for me to digest today's experience. It's hard for my mind to open up to that.' And he tried to explain to me about different dimensions, frequencies and energetic resonance and what we see is not all there is. He asked if I thought we were alone in the universe.

Vaz & I in San Francisco

I responded with, "I don't know for sure. I'd like to think it's possible, I've read about people having ET (extra-terrestrial) visits and OBE (Out of Body Experiences)." I always said that if films are showing aliens, other life forms, stargates and whatnot, then the ideas had to come from some life experience, and what is this reality anyway? If there are infinite possibilities, then everything is possible. We ended up having a long conversation about the potential of other life forms on distant planets, astral travel, dream realms, parallel universes and the construct of reality.

I was practicing acceptance of the unknown. And it definitely got a little easier after a whole month in Mount Shasta. I met many more souls of all different backgrounds and ages. Random beings, like Golden Eagle the drum maker who felt like my father from another dimension. I could write a whole book about Golden Eagle. What a world he pulled us into.

At some point, we ended up in his pottery room where he spun several drums into existence for us all. A whole ceremony took place in this little room as he worked and we all sang and danced and offered ourselves to each drum with words and blessings. Each drum was uniquely moulded in the moment. It was so beautiful to witness this man present in his art, and our energy definitely contributed.

He said he had never made drums in such a way before. He had made bespoke drums but not with all the dancing, intentions and love we were all pouring into the experience. He worked extremely hard to make all the drums we had ordered. I don't think he even knew how much work would be required. We definitely didn't. His blasé attitude

Golden Eagle the Drum Maker

was challenging at times as he just kept saying it would be possible and on time, but we all had some doubts.

At one point he was exhausted, and we laid him down on the grass in his garden as everyone sat around him giving him Reiki and I deeply massaged his body. I was impressed by his skill and strength. These drums along with Golden Eagle, would accompany us for the climax of the heart calling celebration on the peak of Mount Shasta. You could say we sort of adopted Golden Eagle during the time we were in Shasta, or more likely, he adopted us.

Then there was Christopher of the Wolves. Who would initiate the legendary dance we all shared down by the mountain spring where we would daily fill our watering bottles with this pure elixir of life pouring from the mountain tops. Christopher was playing the hang drum (if you don't know the sound of the hang then I recommend you go listen). Its sound is transcendental for me and it's shaped like a UFO which was apt being in Shasta. In fact, it was the only unidentified almost flying object I saw.

It was pure joy to dance freely as I lost myself in his musical melodies, dancing with all those who joined in.

A few nights later I was dancing again in a local bar and met another unique character who also had a next level name (which I forget now). He had a real cowboy look. He was watching me dance, then came up to me at one point and said, "Hey, you man," I couldn't hear him at first with the music and then he said again "Hanuman, you Hanuman" and started laughing. I was like, 'Handy man? Who the hell is handy man?" He said, "Hanuman, look up the name," and then just smiled at me as I danced on in my crazy free flowing way.

Later that night when I got back home, I googled Hanuman, the Hindu monkey god, who is one of the most celebrated and worshipped figures in Indian religion.

Hanuman is regarded as a perfect symbol of selflessness and loyalty. Worship of Hanuman helps the individual to counter the bad karma borne out of selfish action and grants the believer fortitude and strength in his or her own trials during the journey of life. Hanuman is variously described

Hanuman

as spirited, restless, energetic and inquisitive. One point all the major texts agree on is his mischievous nature. As a youth, Hanuman often abused his powers to pester the saints and holy men living in a nearby forest, with tricks such as beard pulling and the dousing of sacred fires. Sounded like my kind of god and I remember being called a cheeky little monkey quite often in my younger years. I took it as another sign to keep me on the path I had now chosen, I was loyal to this thing called love and moving more away from my selfish nature and you can definitely liken me to the trickster, that's for sure.

The whole trip to Mount Shasta was about healing the heart and global awakening. The whole experience was otherworldly, with diverse beings travelling from all over the world and potentially other planets, to be united in celebration of all life forms. We were innocently exploring the unknown. It was precious. I was devoted to a force far greater than me. I was also aware that this was all about me diving even deeper into healing my wounded heart. As I left this unusual volcanic vortex, I wondered what mischievousness may be on its way for Hanuman next.

The adventure continued and the supposed end of the world was getting even closer. Dun dun duuuun...

FREE YOURSELF WITHIN

I returned from Shasta charged up and inspired to continue sharing the message of love. I woke up one night at 4am and journalled twenty pages about how I was going to create these huge free events and bring people together from all walks of life to show love in action. I was sick of hearing people declare they had the most vital information that all of human life depended on and we could become extinct without it, but it could only be accessed for a certain amount of money.

If the information is so important and the whole world depended on it, why the paywall? You cannot buy love. I wanted the workshops to be free and accessible to all, because love is free and doesn't have a price tag. I wanted to bring people together to share their life experiences, resources, skills and what it means to love ourselves wholeheartedly and in doing so, how we can change the world. I wanted these events to be called 'Free Yourself Within'.

One little problem, I had no money and no venue but

a lot of enthusiasm. So I did what I always do and emailed my contacts for a venue, and again (I'm serious) I received one reply from a woman called Susanne Austin. I'd met her randomly (or not) at a Roger Hamilton Wealth Dynamics seminar when I was striving to be a successful entrepreneur and make millions with Cockolada and property investment.

We had met up a few times and kept trying to sync our diaries to record a talk. She was another ambassador of love on a mission to spread joy around the world through her writing, love of nature and infectious positive attitude. I followed her advice with curiosity and arranged a meeting with this guy named Darius and his business partner, Andrew.

I turned up on the day, enthusiastic to share my recent revelations about my shift into this boundless loving state of consciousness and my mission to spread love like Marmite. I believed I had the solution to the world's problems in the grips of my fingertips and just needed a space to begin the next phase. I shared my vision passionately, as they sat very still and watched me like I hadn't been observed before.

When I had finished my pitch, Andrew sat there with a huge loving smile and Darius looked inquisitive. After a slightly longer silence than I was comfortable with, he replied, "I think you could do with a retreat."

This wasn't the answer I was expecting. I was hoping for them to say they had a space for me to use for my mission. Had they not heard my exuberant spiel?

I replied, "I don't think I need to go on a retreat right now, as there are more pressing things at stake." The world may implode if I didn't spread love now. Like right now!

Didn't they know we were on the path to extinction already?

Darius's response was in fact steering me towards a meditation retreat called Vipassana. He went on to explain Vipassana was a 10-day silent meditation retreat and is offered for a donation or exchange of service. Although I had resistance to the suggestion, this was clearly no coincidence. Lloyd and I were only talking a few weeks earlier about meditation retreats and how many of these events have a highly priced paywall. I asked how to apply and Darius said he would share the web details.

I had already been attending yoga classes and meditating more regularly So I wasn't completely closed to this unexpected answer from Darius. Maybe this was an opportunity and the deeper reason we were supposed to meet? Synchronicity is not coincidence. Time would tell.

Both Darius and Andrew observed me for a little longer to see how I was digesting the invitation.

I sat there pondering and after a few minutes they showed me around the large disused warehouse space they had been refurbishing slowly. It was loaned to them on gift from the owner who planned to demolish it at some point. It was messy and had old bikes and other junk all spread around. After the short tour they kindly said I could use it to do my evening workshops, if I thought it was suitable. This was great news. I was overjoyed. I had a space and it was free to use. Almost an instant manifestation, I'd say. This was the beginning of new friendships.

I decided to begin with small evening circles to get some more experience and had my friend design me a basic website, logo and some posters. I was excited to share my

The Warehouse Soon to Become The Spring

vision. I planned everything and a month or so later held my first ever 'Free Yourself Within' circle.

Four people turned up, two of them friends. You have to start somewhere! Mum said I had planned way too much to share for two hours, but I was keen to deliver the great message of love. It was a little cold in this huge warehouse with just the four of us sat in there, but it happened and for this I was grateful and let's face it four is better than none...

After a few weeks of using the space and connecting more with Darius and Andrew, they asked me if I would be interested in project managing the refurbishment of the whole warehouse. They would name it 'The Spring'. With the invitation that once it was completed, I could use the whole space as a base for meetings, recording conversations and to hold longer workshops and events. I agreed and took on a six-month project to help birth a vision that Andrew, Darius and their friend Derick had for some years.

The Spring Project was all about the future of recruitment and employability and their key principles were how more of us can be brilliant more of the time, in ways that are beneficial to ourselves, those around us and to future generations. Their core values were generosity, curiosity, integrity and responsibility. For me they were messengers of a new world and their message was very much aligned to loving service. I learned a great deal from their mindfulness. Especially this saying from Darius, "How you do anything is how you do everything." I termed 'The Spring' as the 'Spring of LOVE'. A space to drink and fill up your cup from.

The Refurbished Spring

I pulled out my project managing skills and called on friends to birth this derelict warehouse into life. I organised painters, carpenters, electricians and firemen to make it safe for people to enter and enjoy. It was a huge venture and required me to show up most days. I was committed and motivated to birth The Spring into life. I was building my own stage to host these one-day 'Free Yourself Within' workshops.

The new dream was coming alive.

WHO LOOKS INSIDE, AWAKES

I was in Darius and Andrew's acquaintance a lot more and enjoyed their level of presence and integrity. Something in their demeanour was different which I attributed to their meditation practice and this encouraged me to follow the invitation to sit for 10 days. After I had relayed the info back to Lloyd, he dived in and attended the Vipassana retreat a few months before me. On his return, like Darius, he didn't speak too much about his process. Darius eluded at times but never gave any direct or clear explanation. He just suggested it would serve me. I didn't mind as I knew why, everyone has an opinion and those opinions may confuse others and create unnecessary expectations. So often our direct experiences are extremely different from another's. I honoured that in them both.

I also wish to be mindful that my words do not coerce or deter you in any way, as you may one day decide to experience this for yourself.

Here is the description from their website, "Vipassana

is one of India's most ancient meditation techniques. Long lost to humanity, it was rediscovered by Gotama the Buddha more than 2500 years ago. The word Vipassana means seeing things as they really are. It is the process of self-purification by self-observation. One begins by observing the natural breath to concentrate the mind. With a sharpened awareness one proceeds to observe the changing nature of body and mind and experiences the universal truths of impermanence, suffering and egolessness."

This felt like the perfect next step in my development, like it was all divinely designed. I was also fascinated by their exchange policy, which was called 'voluntary donation basis'. The whole experience is given as a gift and you can either donate money at the end of the experience or return to serve on another retreat. Dhamma, as it is called, is the selfless path of service. The course I experienced had been paid for by someone before me who had also sat the ten days. This was a beautiful confirmation that a financial exchange model like this worked on such a large scale. They described that serving on a retreat allows the student to practice the tools they share in day to day life, giving without expecting anything in return. Some call this Karma Yoga. I have learned that any form of selfless giving is wonderfully gratifying on all levels.

As I travelled into the unknown on trains and buses, it felt like an initiation was in process, just by being alone on the journey and reflecting on the past months. The journey to the retreat was giving me a lot of insight, even as I headed into more solitude. I sat at the front of the last coach which carried a group of thirty or more random souls up this narrow road with trees either side, farmers' fields all around, no buildings in sight. I felt curious, present and alert. We slowly arrived at the entrance to the Dhamma Dipa Vipassana Meditation Centre. My home for the next ten days.

Home for 10 Days

Apprehensive and uncertain of what I was getting myself into, I trusted Darius and accepted that this was where I was supposed to be. After registering, they explained the daily routine and rules to me.

The gong would sound every morning at 4am, meditation began in the main hall at 4:30am, and throughout the day I would be required to sit in meditation for approximately 10.5 hours, (that's a lot) the longest sit being approx. 3.5 hours. I thought my bum is definitely going to go numb! I was told I must honour noble silence for ten days, no eye contact or physical contact with other meditators, no writing, reading, phones, or anything that could distract me.

After this briefing I then locked my valuables into a locker and was allocated my room. It was a simple dormitory room with a few beds in. It was very clean and sparse. It reminded me a little of being in jail.

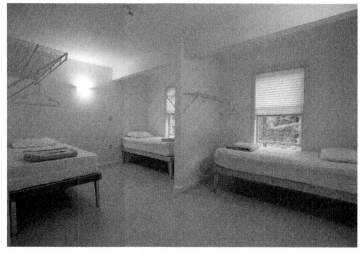

The Vipassana Dormitory

Discipline was not a problem for me, I enjoyed continuity and having structured days. I had a little concern about the food though, would I get fed enough? Would I starve to death? My monkey mind was already in overdrive. I noticed how the mind is always looking for problems or fearing the worst-case scenario.

On the first day, it was clear the food was more than taken care of with two vegetarian meals. However, no caffeinated drinks were provided for stimulation, so I had to say goodbye to the good ole English tea for ten days. How would I cope without my rosy lee? The whole experience was about renunciation of the habits that cause distractions and attachments to the mind and body. Silence and stillness were the tools being used to see and hear clearer.

"Diligently, ardently, patiently, persistently, continuously. Your own hard work will give you the fruits of your stay here, nothing else. From 4:30am until 9:30pm, keep on working, very diligently. May all beings enjoy real peace, real harmony, real happiness." Then the sound of Goenka chanting mantras would reverberate through the room as the hour-long discourse of the evening of the first day came to a close. These words would be heard multiple times in various ways from SN Goenka, the revered meditation teacher who had spread Vipassana globally. His voice would be the only voice I heard for the next ten days through the evening discourses as he invited us into the philosophy and science around the teachings. Sharing simple truths through stories, some of them funny, to describe how the human mind creates reality. I resonated with the teachings from what I had previously been reading and researching.

Renunciation and minimalism were new core values to release me from contributing to my own and others' suffering. As you know, I had already been naturally renouncing over the years, and even more so from all the documentaries I had been watching. From TV and newspapers, to certain foods, chemical cleaning products, deodorants, creams and perfumes that I put on my skin, fluoride toothpastes, branded clothes, certain words in my vocabulary, especially swear words. It felt freeing to let go of the attachments to these behaviours and things.

Every group that attends this retreat is invited to practice a code of conduct with a number of precepts.

One is termed Sila:
to abstain from killing any being,
to abstain from stealing,
to abstain from sexual misconduct,
to abstain from wrong speech,
to abstain from all intoxicants.

These seemed doable, especially the first one. It felt like I was definitely in the right place. Love had already shown me these things had to stop. I hadn't been killing people of course, but killing myself slowly, yes. Intoxicating myself, lying had been my default state and sexual misconduct had definitely been a large part of my life.

In late 2007, just before that explosive meeting with Alice, I had been trying to make a final decision to stop drinking alcohol and drugs, but it wasn't fully embodied. The binge-drinking and drug-taking had stopped but I was still drinking wine now and then.

In 2008, I made a decision to not drink alcohol for 15 years as I had started with my first sip at 15yrs old and I thought why not now experience 15 years without alcohol and drugs in my system. There were a few small occasions during the making of AO when the director was persistent in me drinking with him and the crew as a form of camaraderie. That was a hard lesson in standing by my 'no'. I let myself go a few times but felt disappointed in myself after.

One time he wanted the whole team to drink a large shot of absolute vodka, he looked at me and said to me in his deep French accent, 'Simon you join us?' I felt pressured by his request and felt some guilt that I hadn't joined him numerous times before. So, I said, "Yes let's do this Jacques!"

His smile widened and his eyes shone. And as everyone drank their shot I acted as if I was drinking but launched the shot behind me and proceeded to make out that I had just drunk a very strong one! I even made the sounds to go with it. I was an actor after all! The costume designer next to me, who I had a great connection with, saw what I did and looked at me mischievously and I just winked and smiled back. She understood my actions and knew the director's persistence was a challenge at times. I was learning that it's not always easy to say no and I also saw the joy and innocence in his eyes, he just wanted everyone to enjoy and join him in his celebratory way.

In hindsight I can only say that the decision I made to renounce drink and drugs has been one of the greatest self-loving acts of my life. Anyway, back to the retreat.

Another two precepts of the practice were;

The Four Noble Truths:

the fact of suffering

the origin of suffering (craving)

the cessation of suffering

the path leading to the cessation of suffering

which linked to,

The Three Roots of all Mental Defilements:

– craving

– aversion

– ignorance

I got to face myself like never before. This time, I was in confinement because I had chosen to be. It was not easy to quiet myself to listen and observe all my mental defilements, but I gave it my best for those ten days. It didn't take long to witness how difficult it was for me to slow down and just be still. I'm a very animated and active person. To feel the resistance and agitation just to the idea of stopping the 'doing' persona was not comfortable for me, let alone actually sitting completely still for hours on end. I made a decision after day two to get up as soon as I heard the gong and get into the shower rooms first, one, because the cold water woke me up and kept me awake for the first meditation and two, the queue would get too long and I could miss the beginning. The mind wanted to sleep much more than normal. Sleep was the minds way to drop out.

Vipassana Mediation Hall

There is one part of the day where you can meditate in your room if you want to. I tried this once and slept the whole time! It was too easy to give into the resistance and not be disciplined. After this I made a decision to always sit in the hall with the group. That's not to say I never slept there either, because trust me it happened. My body would start to nod off, leaving me thinking I had dropped into a deep meditative state and reached Samadhi, when in fact I was just asleep like a nodding dog. Concentration is indeed a skill to hone. I must say though, it was funny observing others falling asleep as their heads were nodding up and down and now and then they would realise and make out they hadn't been sleeping. Just like me!

My body wanted to move so much on that first retreat, so much inner turbulence as I tried to find different ways to sit, propping my legs up with cushions and running away from facing the pains of the body, the restlessness, the over-active mind. It was quite something. This was another funny thing to witness as further on through the retreat, meditators would add more and more cushions to their area for comfort, as the days went by little cushion mountains continued popping up throughout the hall.

When all my daily distractions like my phone, books to read, writing paper, and conversation were taken away, I had no option but to listen. I began noticing that when I closed my eyes I could truly see. I began seeing so many visuals from my life, like film strips flying through my mind's eye. This experience taught me what it really meant to sit and observe.

BECOMING CONSCIOUS OF MY UNCONSCIOUS

I noticed how my mind so often needed problems to solve and kept thinking of worst-case scenarios. I was constantly wondering if I was meditating properly and concerned about other people's experience. A lot of outward projection. After a few days it seemed my mind gave up a little and I was able to focus more towards what was going on inside of me.

I began reflecting on my past actions, some key events and relationships with those throughout my life. Memories were triggering emotions from past experiences of domestic violence and the abuse my mum had endured. She and my stepfather argued a lot and these arguments at times moved from verbal abuse to physical abuse. I don't recall every time she was slapped or hit but one moment stuck in my head, the time I came out of my bedroom and saw my mum in the bathroom all beaten up with blood on her face. My mum had been mentally abused most of her life, and not just within her marriages. Her parents were abusive to her as a child, so it was inevitable she would see herself as the weaker person, and put up with people walking over her, and not giving her the respect she deserved. I could see how Mum lost her sense of self after being told so many times that she couldn't be who she wanted to be or do what she wanted to do.

I recalled my mum telling me how getting beaten up by her parents and her partners through verbal threats and slapping, had shattered her self-esteem. It wore her down and killed her confidence. She was traumatised, both physically and emotionally. I believe for a good part of her life, she was suffering from post-traumatic stress disorder. Some of these memories were locked away but began surfacing as I delved deeper within.

I witnessed the patterns that had played out throughout my life through different relationship dynamics. As if I was repeating the actions of my parents and peers. I remembered times when I too had abused women through my ignorant attitude. The mission to sleep with 100 women was present with me, how I had treated women as sex objects for my gain without considering their feelings. My cock was hungry, like some dysfunctional sex addict.

I had never raped anyone, but I could feel that energy and how possible it could have been. I was stealing energy from the women I slept with. Why was my subtle abuse any different to how my fathers and my mum's boyfriends had treated her? My ex-partner Julia kept popping up into my awareness, flashbacks of our time together and how I had mistreated her and other ex-partners through my unconscious behaviours. I was not fully aware of the effect my words and actions could have had on them. I was noticing how powerful words and actions were and how they impacted so much more than just myself and the person I was connected to. Our actions and words really do have an energetic invisible ripple effect that touches the whole of creation. As I sat there in silence, I considered the abortions that I had been a part of. The one with Natalie, while I was in jail, and another with Louisa, a few years after I came out of jail. She had just birthed a baby when we met. The father of that baby left her while she was in hospital giving birth. It was traumatic for her. Into our second year together, she wanted another baby, and again I was not interested because I didn't want to follow my father's footsteps and be an absent father. I wanted to be an actor. Some months later, even though she was taking the contraceptive pill, she fell pregnant. It was not easy for us both, and I chose to leave the relationship as I had my focus elsewhere and wanted to stick with my decision of not wanting to be a father. I heard later that she reluctantly decided on abortion. It's understandable, as she had already been abandoned by the first father.

It felt like I was having to face all these challenging times and feel them all while noticing how they were subtly still impacting me on some level. So many mixed emotions were moving through me, and my job was to just observe them. Witness them rising and passing. Stay focused on the breath in and out and witness the craving, aversion and ignorance. I felt like I was clearing the past pain as a result of my unconscious behaviours from my days as a criminal, my mother's suffering throughout her life and the hostile life I had endured in Castlefield. My father abandoning me at nine months old and why we never met again. Past relationships where I was unable to communicate my truth and lied instead. My relationship with Steve, and how he only ever tried to support me, and love me, but our relationship diminished through several misunderstandings and futile judgments and how this also impacted my relationship with his son, my nephew.

I saw the consequences of me sending my mum and Lloyd away and the rift caused by the dysfunctional relationship I had orchestrated between her and Craig. I had a vision that Lloyd's illness was also birthed during those years of separation from his family and how my decisions may have contributed to that.

I saw the whole web of dynamics playing out with TC, Jason, Diana and other gang members, the stupidity of my criminal acts, and how we were all lost in our own fears, doing the best we could to survive. And how in a warped sort of way we all just loved each other and needed each other to stay alive. I was thinking back over my relationship with Jason and Diana, and wow what times we shared. I saw how we had slowly drifted apart and went our separate ways, but that he was also always there for me, often popping up throughout my life. He ended up getting sentenced to three years in jail. I recall visiting him a few times. I could hear his words from our younger days, 'I will only stop when I get sent to jail'. While in meditation I had flashbacks of me trying to help and support him as best I could. I know he wanted to change, but he knew no different. I knew that it could easily have been me getting longer sentences if I stayed in those circles.

I was observing the many different perspectives, many that had slipped from my conscious memory but were clearly part of my subconscious blueprint and were arising as I sat in silence. I was even going as far back as my grandparents' grandparents, and the struggles they lived through. Honouring and acknowledging it all. I felt the pain move through me that had been numbed for years.

Shame and guilt could be names for this energy, but the key to the practice is not to name or create dramatic stories that the pain-body may like to feed on but just witness the sensations with equanimity. It was immense and not easy to relive some of the experiences.

I remembered a best friend who had been violently beaten in a gang fight that got out of hand. His face was caved in from a scaffold bar being slammed into his mouth, breaking his jaw that would require years to heal. I had decided not to go out that night with the boys and woke up the next day to the news of the fight between two different groups, both of which I knew. My friend was in hospital seriously harmed. I was close to all his family and this was a brutal outcome from a stupid alcohol-driven argument that escalated out of control.

Unconscious actions happening from boredom and alcohol abuse of sexually starved young men upholding false identities with a need to prove something. My mind kept wandering, asking why, what did it serve and how could it have been different. Our friendship slowly deteriorated after this. Many other friendships also ended with no recollection.

Thankfully it wasn't just the painful events I witnessed, that would have been like a bad trip. I also saw the divine perfection and how every single thing that had happened to me had to happen in that way. There were beautiful outcomes that I also got to witness as they moved through me. I was gently reminded of the time I was walking through a park and coincidentally or not met Louisa years after we had parted. She was walking with her mother and her baby twins in a push chair. When I walked away from them that day I felt such a relief in my whole body, as if my guilt fell away. I was happy to know that she got what she truly wanted and my choice to follow my truth however hard it may have been, was in fact perfect.

As I continued to observe, I witnessed so much beauty that had occurred because of the choices I had made. From the many friends who supported me along the way with love, money and kind favours. Friends who employed me when they didn't need to just because they wanted to help and believed in me and my dreams.

Wonderful flashbacks to times with my stepfather when he took Lloyd and I fishing along the riverbanks and lakes and the fun we shared together and other times I worked with him, helping him load up his lorries with the furniture we would deliver across the country. There were moments with my mum and the whole family camping together at events where we would watch my stepfather fly remote control aeroplanes, which was one of his favourite hobbies. These moments had not been present before. I could see how he had actually taken on two children that were not his own and was doing the best he could with what he had. Not without struggle of course, but he did show up. This was something I hadn't been able to do for any of the children that had come into my life.

I was also following the past memories of many amazing experiences I shared with friends, from travelling to other countries, lazy days hanging out playing around, to the crazy nights getting high and dancing to the early hours in nightclubs.

What a wild ride I had been on. I could recognise the love and support we all shared and within the deep sadness there was also great joy. The funky paradox of life. I was overwhelmed at some points with tears of gratitude for all of it. But again, no matter whether the experience seemed enjoyable or not, or had a conclusion or not, or I tried to work any of it out, the practice was to just observe sensations without craving or aversion. It is in craving a good experience or averting a bad experience which creates the suffering. Pain is inevitable, suffering is optional.

Vipassana is and will always be different for all. Everyone has unique battles I know nothing about. I was witnessing mine on many subtle and gross levels. For me this was an internal energetic and physical cleansing through observing the breath and witnessing with conscious awareness the subtle sensations of the body. Quite profound.

I saw how I had taken the weight of the world on my shoulders. I didn't want to contribute any longer to the suffering in the world, but I was still subtly acting from guilt and shame. I was on a mission of love, but still going against society. This was still conflict.

My attitude was still rebellious, and this was causing strain on my relationship with Alice. I could see the magic in our alchemy and all that she was a part of, I could also see my attachments and the projections that I had put onto her. I could see how I was in fact subtly causing harm by not being clear on what I wanted. I was not able to give her what she wanted or needed in a partner.

Could it be that we weren't supposed to be together? We had shared a beautiful partnership, not without our challenges, but those challenges and adversities helped us grow. We had a lot in common, but I could see how our paths were parting. I could see it in the ways we were communicating, our behaviours, the subtle arguments and dismissive attitude.

The love we shared for each other was real, but our unique creative expressions were being stifled with financial struggles and what seemed like an unclear direction. I tried not to make this into a reason to feel guilty, but I was feeling confused because I did not know the outcome. My mind wanted the outcome.

It was hard to imagine that we could part after the impact Alice had on my life. But this story or belief was potentially creating an unhealthy attachment. The more I sat the more I allowed conscious awareness to act like a magnifying glass showing me the consequences of my actions and habitual traits, many I hadn't seen before. The quote, "We do not see the world as it is, but as we are." sprang to mind. I see in others what I do not see in myself. Everyone really is a reflection of my projections.

I was interested in helping others and the world, but my perceptions would be clouded if I did not face up to and get real with my own painful struggles. I was pretty broke financially, but also resisting selling anything in this consumer reality that I deemed to be wrong. I didn't want to market love and I was caught in the belief that the world needing saving by me before it was too late.

The greater picture had become more important than me taking care of my needs. I noticed that I was worn out and disconnected and I could sense the wounded healer archetype was active in some of my actions, as they had the smearing of subtle ego trips masquerading as love in action.

Shit! No wonder Darius smiled at me and said, "I think you need a retreat." He was not wrong. I was being humbled in a very gentle way. I got to really taste what it means to see beyond the seeing. As I closed my eyes, I was able to open my real-eyes and realise what was happening inside of me through heightened awareness. I could feel the potency and potential that silent meditating held and concluded, and that this would not be my last retreat, that was for sure.

Among the many insights those ten days held, was the awareness of the extent of suffering that occurs through sheer ignorance, and the power of forgiveness that could be accessed through conscious loving awareness. I left feeling more optimistic, excited and inspired with my new meditation practice and the clarity I obtained from this initiation. I now wanted to share this practice with the world. I was ready to continue on my mission of love and eager to meditate every day for the rest of my life! No expectations, Simon, no need to set yourself with a task you may not achieve. Which could create even more suffering from craving and aversion. Hadn't I just learned some key lessons? Oh, how the mind likes to control and ping back into its comfortable place.

I was encouraged to meditate two hours per day, one in the morning and one in the evening. I was devoted and wanted to try my best to keep this up. Meditation was a great tool that was going to assist me along this noble path I was courageously walking. I was deeply grateful to Darius and Andrew and excited to go back to The Spring and continue my service or Dhamma. I appreciated these words from Carl Jung, "Your visions will become clear only when you can look into your own heart. Who looks outside, dreams; who looks inside, awakes." If I wanted to truly free myself within, I would have to continue looking inside and face my shadows, feel my pain and heal my past emotional wounds. Meditation would assist me in becoming conscious of my unconsciousness.

The Dalai Lama said, "If every eight year old in the world is taught meditation, we will eliminate violence from the world within one generation." I could see how this could be possible because meditation has the ability to rewire the whole predominant operating system we function from. I was being taught the art of letting go.

It was my quest to practice equanimity daily. I knew that those ten days were allowing me to scratch the surface and it wouldn't be easy once I headed back to my normal daily life, but I was committed to give it my best. I now knew that meditation works subtly through consistency, repetition and trusting the unknown and I began repeating this Zen proverb when I noticed myself procrastinating and finding 101 reasons why I couldn't meditate: "You should sit in meditation for twenty minutes every day – unless you're too busy. Then you should sit for an hour."

THE LANGUAGE
OF LOVE

Once the The Spring was completed (which took a little longer than anticipated) we opened the doors to the public. It was a proud moment and the space was all cleaned up and ready to serve as a loving container for transformation. I decided to change the name of my events to 'The Language of Love' and the first one began during the spring of 2012.

That was a big step into discomfort, but also extremely empowering. I had created my own arena, and it felt like I had built a stage, but not in the theatre, playing a different character, it was now me playing me. I prepared more than I needed to, as always, and had all my printouts and exercises ready to go. I had selected the music to play and videos I wanted to share. Pedro was still by my side and we had a small team of friends who were helping out. The event had a great turn out, with about thirty attendees, which was thanks to Vaz who shared the event details with his LCS community.

As everybody arrived, I could feel the butterflies in my

belly. Some friends who I knew were coming through the doors as I watched from the back. They were greeted by the team and invited to choose a seat in the circle of chairs we had laid out. The smell of incense floated in the air of this huge warehouse. The anticipation was palpable. I then walked around the circle, taking a moment to connect with the eyes of each person and say hello and make them feel safe and welcomed. I knew the importance of people needing to feel relaxed in order to open their hearts.

Ready to Open My Heart

This was our brave playground to reconnect to our innocence. We danced, cried, faced our fears vulnerably and bravely shared our truth. I really can't remember everything that happened after it began, I just jumped into the arena, took the stage and let whatever wanted to happen take over.

I had some idea of where I wanted to guide the group, but I had never done anything like this before, so it was all new territory. I was in the moment, navigating through the day, feeling into the different relationship dynamics and the emotions that would spontaneously arise. I was holding it all and doing the best I could.

It seems I was funny too, and much of the feedback was, 'Simon you are so entertaining'. Many said they hadn't laughed that much in a long time. I loved seeing all these unique and varied humans smiling, laughing and moving through their own transformation.

You could literally see the difference in their energy field from the beginning to the end when they were all glowing and pulsating from all the loving connections. New friendships were being formed, and love was casting its magic. It was beautifully enriching to witness and experience.

Language of Love Circle

At the end of the event I was completely wiped out yet elated. We all cleaned up the space and went out for a celebratory meal. A few days later as I came down from the high, I was understanding the amount of energy required to hold such a space. The first event was a huge success in my opinion. I offered the whole day as donation-based exchange, and people couldn't believe it because I think it was quite rare at the time. We asked them to leave their donations in the envelopes we provided in the glass bowl. I wanted these events to be as free as possible, but I wasn't at the stage to just let them be completely free. Implementing this model of exchange was a compromise but felt right. But it was also going to be very challenging.

Language of Love Dancing

Despite my intentions, I did have expectations and was not financially stable. That first event only gave us a small income and I wanted to give to the team a small contribution too. One of them had two children to feed. It wasn't like we had big overheads, so we all got something, but I could feel the egoic part of me which wanted more and wanted to give more.

This wasn't going to deter me though, I was determined, and I kept hearing a little voice say: this is the way, love is free. Trust.

Yes, I had some doubts, but I wasn't going to let them oppress me. I was on the scout for other facilitators using different exchange models for their events, but I couldn't find any. Until one day, I can't remember who it was, but I was told about a workshop happening in April 2012 with a quirky Canadian guy called Tad Hargraves, who had a company called *Marketing for Hippies*. It just so happened he was on a European tour and visiting Brighton.

I was looking forward to his workshop and when the day came it was jam packed with wisdom and insights on how transparent marketing can be conducted. He said marketing is about establishing the value beyond the immediately apparent, which resonated completely because I could see how I knew the price tag of everything and the value of nothing. He brought up some inspiring viewpoints on the fear that arises with the struggle of wanting to do good and make money at the same time.

He said we do have genuine needs for food and shelter, we do want to be seen and valued, and we do need to sustain ourselves, but we also want to be giving to the world and contributing to the bigger picture. How do we sustain the world while also sustaining ourselves?

This was exactly what I was struggling with. He had hit the nail on the head. He highlighted the conflict between not being able to communicate our needs and how this creates these covert marketing tactics, that get wrapped up in heart centred, loving, transparent or conscious wording, but actually they are still communicating from panic, which creates a culture of fear, scarcity, new age guilt and distrust.

Among so many other gems, he quoted the words of Gandhi which would strike a chord in me for the rest of my life: "There is enough for everyone's need but not enough for everyone's greed." He was definitely walking his talk as he offered his workshop in what he termed the 'pay what you can afford' model. Yes! This was it, this is how I could move forward. After this expansive workshop with Tad, I felt there was indeed an alternative way that was aligned to my heart.

Naturally, I invited him onto Simon on the Sofa and we grabbed a short, but pertinent conversation the next morning by the sea, just before he left for his flight back.

For the next event, I changed the term to 'pay what you can afford' instead of donation based because I was learning that the word donation actually meant for some people that you don't have to give anything.

This 'pay what you can afford' model seemed to be working for Tad so I wanted to give it a go.

I didn't want there to be a paywall and wanted to be able to offer these amazing experiences to those who genuinely didn't have money. I wanted it all to be accessible. Those who were able could pay what they could afford and if a person could not pay anything, that was okay too. The mission was more important than the money to me. I picked up a great saying from Preston Smiles, a guest on Simon on the Sofa, he says, "Love finds a way, and everything else finds an excuse." This was music to my heart.

We decided to host The Language of Love as a monthly event. I wanted each one to have a theme and highlight the importance of mastering how to rewire our dysfunctional false beliefs and consciously reprogram our subconscious minds. To speak our truth and face our fears while uncovering the pain-body that lives within us all. Just how the path of love had invited me to uncover my blocks and disturbances or as Rumi said so eloquently, "Your task is not to seek for love, but merely to seek and find all the barriers within yourself that you have built against it."

FEAR KILLS & LOVE HEALS

I called The Spring my laboratory to explore with others these methods and tools that I had accumulated from my own path. I was designing my own map and learning how best to share that map for others to use if they chose to. Fear and the pain-body was obviously a core topic and breaking it down was beneficial for those who attended. Many hadn't even contemplated what I was sharing or considered that they had a pain-body but totally comprehended it when it was explained. I shared that we have a natural fear response mechanism, which is extremely important to guide us away from real danger like a tiger about to attack us, but our problems arise when we mix up the false fears created from our false Beliefs Systems (BS = our own BullShit) and then believe them as truth and create false stories to justify them.

This is a dangerous feedback loop or as Mark Manson in his book *The Subtle Art of Not Giving a F*ck* terms this 'the feedback loop from hell'. These false limiting stories keep us caged in self-perpetuating invisible prisons created from illusionary false evidence appearing real. I used my own past experiences and explained that as a criminal, I was living in a constant state of fight, flight or freeze, functioning from fear and stress which continually released cortisol into my body. These behaviours and chemicals only lead to disease, pain and suffering on all levels and when we live in fear we become destructive and tell lies as our default state.

I backed this up with wisdom from Bruce Lipton who wrote *The Biology of Belief.* He describes so beautifully how the cells in the body function and his discoveries linked perfectly with my desire to show how we can become the healing balm of love across the planet. Bruce shared that the thoughts we have fire emotions which then drive our behaviours and moods. He found that no two cells can be in the same place at the same time. A cell which is in growth, openness, expansiveness, and functioning coherently while filling itself up with nutrients, is a well-functioning cell. And a cell which is in protection, closed off, depressed and not functioning to its optimum, allows in toxins. A cell in growth is a cell in love and a cell in protection is a cell in fear. If our cells are in protection (fear) they cannot be in growth (love) at the same time. Bruce simplified for me on a cellular level how we react to our dominating thoughts, feelings and environments. Our bodies are created from trillions of cells and these trillions of cells make up a community of cells which creates an organism such as a human (me or you) and therefore a community of humans also collectively represents a larger living organism.

A community of humans, or this larger 'organism' of integrated humans, expresses the same behaviours as organisms comprised of cellular communities. Micro macro, as above so below, as within so without.

If I am living in the energy of fear then clearly I shall attract more fear-based survival emotional states, and attract to me the cells that are of my same frequency. We are made of energy at the core and energy attracts energy. Where focus goes my energy flows. This is the nature of our biology and how dis-ease is created. When my body is in stress, protection and fear, I am at a higher risk of my immune system shutting down.

I never realised how all this was connected and how the chronic release of stress hormones resulted in an elevation of the amount of disease and sickness within ourselves and thus within the wider organism, which is our whole planet. If I am functioning from fear then I am the disease on the planet, you could even say in that moment I am the cancer. This is how important it is to do what it takes to rise out of the false fears, the lies and unsatisfying emotional states because they are literally killing us through compromising our wellbeing. It's as simple as that. Fear kills and Love heals. And it's entirely my choice which state I live in. Love builds trust, and in love I become constructive. I can feel it in my whole body. Love in my mind produces love in my life and the beautiful world I now knew was possible could be called something we have all heard before – Heaven. I perceive there is no heaven or hell outside of me, there is no place to go to. It's right here right now within me. Fear in my mind produces fear in my life. This world of fear I was exposing could be called something we have all heard before – Hell.

THE LOVE DRUG

As much as I shared the results and effects that cortisol (stress hormone) had on our bodies I also spoke about oxytocin (aka the love drug). I explained how the use of man-made drugs and mostly MDMA was actually balancing out the intense stress I was experiencing by activating the release of oxytocin, serotonin and dopamine into my body which is what connected me to the feelings of love, presence and connection. They were sort of helping me to some extent deal with the extreme environments I was living in. But now I no longer needed those recreational drugs to do this because I had discovered the power of the natural pharmacy in our brain and body and how to activate this resource.

Oxytocin, (the love hormone) could be activated naturally and far easier than I thought. One way was hugging and especially for twenty seconds which could activate oxytocin for up to forty-eight hours. Another way was through movement and dance so of course I got everyone moving their bodies through dancing, shaking, laughing and shared my experiences of 5Rhythms ecstatic dance which was my new passion. I combined this knowledge of oxytocin with sharing the wisdom of Chinese medicine which shows us that the heart meridian runs through our hands and digestive systems. This is why when we are in love, we want to hold hands with our lovers, and why children feel safe holding their parents' hands. We are actually holding each other hearts. And also, during birth it is oxytocin that is released to support the vagina to open and guess where the first place a mother puts her child after birth? Straight into a hug on the chest, so that the baby can hear the heartbeat and gets a boost of oxytocin which makes them feel loved and safe. You see, it's all naturally there in front of us, we just have to open our eyes. I was in awe when I discovered all these simple truths and I loved weaving them together and then seeing the responses from those I shared it with. I was so fired up when someone else got it and was amazed with awe and wonder.

WORDS HOLD POWER

"In the beginning was the word..." This is the powerful opening of the Bible. I have never read the bible but these words highlight for me the true power of communication in the universe. Words are spells, which order creation according to our speaking. The ability to speak my truth with conviction and honesty is an incredible power that structures my reality. And I noticed that we often forget that the first person we are influencing with words is ourselves.

I wanted to link together and emphasise the major importance of our words and water. Water is a carrier of information and is impacted by our words. In some organisms, up to 90% of their body weight comes from water and in adult humans it's up to 60%. We consist of a high percentage of water and the words we use are frequency and energy, and these frequencies impact our molecular structures. If our words then are toxic, we become toxic.

At the time I presented the work of Dr. Masaru Emoto, the Japanese scientist who revolutionised the idea that our thoughts and intentions impact the physical realm. He demonstrated how water exposed to loving, benevolent, and compassionate human intentions results in aesthetically pleasing physical molecular formations in the water. While on the other spectrum, water exposed to fearful and discordant human intentions results in disconnected, disfigured, and 'unpleasant' physical molecular formations. He did this through Magnetic Resonance Analysis technology and high-speed photographs.

Though his experiments have never been verified and there is a lot of conflicting drama associated to the whole topic, what he was pointing to I totally resonated with, because I knew how damaging and powerful words had been in my own life. It made sense to me that words effect our physiology. I came across an article from Margie Meacham, 'The Brain Lady'. She is a scholar-practitioner in the field of education and learning. She explained Neuroplasticity which describes how the brain continues to re-invent itself by older, unused pathways falling away, and then through repetition and focus, new ones emerge.

"What we think about actually rewires our brains—for better or worse. We now know that our choice of words has a direct and immediate effect on our emotional response and makes our brains inclined to respond in specific ways. This is true whether we are reacting to spoken words delivered by someone else, or to the inner self-talk that we hear ourselves 'saying' inside our heads. Language doesn't operate simply at the newer, conscious level of the brain. We respond to words at a visceral, autonomic level as well."

The Language of Love workshops were really having a

positive impact, and after the first few I wanted to collaborate with friends I had met through Simon on the Sofa to co-facilitate and share their wisdom and life experiences.

Rasheed Ogunlaru, who had become a close friend through the multiple conversations we had shared, some of them recorded on the Sofa, joined us for the day and shared his wisdom and insights into putting the soul back into business. He is an influential coach, speaker and author of the book *Soul Trader,* which ended up actually featuring me in the topic on conversations. Then there was Tom Fortes Meyer the hypnotherapist who has this amazing ability to use music and guided words in such a way that they can heal past trauma through hypnotic guided meditations. And I was thrilled to invite Anaiya Sophia to share her amazing vision to empower women through the wisdom of the womb. She took us all into a number of tantric practices to open our hearts and connect us more deeply to ourselves and each other.

On the Sofa with Steve Nobel and Rasheed Ogunlaru

These brave community spaces were created for us to feel safe to embrace the trauma and suffering inside of us. To come together in truth. A loving place to be held, heard and healed. We were naturally high on speaking our truth, presence, touch, connection, breathing, dancing, laughing, and lots of hugging. People from all walks of life were struggling with personal and collective fears and all craving real, authentic connection. As I continued to transparently share my own life experiences, I witnessed how touched people were by my rawness and how it supported them to open up and share their stories. When I was vulnerable it enabled others to meet me in that vulnerability. The more personal I became, it seemed to plug into the universal. I could feel how similar all our stories are. The struggles and tribulations, the highs and lows. So unique yet so comparable.

This playground was proving to me why the absence of love is so prevalent in our species and why it can be so difficult to love ourselves wholeheartedly and communicate truthfully. Of course, I wasn't surprised to confirm once again that fear had masqueraded itself as love. Trust was absent. The pain-body was in the driving seat and I was now the pain-body slayer and loving awareness was my lightsabre. Darth Vader you better watch out! I've got Yoda on my side, and as Yoda would say, "Fear is the path to the dark side. Fear leads to anger. Anger leads to hate. Hate leads to suffering." And I could feel the force was strong in me.

CELEBRATE THE CATCH

I know I have mostly been speaking about my pain-body and the collective pain-body, but I want you to know there is a joy-body too. The activation of our joy-body is the by-product of facing, feeling and healing our pain. The joy-body is actually our natural state of being.

Once the layers of false fears, false beliefs and past wounds are no longer running the show, we get to feel a heightened sense of joy. What I would call real joy. Don't get me wrong, an activated pain-body can experience some elevated states, I certainly experienced a lot of fun back in the days of being in fight or flight mode, but this type of joy is short-lived and bittersweet. It's not sustainable, because we have to keep chasing an outside experience to feed the sensations. There can be moments of fun, laughter, and an enjoyment for situations and circumstances, but this is not the depth of joy that arises from real inner peace.

I began tasting this inner peace more frequently and noticed when in this state many situations no longer bothered me as they did before. I didn't need to hold onto anything if I chose not to. I could notice, feel and observe the feelings and the many thoughts forms pass by without attachment.

As I've mentioned before, so many of the programs and systems in our western culture are in fact created by pain-bodies for pain-bodies, and I got to the point where I chose to no longer feed those realms with my energy. Of course, unexpected circumstances happen most days for me and these can often bring up uncomfortable feelings. Vipassana taught me these feelings come and go, and I can feel these emotions (e-motions = energy in motion) but I am not the emotion. Therefore, with conscious awareness I can catch myself being activated (because it happens) and then do what I call 'celebrate the catch'.

This is a really important part of the process because when I acknowledge my pain, feel whatever I am feeling and do not let the response to the pain create destructive behaviours and reactions, I am celebrating the catch. In this action I am consciously rewiring the subconscious to become familiar with this newer state of being, which is joy, acceptance, and love. As I welcome in more joy and present awareness, this process helps rewire the neural pathways that trigger my emotional states. This actually triggers the reward system in the brain which releases dopamine and in essence allows my body to feel encouraged to do it again. I guess you could say I am training myself to be in a more loving, accepting state rather than being angered and frustratingly triggered which was more like my previous default state of being.

Feelings are neither right or wrong, good or bad, they are

just expressed or suppressed. A suppressed feeling becomes toxic and begins breaking down the nervous system. If I identify with the feelings and thoughts associated to them and begin making up stories to justify my pain and begin blaming myself and others, then I can be taken into the 'toxic feedback loop from hell'. Or I can allow the energy to move in a safe way. This can happen through witnessing, but I have found that movement, shaking, and other forms of expression support these more dense energies to be transmuted into more elevated, creative and alive life force energy.

This is what I call Energy Alchemy, where I change and transmute dense matter into creative free-flowing wave frequency. The more aware I am of the difference between feeling heavy dense emotions related to my pain-body or the more heightened and enlightened emotions connected to my creative joy-body, the more I am the one in control of my state of being, rather than being thrown all over the place in reactive mode. I consciously transmute and respond to what is happening in any given moment without the need to unconsciously react to life situations.

All unsatisfying feelings are actually showing me where my core needs have not been met. This process is what I call 'parenting myself'. That way I can be gentler with my wounded tenderness (as Jeff Brown calls the painful parts of ourselves) and learn to better parent my wounded self and be patient with little Simon who needs loving attention.

I am not saying I have mastered this because it takes repetition to achieve excellence, but I am better now than I have ever been.

Just the other day, I overreacted and responded in a way that felt out of alignment, and I was feeling frustrated, hot and bothered. I had gone past my boundaries and had a whole heap of expectations on a particular person to act differently, and then I let all my unsatisfied feelings build up inside without expressing my needs. I call this the 'anger tower' that keeps building until it has to crumble which often results in reacting in ways that just create more conflict and separation. This is how the 'little me', the wounded ego, or small self, creates unnecessary drama. One of those moments where a silly little thing creates so much trouble, like the toothpaste lid being left off or some insignificant occurrence, but you or the other person explode, and it feels totally out of context.

This is the pain-body being activated by a series of smaller triggers which accumulate and then there is nowhere else for the energy to be stored so it has to move outwards. If you don't have the tools and practices for safe emotional release, then unfortunately it gets transferred onto others and then activates other people's pain-bodies and that creates a mess.

Even being aware of my pain-body, I still get triggered, but the time in which I stay triggered has progressively decreased and that also means being able to say sorry when I do act in an egoic manner that is not in accordance with loving kindness. The shorter the amount of time I spend in my activated emotional pain without bypassing the feelings, is how I continue to measure my progress. I see every trigger as a gift when viewed from this perspective. Instead of allowing myself to get lost in the triggered state, I now pose a question to myself in any tense moment: 'Do I want to be right or do

I want to belong?' I see it as my older self, making friends with my vulnerable younger self, who felt lost and confused, who wanted to play and make sense of the world, but very rarely had the true support it needed. It's like my two selves are both learning to trust each other again and through this trust, a merging takes place into wholeness. Then I can enter paradise, which is not a place, it is a state of consciousness, where all I need is less...

GLOBAL LOVE LETTERS

On the 15th February 2013, I got an excitable call from Miguel, he was a friend of Pedro's and had attended some of The Language of Love events. He was training to be an actor and mime artist and I loved his playful energy. He was excited to tell us what happened to him the night before on the way home from an event I hosted, called 'Who is Valentine?' The event was an invitation to those who attended to realise that Valentine's day is just a commercial date and that love is within each of us. It's everywhere always, in all-ways. We are love and no seeking of a partner to complete us is going to make us any more whole.

Of course, this is not an easy concept to embody in a society that feeds off our belief of unworthiness. We had a beautiful evening of authentic connection and everyone left feeling loved up. As Miguel headed home, he found an envelope on the floor outside the tube station he was entering which said, 'To You'. Intrigued, he picked it up, curiously looked around to see if anyone had dropped it, then decided to read it. As he pulled out the letter, the first line read, 'Even though I do not know you...'.

He was feeling excited and continued to pull the note out very slowly, reading the next line. What he continued to read touched his heart so profoundly that the next day as soon as he woke up he called us to share what had happened and how he felt. I wish I could have recorded the phone call.

Miguel with the Original Love Letter

His excitement was contagious. It turned out the love note was anonymous, it was a loving note to whomever would have found it. After he had read it to me on the phone I instantly said to come and visit us in Brighton the following weekend, and film his story and go out on the streets to pay forward this wonderful random selfless act of loving kindness. I know you are wondering what the letter said, so here it is:

"Even though I do not know you
and even though I may never meet you,
laugh with you, cry with you or kiss you…
I love you. With all my heart, I love you."

That following weekend, Pedro, Alice, Miguel and myself went out onto the streets of Brighton and had so much fun. It was so simple, so enriching and touched our hearts deeply. We didn't know how profound this act truly was and none of us had ever written anonymous love letters in this way before.

We filmed ourselves dropping them anonymously around the streets, in bus stops, people's bike baskets, in cafés, posting them in letter boxes, wherever we felt compelled to drop one. A touching highlight was when we saw a person

Love Deposits and Withdrawals

find one that we had hidden and could watch them read it. Wow! This is hard to describe, but it felt like pure love in action.

What was also apparent for us all was when you dropped one, you felt really mischievous and slightly nervous as you drop the love bomb without wanting to be seen. Almost like you are taking something when in fact you are giving unconditionally. This loving act of kindness became a regular practice, dropping them along my day to day travels.

At times, I had strangers bring me the letter I've dropped saying, 'Excuse me, sir, you dropped something' and I would just keep walking saying, 'No no, no, it's not mine, it must be for you!' hoping they would open it. After that initial weekend, one thing led to another and we began sharing this love story online through videos and photos.

This loving force was taking me on a journey, not the other way around. It had a life of its own, it wanted to spread itself, and it had its own intention.

What happened next fuelled me to continue this simple act of love. Pedro and I were on our way to film Simon on the Sofa and to meet two editors for Prediction Magazine, a UK Mind, Body, Spirit publication with a focus on astrology and psychics. We arrived, set up and filmed another inspiring conversation. After the conversation we excitedly shared our experience with dropping anonymous love letters all over Brighton the weekend before. They loved the idea and said they would feature it in their magazine and share with friends.

We left feeling accomplished, jumped on a bus from Stoke Newington (North London) back to Victoria Train

Station (South London).

On the way, I wrote another anonymous love letter and filmed a short video. When we were leaving the bus, I dropped the letter on the back seat, and we went on our merry way.

Leaving Love Letters on the Bus

The next day, when I opened my Facebook account, the first message I received was from Gemma, one of the women we filmed on the Sofa the day before. The message read, 'Si I think you'll like this' and she added a link to the picture of the envelope which looked familiar, and the text underneath the image read:

'I just had one of, if not the hardest and most emotionally draining afternoons at work ever. I get on the bus to find this waiting in my seat. Whoever left it, I FUCKING love you too.'

As I read the whole letter, multiple waves of energy pulsated and tingled throughout my body, I felt elated. I was literally blown away by this love in action. That love found exactly who needed it most. To think that the letter which I dropped on the back of the bus had to go all the way back to Stoke Newington where he had boarded the bus, so the busy bus had travelled another 35 minutes at least, stopping at many stops along the way and letting on multiple passengers and yet nobody else opened the letter. What were the chances?

This, among many other stories alike, compelled me to continue this simple anonymous loving act. I created a Facebook page and purchased a domain called 'Global Love Letters'. Lloyd built me a basic website with a message saying: 'Global Love Letters' is a global movement with a simple intention to spread loving messages across the globe by writing anonymous love letters addressed "For You" and signed "I Love You" and then go drop them absolutely anywhere and everywhere.'

People started doing this all over the globe, and we had connections with people in America who took the practice into schools. Others began writing them in their creative arts workshops, random people got onto the streets with their children, dropping them off and posting their pictures and videos. We were invited to the Mind Body Spirit Festival in London, and they kindly supported us with an area to write anonymous love letters and drop them around the festival. It was so organic and innocent. I thoroughly loved it.

A few months after launching, we received a message on one of our YouTube videos from the mother of the girl who wrote the actual note which Miguel found. How amazing was that? It turned out that every Valentine's day and Christmas, both her and her friend go out with many anonymous notes and drop them around the city. She had been doing it for a few years. It was amazing that she got to see how her ripple of pure intention had spread across the world.

After a while, people started contacting me having shared it on their blogs or in community events. I was invited to speak on the radio and on podcasts to share this simple love story and to encourage others to start in their country, town, city or communities.

The adventure was beyond words. The testimonials and feedback from people all over the globe were humbling as they shared their experiences of feeling deeply loved and connected through the process. Many felt they had a purpose to support the global awakening of love and a few ambassadors of love, (that's what I called them) decided to write them daily and drop them all over the place. I recall specifically Ed Crouser from USA, who was on a mission, Jason Walker from London, and then Laura from Liverpool who has written thousands, it just became what they did to pay it forward. Some of them still do it without need for any

You Are Amazing

accolade or following in life. Just for the love of it. I even had a message from a woman working with suicide survivors who was using the letters to reconnect them to love.

I know writing a love letter isn't a new idea, but doing it in this selfless way was unfamiliar for people. It was activating deep emotions for those who wrote and read them. It can be very difficult for some to write a universal love letter and receive that love too. Often people would say, "Who am I writing to? What do I write?" I would reply, write what you would love to receive.

This is the language of love in full flow. Think of the ripples of unconditional giving we can all create if we choose to.

Love can only do what love does and that is be that which it is. For a global shift in perception to occur on a mass scale it is simple loving acts which have the most profound impact. Less is more. When I move into a simpler, gratified and consciously aware space of reality, everything changes.

More Love Letters

Writing an anonymous love letter and dropping it anywhere in the world for somebody to find is pure unconditional love in action. The beautiful thing about this act is, when I write it to myself and it comes from truth, it resonates to all because we are all the same at the core. We all know truth when we feel it. I was blown away. I continued to share these anonymous love letters in various ways and at times combining it with dance walking on streets while dropping anonymous love letters along the way. It never ceases to amaze me how much joy is felt from those who find one.

I am forever grateful to Miguel and the little adventure we had from his excitable innocent desire to share what he received and continue the ripple of loving kindness across the world.

I DARE YOU TO BE GREAT

I heard that the author and great thinker of our times, Charles Eisenstein, was coming to London to give a talk called 'The Revolution of The Gift Economy'.

I contacted the organising team to ask who was filming the event. Surprisingly, it seemed like nobody was booked in. Here was a man whose voice needed to be heard and they were not filming it? I grabbed my trusty camcorder and headed down to record the event so this could be shared with others. When I arrived at this great church in central London, there was in fact another camera man there, but he was very happy for me to record as well, the more the merrier.

Mark Boyle, the author of *The Moneyless Man: A Year of Freeconomic Living*, was there to introduce Charles.

Mark was an activist known for founding the Freeconomy Community called 'just for the love of it'. The community was created to allow people to share their skills and resources and was moving away from familiar exchange economies towards a 'pay it forward' philosophy. When I met Mark, he had been living without money for two years. I loved this concept of a 'Gift Economy', plus I adored the heart touching movie *Pay It Forward*. This was how I saw love giving unconditionally.

I was keen to learn more and this was a beautiful opportunity and a gift in itself to meet Charles in person and hear his alternative perspectives on how we can shift our world views, from an old narrative which he calls 'The Story of Separation' to a new and ancient story called 'Interbeing'. I was soaking up his words as he eloquently spoke about our ability to live in a gift culture and reconnect to the sacredness of all life.

After the event had finished, I felt grateful to be in the presence of great change makers and in service to something far greater than me.

One thing led to another, and that night I was invited to another meeting a few days later at The School of Law with Charles Eisenstein in conversation with Polly Higgins. The talk was called 'Sacred Economics meets Sacred Law'.

This time, I invited Pedro to come with me and record the event, as I didn't want any unexpected hiccups. These were two great messengers of our times, pioneering visionaries in their own right, and their message needed to be heard far and wide.

After the talk I eagerly wanted to speak to them and invite them both onto Simon on the Sofa. Getting to know their work revealed broader perspectives of how we the people really can be the change. Their messages were so similar at the core, that all of life is sacred and that we should 'first do no harm to planet and people'. This for me is loving kindness.

Polly was diving deep into ecocide and rewriting the criminal law. She was a professional barrister. If you are not aware of what ecocide means, ecocide is serious loss, damage or destruction of ecosystems, and includes climate and cultural damage. Polly believed that ecocide should be recognised as an atrocity crime at the International Criminal Court - alongside genocide, war crimes and crimes against humanity. To say she was on a mission, would be an understatement. Her book *I Dare You To Be Great* touched my heart deeply. Polly emanated the voice of Mother Earth. A true earth angel.

A conversation with Polly Higgins and Charles Eisenstein

That 'dare' felt like a great call from the whole of existence. Can I dare to lead? Can I dare to be all of who I am? Can I dare to speak my truth? Can I dare to live fully and express my gifts freely? This is what Polly evoked. She also had great humour, strength and clarity.

Polly and Charles ignited the impossible within me. It was a blessing to become friends with them both. They lived for the potential and rise of a new humanity. In his book, *The More Beautiful World Our Hearts Know is Possible,* Charles highlights this transition with depth and courage.

Polly died in April 2019. I was stunned and deeply saddened when I was told of the sudden fierce cancer that was spreading through her body and gave her just a few weeks to live. I had the great blessing of sharing some beautiful moments with her, and sitting with her in numerous conversations, some of which we recorded on the Sofa. During those years, I supported her mission the very best I could on social platforms and hosting her at our home and assisting her during her tour around Europe to spread awareness of ecocide and ways we could make a stand and create great change for the next several generations. She not only empowered me, but also thousands, if not millions of others to dare to be great. I miss her powerful energy, her joyous laughter, and unending support and encouragement. But I know her spirit lives on within me and many others across the planet. She left a great legacy and may we all hear her call and dare to be the greatest version of ourselves.

OUR DEEPEST WOUNDS ARE THE GREATEST GIFTS

I first read these words by Julia Cameron in her book, *The Artist's Way*. And I agree, that these deep wounds are the doorway into the greatest gifts we have to give the world.

If I was going to dare to be great, then I needed to continue sharing my deepest wounds and unique story with the world. I had been sitting and listening to so many stories from all who sat on the Sofa, and I wanted to take the next step of showing up and sharing mine.

It was time for another layer of the onion skin to strip away. Meditation was showing me that I was not my story. I was not the stories I told myself, I was not my past experiences.

But how could I weave all that I had experienced and deliver it in a way that would awaken others to see beyond their false stories that have kept them imprisoned? So they too could rise like the phoenix from the flames and realise that loving ourselves wholeheartedly is easier than we care to think because we *are* love. With this loving awareness our actions, words and behaviours naturally contribute to the more beautiful world our hearts know is possible.

It appeared to me that people didn't simply want information, they wanted guidance and I knew I could offer that through sharing my story transparently. It was not my intention to seek egoic recognition, but to show the potential we all have for personal transformation and what is possible when we can let go of the stories that hold us trapped in painful cycles. I really believed that if I could do it, anyone could.

I called up Vaz and told him that I wanted to share my story in a fun and motivational way. He said why don't I offer an evening event to his community. In the meantime, Alice supported this new idea and also felt it was time to share my story to a wider audience and that I should write the book I had been talking about for some time. She had an inspired idea on how to show my story, and asked me for pictures from my past and to write my story in an abbreviated way that would be used as a voice over.

A few months went by with life's usual unexpected twists and turns while we prepared for this new direction. I arranged a date with Vaz for the 8th Nov 2012. He was using a new venue space near Holborn in central London. I began writing the promotion blurb to share online.

'Burglar to Buddha, Breaking and Awakening:
One man's transparent tale from a burglar (somebody who is asleep and takes without asking) to a Buddha (somebody who is awake and gives unconditionally). We are alive at very interesting times of evolution,

so much information being shared. So many theories as to what is happening on the planet. We are experiencing financial, economic, ecological, energy, health care crisis and psychological collapse. Some people say we are on a knife edge of existence and depending on our choices as a collective will determine our continuation or extinction as a species. As the truth continues to emerge, systems of society are crumbling. Cultural values need re-evaluating so that the ills of our past do not repeat themselves over and over again. We are literally writing history in this very moment. We must all take universal responsibility to create new stories, for

it is our cultural values and failings as a society that leads us into crime and violence. Burglar to Buddha is one man's answer to the question 'Will you be part of the cure or cause of humanities extinction?'

I was fired up, planning was in process, and a few weeks before, Alice had completed her beautiful creation. Months of energy and preparation went into this project. She created a photo shoot with me dressed like a criminal on an ID parade, recorded my voice over, then pulled together my whole story in a fun, concise and visually creative way. She even asked Paul to add some motion graphics for extra effects. The completed video was nothing short of a

masterpiece. I was touched. I could never have imagined such an innovative way to tell my life story.

It was epic and I wanted to use it as the introduction to the talk and then I would interact with those who attended.

The evening of the first event came around. I was with Alice and my friend Michelle. Vaz came down to introduce me to his community, there was quite a few attending. I felt the usual nerves of being on stage but I was ready and eager to see how this evening would unfold.

As I sat there in the audience I could feel the adrenalin pumping as I watched Alice's creation shared for the first time on a big projector screen. Apprehension, vulnerability and butterflies took over my belly as I sat there. I felt naked in the true sense of the word. I was revealing my past personas, my life of crime, and my new desires. I was being seen like never before.

When the video ended, many began clapping, which I took to be a good sign. The lights were switched back on and I took to the stage.

This was a familiar place, and when I get on stage something takes over. It's as though I plug into a different part of me. I rarely had a fixed plan or memorise a script because I love spontaneity. The present moment has its own rhythm and truth always arrives uninvited. I was learning that all I had in the moment was all I needed.

I began with taking questions from those who wanted to ask them, and then I free flowed with what wanted to come through. I trusted that like the Language Of Love events, if I showed up transparently then it would allow others to do the same.

It was so much fun and all the elements merged beautifully together. I felt aligned and purposeful. This was me daring to be great and courageously stepping into the next stage of speaking my truth. The whole exchange was energising, I was buzzing after the event and so grateful for Alice's contribution which she felt was a success too. Michelle said, "Yes, yes, yes, I was mesmerised, I have never heard anyone speak so truthfully."

That was my intention, if I want to see truth in the world, I have to be brave enough to speak my own. A few days later I was sent a few messages of appreciation from those who had written to Vaz: "Wow, wow, wow wow, Simon, your transparency blows me away, thank you for creating a space where the truth can be nourished in a brutally honest and liberating way."

"Thanks, Simon, for reminding us how important it is to be our beautiful authentic selves and not worry about others' reactions, all we have to do is come from our heart centre and be truthful and everything wonderful springs from there."

"Superb event, really enlightening talk about how we humans can advance as a race."

These are just a few of many messages that came to me, some people really opened up and sent me long emails with almost their entire life story. I was humbled by the response and as Vipassana teaches me, everything is temporary. It is rising and passing and I was not to get attached with my craving and aversion. I welcomed the feedback as fuel to continue and clearly I had touched a nerve within many who had attended.

All of my events had proved to me that humans want to speak their truth, they want to open up as love, but due to so much fear they have suppressed themselves. It is time we all awaken to these greater truths and free ourselves from the shackles of our past stories and rise up and write the new stories of our liberation from fear and into love.

I read this quote from Lao-Tzu, author of the *Tao Te Ching*, born in 601 BC. "If you want to awaken all of humanity, then awaken all of yourself, if you want to eliminate all the suffering in the world, then eliminate all the dark and negative in yourself. Truly, the greatest gift you have to give is that of your own self-transformation."

My imagination was ignited with a passion to inspire millions. I arranged another talk in Brighton. After each talk I was blown away by the response and the way that just by sharing my story I was giving permission to others to empower themselves.

What if I could inspire the youth of today to make awakened decisions and for them to realise the power and influence they have on culture and society? Because it is the children, the youth of today and the choices they make which determines the path forward for our species.

I was being reminded of the younger me, the me that had desperately needed this support. I knew that if I could educate and empower the youth and especially those from deprived backgrounds, to live with awareness, compassion and integrity, this would create great change for future generations. And their story would not mirror mine.

I asked Lloyd to create a website, where we could share this exceptional, imaginative, artistic venture that was now developing. I was calling it a bridge between crime and consciousness. I had a new mission and wanted to tour the globe sharing this unique transparent story through a medley of live theatre, visual entertainment, inspiring storytelling and empowering speech.

I would highlight the power of transparent communication as the cure for the foundation of lies our species currently communicates from.

The idea just kept growing with a vision to produce a documentary, a book, and then a movie. And it wouldn't just be another rags to riches story. This would be a life-changing tale. We all know the power and influence film has on society and culture, and I was tired of seeing the glorification of drugs, crime, sex and violence. We must all take universal responsibility to create new stories, for it is our cultural values and failings as a society that leads youngsters into crime and gang violence.

I was dreaming of the film we would create and how it would touch the lives of the younger generation and create responsible role models with integrity and compassion.

I clearly had another big vision (nothing new there) and I was going to need a lot of support and funding for such a venture. I was a little overwhelmed to say the least.

I took one step at time and began bouncing ideas around with Lloyd and Alice and wrote the copy for the website. We used some of the images Alice had already created and of course the beautiful video. It was full steam ahead.

After one of the talks, someone asked me if I knew of an organisation called 'A Band Of Brothers'. It's a UK charity working with young men involved in the criminal justice system, who provides the support they need to make the transition to an adulthood free from crime and filled with a sense of belonging, connection and purpose.

It sounded like the perfect place to present my Burglar to Buddha talk, so I got in contact with the founders. It is never as quick as just calling them and getting invited in as there are always steps that have to be taken, but they were now on my radar and it was great to know that organisations like these existed. I stayed in touch and after while a little spontaneous opportunity arose. The founder reached out and said they were having their yearly Charity Gala for existing funders and new investors. They often invited speakers and asked if I would I like to present my talk. I would have fifteen or twenty minutes.

Of course it was a 'yes'. I had a lot of doubts rising, as this was a big event at the grand hotel in Brighton, and a few hundred or more people would be there and I wouldn't be able to screen the video as it was too long so I would have to just talk with no interaction. This was a new challenge. I should have known by now that life always does that to me. Just when I'm getting comfortable, I am asked to step out on the edge. I heard my own words, 'you only grow from being in the arena'. I knew this but sharing myself in this raw way was still not familiar. In the beginning, every time that moment came, I would sweat profusely, as the adrenaline released and the fight and flight response got activated. I was out there in the amber zone getting ready to rumble. It definitely kept me feeling alive, that's for sure.

Alice accompanied me. I was both excited and nervous to get on stage and speak. There were people in the audience who would really know and understand my past as some of them had lived in far greater depravity than me, and many of them would have served much longer sentences. This made the whole experience a little scarier. How would I be received?

A lot of fear was present but I knew that it was simply false evidence appearing real.

Everyone was sat together in the big hotel conference room with round tables all set out elaborately with champagne and all the trimmings. The night began with the founders sharing a beautiful video explaining the project and what great success they had been achieving with the groups of boys that go through the program. There were some other keynote speakers and some entertainment.

Soon, I was up and stepping onto the stage and waxing lyrical. I like to bounce off the audience and so I asked a few questions and was able to engage with them in that way. I was in this surreal moment where I was sharing my story and at the same time somehow witnessing myself in this situation and kind of judging myself too. I didn't manage to share my story in a very linear way and felt a little all over the place. I got lost in parts of the story and was worrying about how much time I had and felt extremely uncomfortable. I winged it and did my best in that moment, and the audience were laughing and engaging with me. But the critic in me was quite harsh. I left the stage feeling slightly deflated.

I let my activated pain-body beat myself up for not planning my talk better and having some structure. I disliked structure and yet without it, I felt like I couldn't express what I wanted to express. This frustrated me. I made so many notes after the event.

Of course, all of this judgement was just my perspective and as I have described before, the little me, the small Simon, needed to be seen and was feeling let down for not doing it right. But right in whose mind? I began noticing the perfectionist was alive in me again, the persona of the actor. I needed to parent myself through this and I knew I was touching the deeper wounds within me.

It was these wounds that were my greatest gifts, but it was not easy in those first few talks. I had to learn what stepping out in this way and speaking my truth would bring up.

Alice said I did really well, and everyone enjoyed it. She was biased, no doubt. A few days later, I received an encouraging message from a man named Mark who was at the event, 'I just wanted to say how much I enjoyed your speech at the Band of Brothers Gala the other night. Many of your thoughts have stayed with me. You were engaging, genuine and inspirational. A quote that still guides me daily is Henry Ford's classic, "Whether you think you can, or you think you can't, you're right." True that. Thank you, and all the best.'

It was heart-warming and encouraging to receive his words and he shared a quote I so often had read which felt like it was me speaking to myself with an encouraging message to continue and remember that impossible spells I'm-possible. Everything really is possible.

CHOP WOOD
CARRY WATER

It may have seemed like I had it all worked out and knew what I was talking about, but little did I know that love had other plans for me. 2012 was over and there was no end of the world as it may have been predicted, but many of my worlds were about to end. I started writing this book in 2013 just after my second Vipassana retreat. My meditations had fallen by the wayside, I hadn't kept them up as I had intended, so I returned for another sit. London was challenging me and Alice even more.

Many productive things were happening, like sharing my story and being on the mission of love, but you may recall on my first Vipassana retreat that I felt Alice and I would part. By now, it was definitely in process. A few years previously, Alice got some corporate photographic work which required her to travel to the small island of Malta. These type of advertising jobs were never her greatest joy, but they paid well.

On a few occasions I was able to join her as her assistant.

Although it may sound great, I was always in resistance as I thought it wasn't what I wanted to truly do. Alice is a very confident and independent woman, and she had flown out a few times alone and was falling in love with the island for a number of reasons and wanted to live there. She loved the sun (don't we all) and it was much more her type of environment and she felt it offered far better opportunities for herself.

A regular pattern in our relationship was that we would break up from time to time, just for a few days or a few weeks, and mostly stay in touch because of missing each other's presence and then always enjoy the excitement of coming back together again. This happened during some of her visits to Malta and we did our best to have a long-distance relationship. But these patterns were highlighting my fear of commitment and the uncertainty I had felt for some years, which was that our paths were not fully aligned.

I wanted to have a partner to join me in facilitating events and spreading love and Alice wanted to travel Europe in a camper van and share her love in her visually creative way. The more Alice travelled to Malta, the more she made friends and slowly created a life for herself. She began creating more opportunities and shooting her own art, which ignited her own creative spark. This was a big step for her in daring to be great and not having to work for others. She had phenomenal visions of how to use art to expand consciousness, and she could do with images what I was attempting to do with words. I have mentioned throughout this book how challenging financially life has been for me at times. And during 2012 it got quite dire. At one point I created a very vulnerable and transparent video called '£5 and parsnip' which was a call for help to my mailing list because we couldn't pay the rent and I literally had £5 in my wallet and a parsnip in the fridge. We found a way to eat but I was on the edge.

Lloyd said I was Vegan, Sick and Nearly Dead which was his version of the great documentary 'Fat, Sick and Nearly Dead'. He's a joker like me and laughter is great medicine in times of crisis, I found it best not to take the whole situation too seriously or I could go crazy. But even with my more heightened awareness and shift in relationship to what money represented for me, it was still a very frustrating and challenging time, and I felt like I kept making life difficult, like I somehow deserved to struggle. I also had great resistance to the prospect of looking for work back in the invisible prison. I was run down mentally, physically and emotionally, but holding up a great façade.

My relationship with Alice got to the point where we were living with each other but feeling oh so distant. I recall some pain-body activation where it escalated to shouting and I felt really disappointed in my behaviour. Even with everything I knew, I still wasn't able to say I just want to be held, heard and loved and I need help. I was in victim mode and experiencing feelings of unworthiness and failure. My personal practices and positive outlook on life were keeping my head just above water, but my meditation practice had pretty much stopped because I had fallen back into comfortable habits. The 'doing' persona was strong, trying to do more, and having high expectations on myself. Basically, I was caught up in the feedback loop from hell, thinking that by doing more I would get more.

My life in the UK was crumbling in a way, although I hadn't really noticed the struggle I was creating. Remember, when you're in the shit, you can't always smell it. Alice was on her last straw too and was pretty fed up with our lifestyle and told me she was leaving to live in Malta. She had set the foundations to make the move and was now ready. She said I could either join her and we could start a fresh new romantic life in the Mediterranean, and I could write my book and get away from the struggles and striving that London had represented for us or I could stay here. I loved her romantic ideas of how life could be. I just had to decide if I wanted to take the risk to try something new.

For some strange reason, at first, my mind thought that staying in the struggle would be a better option than experiencing an idyllic island. I had resistance from all the false evidence I was creating to justify why I should stay in the UK, but after some ruminating, I decided to make the move. I had nothing to lose really. After all, I could always come back if I wanted.

It was a month or so before we were due to leave that I attended my second Vipassana retreat. After this second sit I came out with a new sense of what it meant to meditate and observe the constructs of my inner landscape. That first time was all good and well, but I was caught up in a lot of inner turbulence. It was all new, so my mind was all over the place. I did come away with great insight and intellectually, I had it all down, but I didn't keep the practice going for long and old habits soon came back in. So it was understandable why I found myself in more suffering. I can't go into much detail of the second retreat because I actually don't remember as much of it. This time, I was more present. I knew what the procedure was so I could just sit and witness and not make so many stories up. I did take away that I was very much at the base of the mountain and I felt like a student of this practice. There were definite moments along my path before this point when I'd had a feeling of being enlightened. I had definitely let go of some of the burdens that were weighing me down and I felt much lighter, but in truth, I was still a seeker.

Alice had given me a book by Jack Kornfield called *After the Ecstasy, the Laundry*. It's a great book about going back to ordinary life and doing the cleaning after an awakening. I read some great insights from many who had experienced unique epiphanies that were all somewhat similar to mine.

Enlightenment, it seems so many are seeking it and I was too, even though at times I didn't really know what I was seeking. I wanted to be free in some way and being enlightened definitely alluded to that. But what does being free mean? In this book, Jack describes enlightenment as being the beginning, not the end destination, which many believe they are trying to obtain. Although awakening changes everything, simultaneously it all stays the same.

I experience enlightenment as being more weightless, meaning lighter, because many burdens and false beliefs no longer weigh me down mentally, emotionally, physically or spiritually. And the lighter I am in weight the freer I feel and the brighter I shine, so it has many meanings for me. The brighter I am, the more illuminated I am. The clearer I am. The more present I am. The more loving awareness I am. It really is like I am in this world but not of it. Aware of the different frequencies I can attune to and through this awareness I have more compassion for myself and others. And I love making this joke when I find myself in conversations about enlightenment: what's the difference between an enlightened being and non-enlightened being? Then I wait for all the answers, and up until this point no one has ever said the one I respond with, which is: The enlightened being knows there is no difference!

We are all divine expressions of the same thing. There is no hierarchy in love. Being enlightened and more aware literally means I can see beyond the seeing. Life continues as it is, but my perception of what I see changes dramatically. 'When I change the way I look at things, the things I look at change.' And that leads me into a few other examples that describe this state of being. You may have heard the famous Zen Proverb which describes it as, 'Before enlightenment: chop wood, carry water. After enlightenment: chop wood, carry water.'

Or there is this other phrase too: when hungry, eat, when tired, sleep. I also appreciate the Buddha's simple definition of enlightenment as simply – The End of Suffering.

It was clear all my suffering hadn't ended, and I had some more cleaning to do. And I knew I was going to be tested to see whether I could live what I preached.

I had read that 'knowing thyself is a lifelong path' and realised that I am a little impatient at times.

During Vipassana there is a constant reminder from SN Goenka at the end of the discourses where he says, 'Start Again'. Whatever I am experiencing or whether I think

I have realised a great revelation from the practice, 'Start again'. Which I understand as a reminder that there is nowhere to get and nothing to understand. It's all craving and aversion, just let go of needing to know or searching for some outcome and all will be revealed. My job is to just practice equanimity to all that is rising and passing.

It was Krishnamurti who said, "in meditation, every form of search must come to an end." Which also reminds me of Rumi who says, "what you are seeking is seeking you." Some of these sayings are great, but in the beginning when they are just concepts, they often feel cryptic and the mind cannot properly understand them, which is the point. It's all about letting go and being here now. To realise we are love, beingness, consciousness or whatever term sits best with you. However, letting go and accessing this state of being really is a practice of consciously rewiring subconscious programs and habitual behaviours. I found this story of the Two Monks to be an amazing anchor for me to practice acceptance to what is, because as you know, my mind-made selves still try to hold onto FBS (false belief systems) and my pain-body still gets activated.

"Two monks were on a pilgrimage. They had already walked many miles, avoiding when they could, the society of people, for they were from a particular order of monks that were forbidden to speak to or touch women. They had no wish to offend anyone so they kept to the by-ways and lived off the land. It was the rainy season and as they walked across a broad plain they were hoping that the river they had to cross would not be impassable. From afar they could see that the river had burst its banks; nevertheless, they were hopeful that the ferryman would be able to take them across in his boat. But as they neared the crossing point they could see no sign of the boatman; the boat, it appeared, had been swept away in the current and the ferryman had stayed at home. There was, however, a woman. She was dressed in fine clothes and carried an umbrella. She implored the monks to help her cross, for her mission was urgent and the river, though wide and fast, was not deep. The younger monk ignored her and looked away. The elder, however, said nothing but swept her up onto his shoulder and carried her across, putting her down, completely dry, on the other bank.

For the following hours as they journeyed on through thick and tangled woods, the younger monk berated the elder, heaping scorn upon his actions, accusing him of betraying the order and his vows. How dare he? How could he? What was he thinking of? What gave him the right to? Eventually, the monks entered a clearing, and the elder monk stopped and looked square into the eyes of the younger. There was a long moment of silence. Finally, in a soft tone, his eyes bright and gentle with compassion, the older monk simply said: "My brother, I put that woman down over an hour ago. Why are you still carrying her?"

Such a simple example, but for me it beautifully illustrates how the mind likes to hold on and keep us entangled in the past.

So I was plugged back into my meditation and headed to Malta with curiosity. Alice welcomed me into her quaint little flat that she had acquired through a random synchronistic meeting with an old quirky scientist and inventor. They seemed to be destined to meet. Slowly, Alice introduced me to some of her new friends and showed me around the island. Of course, like any new place it was unfamiliar, but it felt right to be making this move. I had a funny moment of confirmation when I met a friend of hers at this newly opened vegan healthy living café and within a few minutes of speaking she was talking about Hanuman and the *Book of Ram*, I shit you not. In that moment I am certain I could hear the divine laughing with me, great big belly laughs of synchronicity. I danced away from that encounter like Hanuman, thinking, I must be in the right place.

While in Malta, I continued recording conversations on the Sofa, and also created evening transparency sharing circles which were enabling me to meet new friends from within the local communities. I began writing this book as intended and Alice, as always, was supportive in so many ways. We were experiencing highs and lows, but something still felt off. It was not all as romantic as we may have hoped it would be. We were in a new environment, which helped, but the same internal struggles persisted and needed to be addressed. Our paths were still drifting from one another.

I cannot even explain how difficult and surreal it was to separate from a woman whom I loved so much. Especially when there really wasn't that much at fault with either of us, but something deeper within was pulling us apart and there was a greater picture playing out. Relationships are, in my opinion, our greatest learning arena. Alice and I shared many mature conscious transparent conversations and did our best to attempt to consciously uncouple. This is a modern term for breaking up without having to create unnecessary suffering. I would love to say that we accomplished this, but the parting, let's say, was not as grand as the meeting. There were many elements at play and a lot of attachments to the fantasies of what could have been.

We were in the process of dying to what we had shared, dying to the future projections, and dying to all that we had dreamed could have been possible. Our cycle was coming to a close and although these partings are never easy, I know from great experience that when one door closes there is always another that opens. Through a series of events and me clinging on at times, Alice was not happy with some of my actions as our relationship ended.

Little did she or I know that her decision to move to Malta was going to support both of our next stages of evolution. She was and still is a constant catalyst to me stepping into a grander version of myself. Meeting Alice showed me what it means to meet another soul with a greater intention for conscious evolution and expansion. It was emotionally challenging on all levels as we departed and each of us dealt with it in the best way we could and were supported by those closest to us and the new souls that would come into the next constellation of our journey.

A death was in process as the new cycle of life was emerging. I understand that not everyone is supposed to stay in my life forever, at times they are only there long enough to teach me the lessons I need to learn. There is a saying that people come into your life for a reason, a season or a lifetime. I realise there is a role for everyone I meet. Some test, challenge and teach me, some have used and abused me, some have just loved me. But the ones who have been truly important are the ones who brought out the best in me. These are the rare and amazing souls who remind me why it's all worth it. This is what Alice was and did for me and I am forever grateful.

A few weeks before I decided to move out and find a new place to live, someone who was close to my heart yet so far away, was also dying...

ALRIGHT SON?

Early in 2014 I had an opportunity to exercise my loving forgiveness through the great teacher of physical death. This sequence of events was something quite spectacular. Steve received a random call from my father's stepson. He said that our dad was dying and had four months to live. He wanted us to call him and left a number. My sister-in-law reached out to me and sent the news with the number. Steve said he didn't want to speak to him. "Forget him, he left us, I have nothing to say to him." But for me it was different, I wanted to reach out and connect. It felt like a clear yes in my body. This was not an easy phone call to make and I could feel a lot of hesitation, but I did it anyway and David (my dad) answered the call. I said

"Hello, is that David?"

He replied "Yes, who's that?"

I said, "It's Simon."

"Simon?" he said, "Simon?"

I said, "Simon, it's Simon, your son."

The phone went dead quiet, and after a long pause I could hear him say to his wife in the background, "Hey it's Simon, it's Simon, my son."

After another breath he came back onto the phone and said "Alright, Son?"

I laughed a little and said, "Alright, yeah! I'm more than alright." We chuckled nervously and I said, "I got a message from Justin saying you said to call you because you are dying, so here I am."

He replied, "Justin? I haven't spoken to Justin for years."

This impacted me, because I realised that my dad hadn't reached out, and in fact Justin had taken it upon himself to find Steve and I to let us know.

Wow. I was so thankful, and also had these deeper feelings arise about rejection.

"Well, here we are," I said. "What's happening, is it true, are you dying?"

He replied that his prognosis was just four months and he had bile duct cancer, which was inoperable, but he was going to have radiotherapy or chemotherapy as it may delay the spread. We spoke for about 25 minutes, and he shared with me how he had happily lived on a canal barge for many years with his wife and worked as a captain of a boat that travels people up and down the River Thames. He shared a little about his condition and the next four months ahead. I could hear fear in his voice. He asked how I had been and how Steve was. He told me Mum was a good woman. I told him they were doing their best. I shared how much I enjoyed life, and the ways I was sharing love around the world. I didn't ask him why he hadn't ever reached out, because I had never done the same. It didn't feel relevant. Here we were in this moment. The main thing I wanted to say was: "I love you for creating me, I am so grateful to be alive and for this I love and thank you and Mum regularly."

Something happened when I said this, the energy changed, I could feel it for us both, it was profound. Maybe I gave him permission to let go of any guilt he may have been holding onto while simultaneously I was able to release any guilt, shame or projections I was still holding onto. It felt like healing had taken place.

My Dad and I

All in all, it was a beautiful, although slightly awkward, conversation. I asked if he would like to speak again and we shared details. Some weeks passed and for whatever reason we didn't speak. I noticed how I had this battle going on within me. Like he should call me. He didn't even reach out in the first place. He was dying and still I had this little wounded boy inside that wanted him to come to me.

It was a great revelation and so I called him again and this time he wasn't able to speak because the chemo had made him so weak. I could feel how I had some resentment towards him for not calling and again noticed it was all mine. I had to do the cleaning. It wasn't his job. He was my guru in those last moments. He helped me heal even though he wasn't aware of it. I was all about love, yet in those moments, I couldn't just love him unconditionally. But together, we got there. I could have called him every day, but I chose not to.

A week or so later, I was sat in a café when I received an email from his wife, letting me know he had died the day before. As I read the email, a strong wave of emotions moved through my whole body and I burst into tears. This was it. Now he was really gone. That hug I yearned for would never come. As I write, tears are with me again. How beautiful it is to cry.

Since receiving that email, a deeper purification began. I was able to feel and heal the more subtle wounds associated to the absent relationship and lack of connection I had with my father. As I allowed myself to feel the grief of him dying and me never meeting him, more cleansing tears of truth were freed. For some years these tears arose each time

I retold this touching story. Every time I shared it, I allowed myself to feel a little more and every time I read this chapter tears would flow. I experienced how tears that are released can bring clarity, compassion and inner vision. I chose not to attend his funeral. It didn't feel like a yes in my body. Those two phone calls were my goodbye, and it was lovely to hear his voice for those few precious moments. I am deeply grateful to Justin, whom I have never met, for getting his number to me, and to this day I still include my father in my daily gratitude as I had before we spoke.

Thank you, Dad, for creating me. You did more than enough.

DIE BEFORE YOU DIE

Life is uncertain, and sooner or later this moment is going to be my last. Death and the dying process has allowed me to embody a deeper acknowledgment and appreciation for this temporary and precious gift of life that is rising and passing moment to moment. I cannot avoid the physical death or escape it in fear. All my fears at their root are an underlying deep fear of death, the fear of losing myself, someone or something. In moments of fear, I actually think I am going to literally die and that is why it's so difficult to move through my fears because my body has to move through dense and often scary emotional states of loss and grief. When I truly embrace death as part of the life cycle, not separate from it, I can then really appreciate all of life. Death is not taking anything away from me, death is actually giving me something, it's giving me a reason to live.

I have come to realise, through the work of Stephen Jenkinson, that we live in a death phobic society. A society scared of death and an unwillingness to embrace it all.

Stephen says beautifully, "Death feeds life, not the other way around. Without death, there cannot be continuation. We have to die to our old stories for new life to be birthed. What has to die is our refusal to die."

When I honour the inevitability of physical death and the uncertainty of life, then I am able to celebrate and welcome the dying process gracefully. If I don't run away from death in fear, but instead face it consciously, then I can engage with its power respectfully and no longer view it as a scary finality, and instead as an opportunity for rebirth and wisdom. When the things I hold onto cease to have importance, they no longer control me.

Embracing death invites me to live life more present and aware of this fleeting moment. I'm no longer the person I used to be. I am not a persona, a label, a career, a gender, a social status, a social category or defined by any colour, creed or relationship. Where there is no identification, there is no attachment. I understood what Zen masters and Sufi poets often point to – that only by letting go of everything that pins us down, that constrains our lifestyles, like destructive thoughts and emotions, can we truly transform ourselves and change our lives for the better. I choose to move through death and the dying cycle with a little more allowing, reverence and surrender. I can even die to the concept of death.

This is what dying to it all means for me. What happens when I can accept what is, let it all in, feel it all, and then let go beyond all my identifications, judgements, expectations, projections into the future or emotional chains that keep me locked in the past? I enter the miraculous state of being, that's what happens. What I accept I go beyond. That's the miracle right there, and when I can witness the miraculous in everything, I know I am right here in this awe-inspiring present moment and it is here that I get to savour it all and flirt with infinity.

In his book *Be Here Now* Ram Dass asks every person to be the bliss of the universe and access the joy and liberation of living in the present moment. "This is it! This is all there is right now!" And I know it's a cliché, but the journey really is the destination. There is nowhere to get and nowhere spells 'now-here'. All this work on the self, all this self-observation, if implemented with consistency and integrity, can lead us into the spaciousness of being. A state of being which is the eternal, ever present source of all life beyond this temporary physical form that is subject to the cycles of birth and death.

Being is that inner most invisible and indestructible essence, and I only get to taste it when the mind is still, when there is not so much turbulence with all the mental chatter, and projecting, assuming and personalising. Love is not personal. Fearful thinking makes everything personal.

Being cannot actually be grasped with my mind, being can be felt but never understood mentally. It is accessible when my attention is totally and intensely witnessing. Vipassana meditation, yoga, qigong, 5Rhythms, dynamic meditations, and many other practices that invite the opportunity to go beyond the mind and arrive into more presence, even if only for a few moments, have all supported this alternate way of seeing life. Through the observation of my own inner energy field and feeling the subtle sensations, aliveness and animating presence within my body, I have become extremely grateful for my existence.

Eckhart Tolle asked: "Can you look at a tree and not name it a tree?" Just observe it without evaluating what is? In his book, *Stillness Speaks*, he brings awareness to the fact we get lost in doing, thinking, remembering, and anticipating a world of problems. "We have forgotten how to be - to be still, to be ourselves, to be where life is: Here and Now."

Nature has a great way of allowing us to taste what it means to simply be here, to be still. Whenever I bring my attention to anything natural, anything that has not been created by humans, I am able to create a distance from the incessant conceptualised thinking and just be with what is without naming it. This is not an easy process and can bring up a lot of pain, frustration and resistance. At first this can create even more mental constructs and the mind trying to explain what is happening and have it somehow worked out. To face the death of my personas is not an easy task. These are personalities that have been constructed over years of habitual behaviours. They are embedded into my subconscious.

You can try this for yourself by bringing your attention to a tree, the sea, a mountain, a shell, insects or an animal, anything really and simply perceive it, hold it in your awareness without thinking about it.

When I do this, I am taken beyond the form into the formless and enter the realms of the ultimate sacred mystery. This is being for me. This is awareness. When I am fully aware, there is nothing to lose and nothing to gain. Awareness allows a deep inner peace, greater acceptance and graceful forgiveness. Death, dying, life and living therefore become a great celebration and a confirmation that everything is constantly changing, moving, rising, and passing through the cyclical nature of all that is. The fragility and ephemerality of my unique physical existence and expression of life force called Simon, has risen and every breath of oxygen, the elixir of life that I inhale, takes me one breath closer to my dissolution in this form. That which gives me life, takes it away. The story of little me shall be a distant blip in momentary time and space, maybe recalled on some future lips from time to time. Back to the formless I shall return. Everything exists and nothing exists, all at once. The dichotomy of existence. I am love. I am that being. I am that space. I am a drop in the ocean, and the ocean in the drop. Everything changes but the essence remains the same. I choose to die before I die so that I can truly live and I learn to love the intrinsic intelligent design of it all, that which is me.

This too shall pass.

ALL I KNOW IS
I KNOW NOTHING

I haven't sat under a Bodhi tree for 49 days. I haven't studied Buddhism or any religious scriptures in great depth. As the story is told, Buddha saw the pain and suffering around him and went on a quest of personal freedom which took him deeper inside of himself. Did Buddha exist in the way we are told? Is our His-story the whole story? There are many contradictory depictions. Everything I have written in this book is a story, my perspective and not the whole picture by any means.

There are thousands of buddhas and in my understanding, Buddha means Buddhahood, not just buddha, a person in form. It's a state, a quality, a fragrance. What kind of fragrance you may ask? It's a pure fragrance. What is to be purified? Purification of the mind. When the mind is purified, the end of that purification is nothing but the state of buddha. It's a formless and nameless state of being. The names are used often as metaphors to create some form of understanding. The words are merely pointers to that which cannot be named. All the words are in themselves tools to play with and paint onto the blank canvas of creation. I see it as trying to define something that is invisible. This state of Buddhahood, or present awareness, or unconditional love, is a quality, a state beyond mind, beyond emotion, beyond body and ultimately beyond name and form. We can experience it but cannot show it. We can taste it with the limitations of our five senses. But we have to dive beyond that which we can perceive and transcend the five senses and then we get to experience that which is beyond them. I cannot prove what I am pointing to and that's where the funky paradox drops in again.

In a State of Buddhahood

I initially used the word Buddha for the title of this book, because Lucy had named me 'Buddha in the bedroom' in her book *50 Ways to Find a Lover*. She described openly her quest for sex and how at the time I was living in her front room and sleeping on the sofa bed and she loved my daily wisdom and reflections to her experiences. So she named me Buddha. Maybe she too could taste that I was offering some of the fragrance of Buddhahood.

I invite you to not get too caught up on the word 'Buddha'; if it's not resonating with you or points you to a religious feeling and you are anti-religion then do as a quote I read once says; "If you meet the Buddha on the road, kill him." What this message invited me to consider was that no matter what my concept of Buddha may or may not be, it's wrong and I can kill it or let go of thinking that I know.

I learned that there are the known knowns. These are things I know that I know. There are known unknowns. That is to say, there are things that I know I don't know. But there are also unknown unknowns. There are many things I don't know I don't know. What I know is much smaller than what I don't know. Not needing to know and not needing to be right has been far more freeing and unifying than proclaiming to know it all. What a burden that would be. Whenever I find myself trying to be right or upholding some belief I may have, I ask myself the question I always ask when triggered: do I want to be right or do I want to belong? The very nature of love is belonging. Love unites, and fear fights to be right. A burglar takes without asking, and Buddha, in my opinion, loves unconditionally.

DIVINE PLAY

So where do we go from here? We end where we began, making a full circle back to being free like a child and playing with all of creation.

This mysterious life cannot be worked out no matter how hard I try and any words I try to use to explain the greater mystery, never do it real justice. I do however have so much reverence and appreciation for all the discoveries that humans have uncovered through relentless adventures, so many losing their lives to explore what seems like all corners of this mysterious planet we call earth.

I am not saying words are not powerful in their own right; they carry energy as I have said before, they help me shape reality, they are a tool that enables me to play and navigate through this mystery and into the spaciousness of being.

In the first chapter of the *Tao Te Ching*, I read 'The Tao that can be named is not the eternal Tao'. Anything that I may want to point to cannot be named. Doesn't this make you laugh? It does me. This is what I mean when I said the funky paradox, or reverse dichotomy. The more I observe the more it seemed to me that everything is backwards. I started saying that we had to 'flip the pancake' in order to truly see the myriad of creative realities all playing out at once. I see these cryptic clues within the design of the words themselves. And you know I love wordplay. Some of my favourites are 'The ordinary becomes extra-ordinary'. Or 'Imperfection is the perfection'. Imperfect even says I'm-perfect!

'Less is more' or 'Let go to receive', 'Certainty is found in uncertainty', 'Vulnerability is our strength not weakness 'or the one I have recited many times: 'The only way out is within'. It's all one big cosmic joke and reality is an impermanent illusion. Are we not all just making it up as we go along? Winging it where possible and hoping to live as long as we can while avoiding all the potential dangers and life-threatening disasters.

If I believe that I think I have the correct image of what it means to be anything, then I can also practice the art of letting things be the way they are. When I am not holding onto my beliefs, needing to prove myself, or making what is into something other than what it is, then I am free. Free of all the nonsense. I can then observe it all without needing to evaluate. And laugh when I take myself and others too seriously. Seriousness is a dis-ease and whenever I have taken life too seriously, I have missed all the heavenly glory and felt sick in the belly. The more playful I become the more I see my egoic traits evaporate. What happens if I let go of seriousness and yet, remain deeply sincere in my truth?

What if I can stare fear in the face and begin to laugh, to know that at my deepest core I see the truth and choose to remain free?

When I can let go of trying to control what is, when that manipulative behaviour falls away, I can laugh at it all. Laughter, therefore, is sincere. And when I say laugh, I mean really laugh, not needing a joke or going to pay a comedian to make me laugh, I mean laughing for no reason by accessing my authentic laughter.

It was Osho who said, "Laughing at someone is sick, laughing for a reason is intellectual and laughing for no reason at all is spiritual."

My friend Marc Itzler describes laugher as such, "Laughter is the greatest expression of understanding. Laughter is our bodies' reaction to a moment of ultimate clarity, it is how we express the recognition of truth itself. That's why when we realise truth, laughter spontaneously arrives. It is what makes satire deeply funny and moving all at once. This is because laughter is intelligence. It is the ultimate expression of rebellion."

The world is a vast playground in a cosmic multiverse potentially flying through space at a thousand miles per hour. The whole play of existence, the way creation creates is so exquisite that bowing down in reverence and laughing in awe is the only true response to it all.

As I appreciate it all as a cosmic joke, I am able to understand the ultimate mystery. A mystery is near impossible to understand or explain. That's the irony. Trying to understand what cannot be understood and explain what cannot be explained. Isn't that hilarious especially when we argue to uphold what we think we know? (That can still happen!)

But when I am not attached, ahhh I can loosen the grip, because I'm just a speck in this grand spectacle. Protons, neutrons and electrons all enjoying the cosmic dance in the space of an atom playing along to the unified melody of the uni-verse (one-verse).

I choose to take life non-seriously, not in the sense of not caring, I care but don't carry. "It's not the load that breaks you down, it's the way you carry it."

Marc goes on to say, "An intelligent, awakened and joyful person is always, always sincere. They are led and guided by a bigger picture, a bigger perspective. And that creates an immense freedom. The laughing rebel, live liberated lives. They live a life of courage and truth."

I move from seriousness to sincerity. From emotional enslavement to personal power, from victim to sovereign hero, where I can care and contribute more than ever before.

Have you ever heard someone laughing so hard, they can't stop, and they try to scream out: 'Stop! Stop! Your killing me!'? Well, there is some truth in that. In order to access the deep belly laughter or 'cosmic chuckle' as I like to call it then I have to renounce seriousness and actualise the power of divine playfulness as a force of my authentic transparent expression. That is what the sages and great mystics of history have always taught. Laugh in the face of fear, celebrate, dance and sing in gratitude, because that generates power and confidence.

Let us all laugh together and play every day and do it with abandon. Whether we are experiencing sadness and adversity, or joy and peace. How would our lives change if we accessed this underlying truthful attitude of real joy for being alive, no matter the situation?

To play like children do, to tap back into the innocence of being, to play with the creative life force in reverence and gratefulness, to commune with this divine energy that permeates all things. As children we laugh hundreds of times each day, delighted by the newness of living. Laughter has been a part of the human mode of expression since before evolution granted us the art of speech. Playfulness in itself is true freedom.

It was Donald Winnicott who said, "Play is the one activity where the whole personality is present." When Donald speaks of the whole personality, he means the whole Self. And in terms of play he meant not only the ways that children of all ages play, but also the way adults "play" through making art, or engaging in sports, hobbies, humour, and meaningful conversation. At any age, he saw play as crucial to the development of authentic selfhood, because when people play they feel real, spontaneous and alive, and attentively interested in what they're doing.

Play, and laughter for no apparent reason, brings us into the present moment like nothing else. When I can laugh wholeheartedly at life's ridiculousness instead of responding irritably, my focus shifts. Anger, stress, guilt, sadness and all that the pain-body feeds on no longer wields any influence over me and instead I am empowered to make light of what I originally feared. Play therefore transports me back into wholeness, and this deeper realisation reminds us that we are already whole, we can never not be whole, and love is effortless and when we access this effortless state of being, we are beckoned into the divine dance of existence. This is the child mind which has been referenced to as Buddha mind.

"The wise person," said Mencius, in the fourth century BC, "is one who doesn't lose the child's heart and mind."

There is a way to recapture the open qualities of a child's mind. It is called 'beginner's mind'. This concept from Zen Buddhism, called shoshin, invites us to experience life in a way that is unburdened by the past and by previous knowledge. One Zen master called beginner's mind 'a mind that is empty and ready for new things'.

So in order to play with what I am pointing to, we have to empty ourselves, and die before we die to the past stories and burdens we may still be carrying. I am so grateful to have heard the call back to being a child again, to dance in the wonder and awe and to awaken to this majestic mystery. And to be reborn and guided by the darkness of fear to the light of love. I metamorphosise from the chrysalis to butterfly.

I love these words from DarPan: "The butterfly is a marvellous demonstration of the power of trust and vulnerability in the miracle of metamorphosis. After all, what is a butterfly if not the flowering of caterpillar beyond its wildest dreams? Emerging from the womb of the chrysalis, the butterfly discards its restrictive silk and shell, to inherit a magical new world of flowers, breezes and sunshine. A world of freedom and delight. A celebration of its divine nature. Spreading her wings for the first time, she has no idea whether she can fly, she simply opens her wings in perfect confidence and is effortlessly conveyed into the spiral dance of graceful flight."

This is what I am talking about, smile inside and belly laugh at everything. The child mind is a magical place to bathe in the sound of laughter as we return to wholeness. We are Gods or Buddhas or miracles or any other name you want to term this powerful creative force.

Supernatural Gods in the flesh as Joe Dispenza would say. I am a co-creator with the universe. I am the dreamer of the dream. I am the one I was waiting for. Many messengers before me said the very same thing; God is within. The Kingdom of Heaven (If you choose to term it that) is inside each of us. Let go of trying to control, let go of trying to plan and just laugh with existence. The messages are everywhere, even in this old Yiddish proverb, "We plan, God laughs."

Every moment I live, is an opportunity to serve and support others to step into their magnificence. To awaken to the wonder and awe of this majestic gift of life, to laugh with abandon as I die-ve into the depths of love and experience real joy and real peace.

I ask myself daily, Can I dare to be great? Can I take full universal responsibility? Can I speak my truth? Can I surrender to what is? Can I face it, feel it and heal it? Can I be grateful for it all? Can I walk this mysterious path and treat everyone I meet as a noble guest? Can I move from me to we? Can I contribute usefully and play as purpose? Can I surrender and let go to the divine design and sacred freestyle of it all? Can I play with innocence and die before I die?

'Flow like water' as Bruce Lee would say. May we all laugh with the knowing that we are the cosmic mystery.

Let's keep it free, keep it pure, keep it simple and dance to the divine awe-chestra that never stops playing for us. Run free, beautiful child, like only you and I know how.

As Buddha said: "We are all Buddhas. Just open your eyes."

'Sentient beings are as grains of sand.
I vow to save them all.
Deluding passions are endless.
I vow to extinguish them all.
The truth is impossible to teach.
I vow to teach it.
The way of the Buddha is impossible to attain.
I vow to attain it.'

Bodhisattva Vow

AFTERWORD

There are theories that say it can take seven years to write a book, and in my case, this has been true. It feels at times I have made it really difficult, or maybe after my next book I will say that's not true and its actually just hard work to complete a book.

So here I am at the end of the October 2020, when we are currently experiencing what is being called a global pandemic. If there was ever a moment for humanity to awaken collectively out of fear, this would be it.

Nothing ever goes exactly the way I plan, and I have learned to accept that. In fact, I no longer make plans. Instead I say I make 'rough sketches'. When I am able to get out of the way of trying to control the outcome, and instead let life reveal itself to me in ways I would least expect, I find the divine design always awe-chestrates it far greater than any of my plans could have.

The small me still gets caught up in personal realities created from fearful thoughts and diminishing feelings, and

I am asked to surrender to what is every day. This book is part of that deeper process of letting go of my story and the mind-made self, called Simon. My story is no more fixed than the self is fixed. Stories can empower or disempower us.

Through writing this book I have been able to see the light of truth though my own make-believe narratives. This book is my perspective and of course, anyone telling the same stories I have shared, from their point of view, would have written a very different book. I have no doubt they would definitely have highlighted parts I have completely forgotten.

What is true for me now may not be tomorrow and this book has lingered with me in the background as I continued to journey through the mystery throughout the last few years. How many times have I started and stopped, aware that I had no structure, and way too many concepts and stories to get into one book? I often read what I had written about my past and wondered if the story even needed to be shared. There have been so many times that unworthiness, self-doubt and fear have held me back from sharing this story with the world. I was feeling resistance to reading the same chapters over and over again during the editing process. I was frustrated at times that it was taking too long and I was agitated when friends would ask, "How's the book coming along, Si?" There were times when I wished I hadn't told anyone I was writing a book. Though despite my agitation, their questions always triggered me back to the writing.

My beautiful editor eventually said, "You have to stop changing things around or it will never get finished."

I've had a constant thought present for years, saying it

should have been completed sooner, but that just highlights the absurdity of the monkey mind and now makes me chuckle with the cosmos. As if it could have been any other way than what it is now?

Friends told me the book would arrive when it was ready, and that I am in fact living the book and if it never gets published, that's okay too.

This book is for no one other than me. It may serve you in some way and if it does, I am thankful. But at the core, this book is a self-loving act to dissolve the programs in me which have held me captive in these pages. I have had to feel so much through writing this book, and for this I am deeply grateful. I thought that during the first stage when I initially wrote hundreds of pages of my past down on paper, that I had freed myself, but I hadn't. I was still trapped by many fearful thoughts and unsatisfying emotions.

Since 2014, I have shared my story with the world at events, on podcasts and on videos, and I have had to practice what I preach and live what I teach.

Through Alice, I was introduced to another magnificent woman called Dara. We had met a few years prior for a very short encounter at a festival. Alice was friends with her for a while but for a number of reasons their friendship drifted. During those years, Dara had given birth to her daughter Maya and had moved through the breakup with her previous partner.

At the time I was separating from Alice, I had been called back to the 5Rhythms dance as a way to process what I was experiencing. There were no 5Rhythms teachers on the island, so I created my own dance events. It was at the second dance, just before I was about to lock the entrance door, that Dara walked into the room. She was somehow strangely familiar with her resplendent presence and magnetic smile, and I was captivated once again as love presented itself unexpectedly.

Little did I know what this alchemical explosion was about to create. This time, literally one door closed exactly as another opened.

That evening's dance and the dances that followed set the foundation to birth an ecstatic relationship bond that has just taken me on another seven-year cycle of living and dying. This has allowed me into a depth of relating that was possible because of our willingness to stand in the fire of truth as our fear burned away to reveal the unconditional. I chose to embark into a co-parenting relationship and it has been of no surprise that Maya also became one of my greatest teachers in loving unconditionally.

Just six months after meeting we launched a seven day retreat we named 'NAKED the Retreat'. We combined our wisdom, passion and desire to show up in service to love by creating radical immersions. Our combined energy is explosive and extremely creative. NAKED is an invitation to strip away all that blocks us from the love that we are. We have toured the world sharing our love through these retreat spaces and a multitude of other events on and offline. I realised some years ago that our focus was actually directed towards what we call the five greatest taboos of our culture; truth, money, sex, death and power. And through the courageous souls we have had the gift of working with and meeting in their most vulnerable states, the more we realised that all these taboos are linked together. Our sexuality holds the key to so many of the dysfunctional relationships we have with ourselves and others, and allows us to uncover great wisdom and insight if we are willing to venture into the deeper recesses of our conditioning.

In 2018, my inquiry into sexuality led me to become a 'Sexological Bodyworker'. This brought many of the tools I had been learning and sharing into a clear intention, to unblock and ignite life force energy using the intelligence of our physiology, without excluding our genitalia (which so often happens in many practices and therapies). By using breath, movement, sound and meditation we go deep into the rewiring of our subconscious false beliefs, shame and guilt associated to our sexuality. We merge and weave the intelligence of the heart with the genitals, or what I like to call the sexual centre.

So many seekers in the world are looking for the holy grail, the elixir of life, or God, and through this training it was clarified to me that a massive factor that disconnects us from life and living is due to the immense amount of suppression and sexual abuse that so many of us have endured.

If we are inviting a greater love of self and we journey back to the awareness of our wholeness, but don't include the relationship with our genitals and sexuality, desire and eroticism, then we are missing a huge part of what it means to be an alive embodied human being. In order to connect to the source of life we must journey back to where we came from, which is the genitals. God then, has been hidden in our pants all along. It is here where so much wisdom, truth and healing can take place. But this, my friends, is the next chapter and who knows, maybe I will attempt to write another book…

Burglar to Buddha could never have been delivered before this moment. As I reflect on my hero's journey, the whole metamorphic process has been absolute perfection. Every single experience, every interaction, every relationship in the exact way it has turned out, every abortion, every gang war and act of violence or crime, all of it has had to happen exactly as it has for me to be here right now in this moment.

It has not always been easy to welcome in the truth that all is well in all of creation. To accept all what I perceived to be violence and ignorance in the world and then shift into the eyes of unconditional loving awareness. To drop my judgments of right or wrong, good or bad. On some days it's still very difficult to let go of, like the wise monks crossing the river. But this is where I sit and play, in the divine dichotomy, and this is how I choose to view the miracle unfolding. There's definitely been a paradigm shift or two.

And it's all happening all at once. My ordinary life has become extra-ordinary. Everything will change but the essence shall remain the same.

I will continue to sit and observe in silence, and to do the best I can to consciously design the most beautiful world my heart knows is possible. In the knowing that nothing needs doing and all gets done. I am already whole and complete. Who knows what's to come next? Not I. But I shall welcome whatever does with an open heart and mind and always ask myself, what would love do now?

Because it's all love and I am that.

All that remains then (for me at least), is to joyously participate in the divine ecstasy of creation while opening my arms wide to welcome in the infinite possibilities that this magnificent cosmic playground has to offer.

Be a light unto yourself
Simplicity is divinity
And so it is…

BIBLIOGRAPHY

BOOKS REFERRED TO IN THIS BOOK

The Last Hours of Ancient Sunlight
by Thom Hartmann

The Moneyless Man: A Year of Freeconomic Living
by Mark Boyle

Born to Succeed
by Colin Turner

The Subtle Art of Not Giving a F*ck
by Mark Manson

The Biology of Belief
by Bruce Lipton

The Miracle of Water
by Masaru Emoto

Freedom From The Known
by Jiddu Krishnamurti

Soul Trader
by Rasheed Ogunlaru

FreeMind Experience: The Three Pillars of Absolute Happiness
by Tom Fortes-Meyer

Womb Wisdom
by Anaiya Sophia

The Artist's Way
Julia Cameron

The Hero with a Thousand Faces
Joseph Campbell

Confessions of an Economic Hit Man
John Perkins

Where Do We Begin
by Nicholas Eldridge

Illusions
by Richard Bach

A New Earth & *The Power of Now* & *Stillness Speaks*
by Eckhart Tolle

Dream Healer
by Adam.

The Keys of Enoch
by Dr JJ Hurtak

The Alchemy of Voice
Stewart Pearce

The Celestine Prophecy
by James Redfield

I Dare You To Be Great
by Polly Higgins

The More Beautiful World Our Hearts Know is Possible
by Charles Eisenstein

After the Ecstasy, the Laundry
by Jack Kornfield

Orphan Wisdom
by Stephen Jenkinson

Be Here Now
Ram Dass

50 Ways to Find a Lover
Lucy-Anne Holmes

Becoming Supernatural
by Dr Joe Dispenza

Tao Te Ching
Lao Tzu

Watch My Back & *The Elephant and The Twig*
by Geoff Thompson

Th Book of Ram
by Devdutt Pattanaik

FILMS & DOCUMENTARIES:

Romans 12:20
Clubbed
Other Side Of The Game
AO The Last Neanderthal
Network 1976
Soylent Green
The Matrix
Revolutionary Rd
The Truman Show
The Celestine Prophecy
The Shift
Into the Wild
Blue Gold
The Cove
A Beautiful Truth by Steve Kroschel
I AM by Tom Shadyac
The Matrix
I Heart Huckabees
Groundhog Day
One Flew Over the Cuckoo's Nest
The Shift
Road to Peace by Leon Stuparich
Pay It Forward
Fat, Sick and Nearly Dead
Finding Joe
The Century of the Self (TV Docu-Series 2002)
Thrive 1 & 2 - What on earth will it take?
Becoming Nobody by Jamie Catto

Kumare
Fantastic Fungi
Kiss The Ground
Social Dilemma

WEBSITES/ARTICLES:

Margie Meacham
www.td.org/insights/how-words-affect-our-brains

Dr William Campbell Douglass
WHO MURDERED AFRICA

Vipassana
uk.dhamma.org

Dar Pan
darpan.com

Tad Hargraves
MarketingforHippies.com

Soul Trader Rasheed Ogunlaru
www.rasaru.com

The Spring Project
www.springproject.uk

Christian de Sousa
glimpsesoflight.net

BOOKS BY NOT
FROM THIS PLANET

LABRADORITE PRESS

Little Something
by Elizabeth Lockwood

THE AMETHYST ANGEL

The Earth Angel Series
by Michelle Gordon

The Visionary Collection
by Michelle Gordon

TURQUOISE QUILL PRESS

Duelling Poets
by Michelle Gordon & Victor Keegan

AMBER BEETLE BOOKS

The Magical Faerie Door
by Michelle Louise Gordon

JASPER TREE PRESS

The Winter's Sleep
by Monica Cafferky

The Girl Who Loved Too Much
by Michelle Gordon

Not From This Planet is an Independent Publisher on a mission to collaborate with authors to create the best possible books that delight and inspire and entertain – and also pay a fair royalty to the author. They treat every book as if it were their own and they have big have plans to take the publishing world by storm.

Follow Not From This Planet on
Instagram - @notfromthisplanetbooks
Facebook - @notfromthisplanetbooks
Twitter - @ NFTPbooks

NotFromThisPlanet.co.uk

Printed in Great Britain
by Amazon